MOVEMENTS OF RELIGIOUS THOUGHT

THE VICTORIAN LIBRARY

MOVEMENTS OF
RELIGIOUS THOUGHT
IN BRITAIN DURING THE NINETEENTH CENTURY

JOHN TULLOCH

WITH AN INTRODUCTION BY
A. C. CHEYNE

NEW YORK : HUMANITIES PRESS

LEICESTER UNIVERSITY PRESS

1971

First published in 1885
Victorian Library edition published in 1971 by
Leicester University Press

Distributed in North America by
Humanities Press Inc., New York

Introduction copyright © Leicester University Press 1971

Printed in Great Britain by
Unwin Brothers Ltd, Old Woking, Surrey
Introduction set in Monotype Caslon

SBN 391 00160 4

72-178660

THE VICTORIAN LIBRARY

There is a growing demand for the classics of Victorian literature in many fields, in political and social history, architecture, topography, religion, education, and science. Hitherto this demand has been met, in the main, from the second-hand market. But the prices of second-hand books are rising sharply, and the supply of them is very uncertain. It is the object of this series, THE VICTORIAN LIBRARY, to make some of these classics available again at a reasonable cost. Since most of the volumes in it are reprinted photographically from the first edition, or another chosen because it has some special value, an accurate text is ensured. Each work carries a substantial introduction, written specially for this series by a well-known authority on the author or his subject, and a bibliographical note on the text.

The volumes necessarily vary in size. In planning the newly-set pages the designer, Arthur Lockwood, has maintained a consistent style for the principal features. The uniform design of binding and jacket provides for ready recognition of the various books in the series when shelved under different subject classifications.

Recommendation of titles for THE VICTORIAN LIBRARY and of scholars to contribute the introductions is made by a joint committee of the Board of the University Press and the Victorian Studies Centre of the University of Leicester.

INTRODUCTION

John Tulloch's *Movements of Religious Thought in Britain during the Nineteenth Century* originally appeared as long ago as 1885; yet at intervals ever since tribute has been paid to its very considerable merits, and there is good reason for believing that it may still provide not only the most compact and comprehensive but also the most stimulating introduction to its subject which the modern reader can obtain. When, shortly before the First World War, Canon V. F. Storr published his own somewhat fuller account of the development of English theology between 1800 and 1860, he included several quotations from Tulloch's work, praised its opening chapters as "the best general estimate of Coleridge's influence on subsequent theology with which I am familiar", and regretted that it was then out of print. Rather more than a decade later the compliment was reiterated by a Scandinavian scholar, Archbishop Brilioth of Uppsala. His classic study of early Victorian churchmanship, *The Anglican Revival*, commended Tulloch's "excellent sketch" of Richard Whately, and went on to acclaim the whole series of lectures — "now unfortunately long out of print" — as "perhaps the best work on the theological history of the earlier nineteenth century in England." The appearance in 1942 of C. R. Sanders' careful reappraisal of Coleridge and the Broad Church movement brought fresh proof, this time from across the Atlantic, of Tulloch's continuing vitality and influence: his judgements upon men and ideas received frequent and approving mention in text and footnotes alike, nor could even the keenest scrutiny of its pages have detected any substantial divergence from Tulloch's overall view of early- and mid-Victorian thought. Finally, in 1961 Dr Alec Vidler added yet another voice to the modest chorus of approval, describing *Movements of Religious Thought* as a "valuable book", and selecting it and Otto Pfleiderer's *The Development of Theology in Germany since Kant, and its Progress in Great Britain since 1825* as the only nineteenth-century works to be included in the short general bibliography of his Pelican History volume on *The Church in an Age of Revolution*.

In accounting for the durability of Tulloch's unpretentious little treatise we must be careful not to claim too much. Based as it is upon a course of popular lectures, it lacks the panoply of twentieth-century scholarship and occasionally displays qualities more appropriate to a sermon than to an academic dissertation. At certain points it is frankly dated. One wonders, for example, whether all our contemporary authorities would describe as "shallow, meagre, . . . quite baseless" a theory that asserted "the derivative connection of Christianity with the Essenes"; and it is amusing to lay Tulloch's idyllic picture of life with the Hares alongside the awesome account which Professor W. L. Burn recently constructed – from the same sources! – in his study of *The Age of Equipoise*. The rather harsh Puritanism of Tulloch's remarks on George Eliot, culminating in the statement that "We do not look to minds of this stamp, into which the arrows of conscience make only slight wounds, for a true estimate of Christianity either in its divine character or origin", calls forth a strongly negative reaction from today's reader. We find it difficult to share his apparent admiration for F. W. Robertson's odd remark that "I refuse to permit discussion respecting the love which a Christian man bears to his Redeemer – a love more delicate far than the love which was ever borne to sister or the adoration with which he regards his God – a reverence more sacred than ever man bore to his mother." And no doubt various other comments might be cited which by their sentimentality or their censoriousness or their indefinably 'Victorian' ring have power to startle, shock, or entertain us. But on the whole he has worn extraordinarily well. Why should this be; and why, in a world so different from his, does he still exert a claim upon our attention?

At the very outset, there is something impressive about his almost uncanny gift for concentrating upon men and movements whose importance has been little diminished by the passage of time. Coleridge; Whately and Thomas Arnold and their associates in the early Oriel school; the Tractarians; Thomas Erskine, Edward Irving and John Macleod Campbell; Thomas Carlyle; John Stuart Mill; F. D. Maurice and Charles Kingsley; F. W. Robertson: within the chronological limits (1820–1860) which he himself set, Tulloch's survey includes nearly every figure whom the present generation would rate as of first-class, or well-nigh first-class, theological significance, and it is quite remarkable how unwilling some of his ablest successors have been to depart from the ground-plan which he mapped out. Storr, for example, had more than twenty-five years of further scholarly research behind him when he made his assessment of nineteenth-century theology, yet apart from sketching in the Continental background he added very little to his Victorian forerunner's basic outline; and one cannot but observe the striking resemblance between Tulloch's chapter-headings and the table of contents in Professor Basil Willey's still more recent *Nineteenth Century Studies*. (In 1885, admittedly, some minnows slipped through along with the big fish; yet the verdict passed on a minor figure like George Combe is thoroughly level-headed, and if Bishop Ewing and Wright of Borthwick do not merit the care bestowed upon them the outlook of which they were the representatives most certainly does.) All this bears witness to a capacity for distinguishing between essentials and inessentials which appears and reappears throughout the *Movements of Religious Thought*, not least in its convincing estimates of systems and parties – their various components and their peculiar strengths and weaknesses. We should have to go far for a more sympathetic or discerning examination of the main thrusts of Coleridge's religious thought than is contained in the opening chapter. The account of the Oxford Movement can bear comparison with most subsequent evaluations, and that in spite of being written well before such basic sources as Dean Church's *The Oxford Movement* and Anne Mozley's edition of *Letters and Correspondence of John Henry Newman* had appeared in print. Even the essay on F. D. Maurice has obvious merits, and may be looked upon as one of the early manifestations of the great and increasing interest which scholars have come to take in that obscure and self-contradictory but nevertheless rewarding and influential theologian.

To his gifts of insight and sure judgement Tulloch adds other good qualities. Note should certainly be taken of the skill with which he traces the influence exerted by men like Coleridge or Erskine or Arnold on their contemporaries, and of the light he thereby sheds upon the complicated network of intellectual relationships in the Victorian age. But perhaps even more remarkable is his ability to recapture the temper and atmosphere of a given period and bring its characteristic features clearly into focus. This ability can be discerned in the remarks with which he introduces his study of Coleridge, and in the brief survey given of Scottish thought as it was before the emergence of Erskine, Irving, Macleod Campbell and Carlyle. It is also impressively obvious in a later passage, where he introduces an examination of the ideas of George Eliot, F. D. Maurice, and Charles Kingsley by describing the distinctive intellectual climate of the late 'forties and the early 'fifties. "There set in", he tells us:

a period of sceptical languor. The failure of the Oxford movement especially produced a strong reaction, which worked powerfully in many minds to the distrust of all religious truth. This was the time of which Mr. Froude speaks in his life of Carlyle, when he and a companion band of truth-seekers were driven into the wilderness in search of something in which they could believe – some certainty on which they could stand. He and others found a refuge in Carlylism, but many found no such refuge. His own early volumes – now rarely met with – *The Shadows of the Clouds* (1847) and the *Nemesis of Faith* (1849); the poems of Clough, who at this time broke away from Oxford and resigned his fellowship; the *Phases of Faith* of Francis Newman (1849) who then also parted with his early Evangelicalism; the struggles after a higher belief which meet us in the lives of Kingsley and Frederick Robertson; all testify to the sceptical weariness which in these years overtook many minds of the younger generation. No finer spirit than Clough's was ever wrecked on the ocean of doubt, and Frederick Robertson, as we shall see, bore to the last the impress of the suffering through which he then passed. It was in the same years that John Sterling's faith disappeared; and Matthew Arnold's first poems, with all their divine despair, although not published till a later date (1853), were born of the same time of spiritual darkness, when the sun of faith went down on so many hearts.

The same descriptive – and analytical – power is again evident in the closing chapter of the book, which is largely devoted to a consideration of Robertson and Ewing but also includes some interesting comments on the new epoch which began round about the year 1860. That epoch, so Tulloch contends, was to be marked – in religious matters, at any rate – by the dominance of two mighty if hitherto unfamiliar forces: the concept of Evolution and the practice of Biblical Criticism. What he calls "the 'scientific' note" began, and continued down to the time of writing, to be sounded by all who indulged in philosophical or theological speculation. "The great idea of Evolution, underlying all processes of thought as well as of Nature, came into prominence"; and the result was a replacement of old conflicts by new ones, "the lines of which are not too strongly marked as Theistic . . . and Atheistic." Following upon the publication of *Essays and Reviews* (he does not mention *The Origin of Species*):

questions of criticism and history were transformed into questions affecting the very existence not only of Christianity but of religion – such questions as the possibility of miracle, and whether any Divine theory of the world is tenable. It is in this deeper groove that religious thought has mainly run during the last twenty-five years, with thinkers like Herbert Spencer, and Professors Tyndall and Huxley, and Matthew Arnold on one side, and on the other a group of Theistic thinkers, of whom one of the most conspicuous and distinguished is certainly Dr. James Martineau.... This deeper conflict was no doubt opened by the Mills and their school within the earlier period we have reviewed, but it has recently passed into wider and larger phases.

The literary and historical criticism of the Bible made its popular début, according to Tulloch, in Jowett and Stanley's commentaries on the Pauline epistles. "Both writers", he says of the Master and the Dean, "mark for us a turning-point in the criticism of Scripture and the *renascence* of Christian ideas nearly contemporary with the influx of new ideas in philosophy and science, which have also acted so powerfully in recent years." And he goes on to summarize their services to theology as follows:

They reproduced in a higher form all that was good in the Whately school, with a richer insight into the essential characteristics of New Testament thought, and a far clearer and more illuminating hold of the spiritual and historical position of the great Apostle – of the true meaning of his teaching, and the development of his doctrine. From this time has greatly advanced that profounder study of the New Testament, which looks beyond its traditional to its real aspects, and its organic relations to contemporary usage and opinion – which sees

in it a living literature, and not a mere repository
of doctrinal texts – and aims to separate the essential
from the accidental of Divine Thought, untrammelled
by later notions and controversial fictions.

The enthusiasm herein implied for the presuppositions,
aims and attainments of Biblical Criticism may not be
shared by all present-day theologians, but nearly every one
of them would agree with Tulloch's enumeration of the
forces which did most to shape religious thought in
Britain in the second half of last century; and credit is
assuredly due to him for providing, thus early, an analysis
of the situation which still commands practically universal
assent.

A great deal of the charm and liveliness of the work
now under review derives from its refusal to examine
ideas in isolation from the lives of the men who produced
them. This biographical approach (as we might call it)
was, in 1885, no new thing for Tulloch: he had already
employed it on several occasions and to good effect. As
early as 1859 he published a study of the leaders of the
Protestant Reformation which achieved sufficient popularity to be re-issued in the 1880s; and not long afterwards he followed it up with a companion work on those
heroes of Puritanism, Baxter, Bunyan and Cromwell.
Much more important, the magnum opus which crowned
his scholarly career – *Rational Theology and Christian
Philosophy in England in the Seventeenth Century* – dealt
in its first volume with such liberal churchmen as Lord
Falkland, John Hales, William Chillingworth, Jeremy
Taylor and Edward Stillingfleet, and in its second with
those distant forerunners of the Broad Church school, the
Cambridge Platonists. The generous measure of critical

acclaim which greeted its appearance between 1872 and 1874 may well have encouraged the author to use the same method in his subsequent examination of nineteenth-century thought: at any rate, when *Movements of Religious Thought* came out rather more than a decade later it too was organized round a series of carefully selected character-sketches.

Outstanding among these is a vigorous and sensitive portrait of Thomas Carlyle, in which the relationship between the experiences and the ideas of the great man is painstakingly explicated (often with the aid of his own incomparable prose) and a modest but not unsatisfying assessment made of his contribution to religious thought. A short passage on the famous "spiritual deliverance" may convey the flavour of the essay as a whole. "It is difficult", Tulloch writes:

> to know how far Carlyle's language . . . is to be taken literally, especially when speaking of himself. No Methodist – not even John Bunyan – clothes his spiritual experiences in more highly metaphorical phrase. His imagination bodies forth his sufferings, more rarely his joys, in figures of intensity and magnitude altogether disproportionate to the experience of ordinary men. The transformation of Leith Walk, in all its prosaic ugliness, into the Rue de l'Enfer, is merely one among many instances of this power of imaginative exaggeration. 'Dragons' and 'Tophet', 'Eternities', 'Silences', 'Immensities', are the familiar imagery of his mind. He sees everything transfigured in a halo of gloom or of sunshine. The truth seems to be that on this occasion peace of mind came to him largely from a temporary access of health. The summer of 1826,

spent in his own cottage on Hoddam Hill, with his mother at command to attend to his wants, and set free from the distractions of the paternal farm, seems almost to have been the happiest portion of his life. He had room; he had work; the translation of German Romance, which cost him little trouble and brought in some money. The view from his cottage over the Solway Firth was unrivalled in extent and grandeur. No other residence seems to have suited him so well, and it was one of the misfortunes of his life that he was unable to retain it. . . . Had Carlyle only been able to dwell on the top of Hoddam Hill with some fair portion of this world's goods, and his strong peasant mother, who knew all his ways, to minister to his wants, instead of the delicate lady whom he made his wife, we might have heard less of 'dragons' and 'Stygian quagmires'.

Tulloch seems to be especially at home with Carlyle. But he also gives us striking portraits of F. D. Maurice and F. W. Robertson; and his evocations, on a smaller canvas, of such men as Richard Whately, Hurrell Froude, Thomas Arnold, and Erskine of Linlathen are in their own way equally fine.

Quite apart from its intrinsic merits, *Movements of Religious Thought* also deserves notice as a characteristic, if exceptionally impressive, product of liberal theology in the late Victorian period. Its author was, without doubt, one of the most distinguished and influential representatives of Scotland's 'Broad Church' school – a man who, along with Professor Robertson Smith of the Free Church, led the way in transforming the Presbyterian Weltanschaung in the years between *Essays and Reviews* and *Lux Mundi* (or, if we prefer to steer our course by

Continental landmarks, between Strauss's *Das Leben Jesu* and Harnack's *Das Wesen des Christentums*). Born in 1823 in the Perthshire village of Dron, where his father was minister, young Tulloch studied Arts and Divinity at the University of St Andrews; and although his performance had not been outstandingly brilliant he was allowed to spend only a short time in parochial work before Lord Palmerston's government appointed him to the much sought-after post of Principal of St Mary's College and Professor of Theology in his old University.

The reasons for this sudden promotion are not altogether obvious. That young Tulloch should, within weeks of leaving college, inform a friend that "I have not resigned my boyish dreams of an academic life. It is still my ambition", is hardly proof of his ability to realize such longings. Yet he was nothing if not determined. While still an inexperienced parish minister in Dundee, he obtained leave of absence to pursue theological and linguistic studies in Germany; he read widely and assiduously; he contributed articles on religious and cultural subjects to a variety of newspapers and periodicals (including the *North British Review*, *Kitto's Journal*, and the *British Quarterly Review*), and gained high commendation for them; he struck up an acquaintance with men of standing in the literary and ecclesiastical world like Principal Sir David Brewster of the United College of St Andrews, Archdeacon Hare, Sir James Stephen, Professor J. S. Blackie and the once-famous Baron Bunsen; and as early as 1851 he toyed with the idea of applying for the chair of Ecclesiastical History at Glasgow. His name began to be known — and then, at the close of 1853, the Principalship of St Mary's College, St Andrews, fell vacant. After some complicated negotiations, a good deal of pressure on

Tulloch's behalf by influential friends like Bunsen, Brewster and Lord Kinnaird, and at least one almost incredible stroke of luck (the details of which are recorded in Mrs Oliphant's *Life*), he received the appointment: the forces of liberalism, already in the ascendant in the United College, had conquered among the theologians of St Mary's also. Almost simultaneously, as if in confirmation of the new professor's worth, came news that the Burnett Trustees − Baden Powell, Henry Rogers and Isaac Taylor − had awarded him a £600 prize for an extended essay on a theological subject; and only a few weeks later both Macmillan and Constable were competing to be his publishers. He had, overnight, become a celebrity.

Tulloch held the twin appointments of Principal and Professor from 1854 until his death thirty-two years later; and almost the only shadow upon his enjoyment of academic office, its duties and its privileges, was cast by the mysterious and desolating attacks of nervous depression which dogged him from early manhood to the very brink of old age. Though frequently lamenting the meagre provision made for himself and his family, and sometimes tempted by the ampler opportunities which chairs at Glasgow and Edinburgh seemed to offer, he nevertheless found much to delight him in the quiet but sociable East Neuk of Fife; travelled far during the inordinately long vacations of those halcyon times; poured out a steady stream of books and articles; dabbled not unhappily in university politics; and lectured with acceptance to his small but admiring classes. He served as one of the commissioners of the Board of Education set up in 1872, and played an active part in the negotiations for university reform which bore fruit in the 1889 Act. For a short time at the end of the 1870s he was editor of *Fraser's*

Magazine; and his friendships came to include some of the best-known literary figures of the day.

In his own Church of Scotland, Tulloch had to endure some early criticism, and even unpopularity, on account of his 'advanced' theological and liturgical views; but the trouble was never very serious, and in the course of time he acquired a standing with Queen and people similar to that enjoyed a little earlier by the great Norman Macleod himself. Secure in the regard and affection of the General Assembly, he became almost inevitably its leader in the resistance to Disestablishment, and in 1878 he attained the highest honour which Presbyterianism can bestow – the Moderatorship. (Now, as in Tulloch's time, the Moderator is chosen annually from among the ministers of the Kirk to preside, *primus inter pares*, over the meetings of its supreme legislative and judicial body, the General Assembly. Though purely honorary, and held for a strictly limited period, the appointment has been graced by a high proportion of the ablest and most respected ministers of the Church of Scotland, and the prestige attaching to it is very considerable.) Such a story enables one to understand how his death in 1886 – not much more than a year after the publication of *Movements of Religious Thought*, and when he was at the height of his powers – seemed to many like the end of an era. It had been an era in which the Auld Kirk, recovering from the shock administered to it by the Disruption, gradually acquired some expertise in dealing with the challenges of urban and industrial society, forged new evangelistic weapons and refurbished old ones, discarded many of the restraints imposed upon it by seventeenth-century Puritanism, re-fashioned its worship on more catholic lines, and set about re-defining its attitude to the system of doctrine whose best-known formularies are the Shorter Catechism and the Westminster Confession of Faith; and few, if any, of its servants could claim a greater responsibility for the transformation brought about in the Scottish religious scene by these enterprises than John Tulloch. He was, it may truly be said, the very embodiment of the liberal churchmanship of his time; and one is hardly surprised to find that the concerns and controversies to which he had given his attention over many years have left their mark on nearly every page of the present volume.

What, then, were his characteristic beliefs and attitudes? Not to simplify unduly, the following must be included in any account of him: a devotion to 'inquiry' and an intense dislike of 'dogmatism'; a conviction that neither undiluted Rationalism nor undiluted Traditionalism is the way to religious truth; an historical approach to all credal formulations; a hatred of 'bibliolatry' and a modest confidence in the methods of Biblical Criticism; and finally, a desire to distinguish between theology and religion. Recurrent themes of all Tulloch's written work, they are stated with particular frankness and clarity in four short addresses – designed for various occasions, academic and otherwise – which mark the development of his thought from the 1850s right through to the 1870s: his inaugural lecture, *Theological Tendencies of the Age*, delivered at St Andrews in 1854; an introductory lecture, without a title, delivered in St Andrews in 1864; an address on *Theological Controversy* delivered to Edinburgh University Theological Society in 1865; and *Religion and Theology: a sermon for the times*, preached in Crathie parish church in 1875. In order, therefore, to deepen our understanding of Tulloch's book and its setting we must briefly glance at some of the things which he had to say in these highly personal, yet at the same time carefully considered, programmatic statements of his fundamental beliefs.

Devotion to 'inquiry' and an intense dislike of 'dogmatism'. Tulloch was always well aware, particularly in the middle years of his life, that the spirit of unbelief – of 'anti-supernaturalism' and 'subjective criticism' – was abroad in Victorian Britain. "There is", he once declared, "much of a doubtful and negative character in the mere literary atmosphere we are all breathing." But he differed from many of his contemporaries in maintaining that against such a foe ecclesiastical condemnation was of little avail, and could in fact do much positive harm. "I must venture to say", he told his young hearers in 1864:

> that the most ominous and saddening signs I can see on the religious horizon are not the spirit of inquiry, whether within the church or without it, but the unreasoning dogmatism with which in many cases this spirit has been met. The spirit of inquiry may be harmful ... but it is not necessarily either injurious or dangerous; while one has only to open any page of the New Testament, or study any century of Christendom from the beginning, to see that a blind and angry dogmatism is no weapon of spiritual warfare, and can never advance the cause of truth.

Moreover, the type of unbelief at work in the 'fifties and 'sixties was such as to render violent dogmatism especially inapplicable.

> The assailants of the old views of Christianity are for the most part of philosophical temper, and of quiet thoughtfulness. They can only be met with any success

in a corresponding spirit, with the weapons of a higher thoughtfulness, a more conspicuous moderation, and a fairer learning. This alone is the becoming attitude of those who are fighting for the better cause. As the 'ever-memorable' John Hales has said in his *Golden Remains*, which contain many precious sayings for such a time as ours, "If it be the cause of God which we handle in our writings, then let us handle it like the prophets of God, with quietness and moderation, and not in the violence of passion, as if we were possessed rather than inspired."

And again:

Christianity claims to be an eminently reasonable faith. It is the 'wisdom' no less than the 'power' of God. It is, if it is true at all, the highest truth; and so it is the business of Christian apology, in the face of unbelief, to show evidence of this. . . . There is no higher task for the Christian reason in every age than to vindicate the eternal basis of Christianity as a truth for the reason no less than for the conscience and the heart, as the highest philosophy no less than the highest expediency. To abdicate this rational ground of defence is to confess the Gospel to be a superstition – to acknowledge a hopeless schism between reason and conscience, between philosophy and religion. . . . No doubt the Church has its rights of utterance – its power to condemn as well as its duty to inquire and defend – but none the less true is it that men no longer heed utterances which are not weighty in argument as well as in tone, nor bow before a condemnation which is not reasoned as well as authoritative.

Readers of the *Movements of Religious Thought* may well feel that Tulloch lived up to his own teaching in the admirably fair treatment therein accorded to such unbelievers as Carlyle, John Stuart Mill and George Eliot. The whole book, in fact, is a tribute to the superiority of dialogue over denunciation, an example of the gentle and level-headed inquiry which its author admired and was ever seeking to commend.

Conviction that neither undiluted Rationalism nor undiluted Traditionalism is the way to Truth. The greater part of Tulloch's inaugural lecture in 1854 was devoted to a discussion, and rejection, of two prominent tendencies in theology and the religious life which he believed to be characteristic of his time. There was, in the first place, what he called Traditionalism, by which he meant "not merely the recognition of an element of traditional authority in theological investigations . . . but the exclusive supremacy of this element in one form or another." One of its chief manifestations was in the Anglo-Catholic school, for whom "the great question in matters of doctrine was not, 'What saith Scripture, under the scrutiny of reason or the Christian consciousness?' but 'What saith the Church?'." Tulloch was not insensitive to the virtues of the Oxford Movement, as he shows in the closing pages of his chapter on it in *Movements of Religious Thought*; and the inaugural also contains a glowing tribute:

> The genuine earnestness of the men who first engaged in it, and the depth of sacred conviction from which it has sprung, will not be denied by any who have given it their candid attention; and we must no less acknowledge the consummate scholarship, the range and

subtlety of intellect, the fine and beautiful comprehension often of the real import of the Church's history, and the deeper significance of certain aspects of her doctrine – especially, perhaps, the exquisite literary skill displayed in the writings which it has called forth.

At the same time, however, he rejected it as being "utterly opposed to our sympathies", and used the phrase "purely disastrous" to describe its effects on Christian theology.

The other manifestation of Traditionalism, which Tulloch found even less congenial, was old-style Evangelicalism as he encountered it in his own country. It too (according to him) rejected the claims of reason and conscience, this time in the interest of a narrowly confessional interpretation of Holy Scripture; and once again the consequences were devastating:

The general evidence of this traditional tendency . . . is a slavish adherence to certain religious formulae – a timid cowering from the glance of Reason as something which it is felt somehow ought to be acknowledged, but which it is not known how to acknowledge. Reason, as it were, stands ever at the door of this theological school waiting to be received. It is never either admitted or dismissed; but there it stands ever – a hovering phantom, a sort of scare-shadow to the theological puerilities which are its delight. However it may profess to acknowledge the right of private judgement, there is nothing less known, and nothing less tolerated by the adherents of this school than any free and fruitful exercise of this right. Authority, in fact, has here, in certain cases, established itself in a far more inflexible, as in a far less dignified and impressive form, than in Catholicism. And, as irresistible evidence of this, we find this school, of all, the most utterly destitute of a living and learned Theology.

One can understand why Tulloch, having condemned Evangelicalism for its basic irrationality, later sympathized with Irving and Erskine and Macleod Campbell (all of whom had run up against it) and with F. W. Robertson (who had thrown it off after a struggle). His avowed enthusiasm for Coleridge also becomes comprehensible, for it was Coleridge who "once more, in his age, made Christian doctrine alive to the Reason as well as the Conscience – tenable as a philosophy as well as an evangel".

But if Tulloch eschewed Traditionalism he felt equally unhappy with the most obvious alternative to it, namely Rationalism. In each and all of its many forms (he himself referred to the 'positivist', the 'intellectual', the 'intuitional' and that associated with the name of Friedrich Schleiermacher) its aim seemed to be "to find the determining element of theological truth in some purely inward or subjective standard"; and with this he could not agree. "If the original revelation of Reason is not to be rejected", he told his students, "the later objective revelation in Scripture must withal remain the standard and arbiter of Truth. . . . The Bible must be acknowledged as not only co-ordinate with Reason, but as forming, in all points of religious truth, the ultimate *determining* authority." And although by the time of *Movements of Religious Thought* he had somewhat modified his attitude to Schleiermacher – of whom he observed, in 1854, that "It is undoubtedly from this quarter that our Theology is in the greatest danger" – his favourable comments on Julius Hare and Connop Thirlwall and other disciples of the great German theologian imply no fundamental change in his position. That, as his criticisms of John Stuart Mill and others reveal, remained to the end what it had been in the 1850s. In his own words, he opposed Rationalism "not because it embraces a subjective element of determination in Theological Science, but because in different forms it embraces nothing else", setting up "the shifting standard of the human spirit" as the sole arbiter of Christian truth and science. And his conclusion on the whole matter was as follows:

> On the one hand, we can have no fruitful and vigorous Theology without the continual, ever-renewed inquest of free criticism – practical religion, even, perishes under its decay; on the other hand, the Bible must ever limit and bind all such progressive inquiries, for here we have no longer the word of man but the word of God. . . . Its light, therefore, must at once guide and circumscribe our onward course.

Historical approach to all credal formulations. As an appendix to the published version of his 1865 lecture to Edinburgh University Theological Society on *Theological Controversy, or The Function of Debate in Theology*, Tulloch printed some notes on the Westminster Confession of Faith which are of interest as condensing his views on a subject which exercised the Scottish mind throughout the greater part of the century. Observing that the propriety of confessions of faith would soon become a crucial question for Christian men, he called for historical and philosophical study of the Church of Scotland's "subordinate standard". "The Confession of Faith", he claimed "in its origin and in its principles was the manifesto of a great religious party which, after a fierce conflict, gained a temporary ascendancy in England and Scotland".

And he went on:

> Indeed, the same thing could be said of every Protestant Confession of Faith. . . . They are one and all historical monuments, marking the tides of religious thought as they have swelled with greater fullness in the course of the Christian centuries; and none of them can be understood aright simply by themselves, or as isolated dogmatic utterances, but only in connection with their time and the genius and character of the men who framed them.

The consequences of such a view were far-reaching:

> The popular ecclesiastical notion of creeds and confessions as in some sense absolute expressions of Christian truth – *credenda* to be accepted very much as we accept the statements of Scripture itself – is a notion in the face of all theological science, which every student deserving the name has long since abandoned. Those creeds and confessions are neither more nor less than the intellectual labours of great and good men assembled for the most part in synods or councils, all of which, as our Confession itself declares, "may err, and many have erred". They are stamped with the infirmities no less than the nobleness of the men who made them. They are *their* best thoughts about Christian truth as they saw it in their time – intrinsically they are nothing more; and any claim of infallibility for them is the worst of all kinds of Popery – that Popery which degrades the Christian reason while it fails to nourish the Christian imagination.

Tulloch's historical approach to all credal formularies is, of course, only one aspect of his tendency to view a very wide range of questions, and particularly Biblical ones, from the historical angle. This tendency, which crops up at many points in *Movements of Religious Thought*, reveals him as sharing in – and helping to spread – a mood which had begun to establish its ascendancy over the cultivated intellect of Britain round about the middle of the century. It was a mood which, to use a phrase from Noel Annan's essay in the G. M. Trevelyan festschrift, *Studies in Social History*, inclined men to view Truth "no longer as absolute, philosophically static, revealed once for all, but as relative, genetic and evolutionary"; and for theology its implications were tremendous. If Tulloch did not see all of them, he at least saw some; and his book is the more valuable in consequence.

Hatred of 'bibliolatry' and a modest confidence in the methods of Biblical Criticism. Few things annoyed Tulloch more than what he called "subjective criticism" – meaning by this an essentially unsympathetic and hypercritical attitude to the Bible. Such criticism, he declared in his introductory lecture at St Andrews in 1864, "partakes of the very spirit of unbelief – the spirit, namely, which refuses to recognise a Divine revelation at all – sets its own light against the light of God, its own reason against the divine reason in Scripture." Yet even here his essential moderation shows itself, for he never falls into the opposite error of 'bibliolatry', never asserts the absolute identity of the Bible with the Word of God. Although he can affirm that "The fact of an objective revelation, and that Scripture contains such a revelation, are primary and constitutive facts of Christianity", he nevertheless also contends that "not only does Christianity not dread – it demands, as a condition of its higher intelligent life, that the several books of Scripture, as the successive media of

Divine revelation through a long series of ages, should be minutely investigated, tested and proved by all the aids of criticism, and by all the growing light of the Christian consciousness." He counsels us, moreover, to learn to distinguish between the Divine revelation in Scripture on the one hand and our inherited beliefs, prejudices and conceits on the other. This relaxed attitude towards the literary and historical approach to Scripture – this belief, as he put it, that "the Christian reason must have room to work" – is clearly evident in *Movements of Religious Thought*. It appears not only in the approval given to Coleridge's liberal views on the subject but also in the complimentary references made to the exegetical labours of Dean Stanley and Benjamin Jowett. "From this time", he says of the year 1855, when both these men published commentaries on Pauline epistles, "has greatly advanced that profounder study of the New Testament, which looks beyond its traditional to its real aspects and its organic relation to contemporary usage and opinion – which sees in it a living literature, and not a mere repertory of doctrinal texts. . . . The text of Scripture has been studied in its own meaning, and not in support of dogmas which were the growth of long after centuries, and would have been wholly unintelligible to the writers credited with them. The spirit has been liberated from the letter, and the very form and pressure of divine truth as originally presented to the world brought near to us." Crudities and inconsistencies notwithstanding, this is a view which would still, nearly a century later, commend itself to a high proportion of theological scholars – which suggests that in reading Tulloch we not only survey the religious thought of a bygone period but also glimpse the shape of theologies yet to come.

Desire to distinguish between theology and religion. In text and title alike, Tulloch's Crathie sermon of 1875 on *Religion and Theology* makes a distinction which occurs and recurs throughout his writings, not least in the *Movements of Religious Thought.* He would not (so he tells his hearers) have them despise or disparage theology. But he wishes them to remember that the welfare of the soul is not determined by theology and its problems: "the antiquity of man, the age and genesis of the earth, the origin and authority of the several books of Scripture." These matters have to be dealt with, admittedly, and in dealing with them there is available to us "no light but the dry light of knowledge"; yet the satisfaction of our spiritual requirements need not await their solution:

> Because I cannot be sure whether the Pentateuch was written, as long supposed, by Moses, or whether the Fourth Gospel comes as it stands from the beloved apostle, am I less in need of the divine teaching which both these Scriptures contain? Surely not. That I am a spiritual being, and have spiritual needs craving to be satisfied, and that God is a spiritual power above me, of whom Christ is the revelation, are facts which I may know or may not know, irrespective of such matters. The one class of facts are intellectual and literary. The other are spiritual if they exist at all. If I ever know them, I can only know them through my own spiritual experience; but if I know them . . . I have within me all the genuine forces of religious strength and peace. I may not have all the faith of the Church. I may have many doubts, and may come far short of the catholic dogma. But faith is a progressive insight, and dogma is a variable factor.

Better than all theological definitions, therefore, is " 'the honest and good heart' which (in the Gospel phrase) 'having heard the Word, keeps it, and brings forth fruit with patience.' " And so his last word on this matter is a summons to rigorous inquiry on the theological level, together with quiet receptivity on the religious level:

> I have no ready answers to your questions, no short and easy method with modern scepticism. Inquiry must have its course in theology as in everything else. It is fatal to intelligence to talk of an infallible Church, and of all free thought in reference to religion as deadly rationalism to be shunned. . . . You must examine your own hearts; you must try yourselves whether there be in you the roots of the divine life. If you do not find sin in your hearts and Christ also there as the Saviour from sin, then you will find Him nowhere. But if you find Him there . . . then you will accept difficulties and doubts, and even the despairing darkness of some intellectual moments, when the very foundations seem to give way, as you accept your other trials; and, looking humbly for higher light, you will patiently wait for it, until the day dawn and the shadows flee away.

There are echoes here not only of Tulloch's beloved Caroline Divines, but also of the views of Coleridge and F. D. Maurice and (still more) of F. W. Robertson and Thomas Erskine.

Those readers of *Movements of Religious Thought* who come by stages to the conclusion that this is something more than a work of unimpassioned scholarship – that it is, in fact, a manifesto as well as a treatise – are surely right. Written by one who was almost equally at home in the courts of the Church and the councils of the University, the offices of city editors and the smoking-rooms of London clubs, its pages are marked not only by an interest in the past but by an eager involvement in the concerns of the present; and its author frequently makes plain his conviction that the story of bygone phases of thought has an urgent message for the men of his own time. What that message was we have already seen. It is, above all else, a summons to humility of spirit and receptivity of mind. Change, Tulloch constantly asseverates, is always at work in the affairs of men, even where the most apparently immutable attitudes or systems are concerned, and in the world of the intellect to be immobile is to be dead. Let us, therefore, be prepared to abandon old shibboleths and to welcome new insights; and let dogmatists – especially Scottish ones! – never forget that God's truth is larger than their imperfect notions of it and that "the movements of Christian thought are for this very end, that we may prove all things and hold fast that which is good." Or as he puts it in the very last sentences of the book:

> What we perhaps all need most to learn is not satisfaction with our opinions – that is easily acquired by most – but the capacity of looking beyond our own horizon; of searching for deeper foundations of our ordinary beliefs, and a more sympathetic appreciation of the beliefs of others. While cherishing, therefore, what we ourselves feel to be true, let us keep our minds open to all truth, and especially to the teaching of Him who is 'the Way, the Truth and the Life'.

But the quasi-missionary fervour which Tulloch brings to the pursuit of his researches and the advocacy of his conclusions should not be allowed to distract us from

the scholarly worth of his achievement as a whole. Shrewd
and sensitive in his observation of the religious world of
his time, fair and lucid in his exposition of its characteristic
beliefs and attitudes, we could hardly wish for a more
sympathetic or better-informed guide to a period whose
importance is seldom questioned but whose animating
spirit often seems to elude us; and there is not a chapter
in this deceptively simple and unpretentious volume but
will assist our comprehension or stimulate our interest
by its exposure of unsuspected relationships, its grasp of
unperceived unities, its penetration (in discussing many a
system of thought) to "the very pulse of the machine",
its wide familiarity not only with the philosophy and theology of the early Victorian age, but with its literature and
social history as well. We have already noted how sharp
an eye Tulloch has for the really significant men and
movements in the epoch with which he set himself to deal,
how deft he is in tracing affinities or highlighting incom-
patibilities, how adept at discriminating between the
superficial and the fundamental in a person or a programme,
how quick to perceive the essential features, the temper
and the atmosphere of an age, how skilled in combining
the arts of biography and historical analysis. After nearly
ninety years, his modest little volume has worn much
better than many more immediately prepossessing studies
(one thinks, for example, of Lytton Strachey's *Eminent
Victorians* or Donald Carswell's *Brother Scots*); and it
looks like wearing almost equally well over the next
few decades. In the amusingly fulsome dedication to
Mrs Oliphant which is prefixed to the original edition of
the book, we read as follows: "I know of no writer to
whose large powers, spiritual insight and purity of thought,
and subtle discrimination of many of the best aspects of

our social life and character, our generation owes so much as it does to you." Without much alteration, and with greater justice, these words might well be applied to the author of *Movements of Religious Thought in Britain during the Nineteenth Century*, John Tulloch himself.

A. C. Cheyne
Edinburgh, March 1971

BIBLIOGRAPHICAL NOTE

Movements of Religious Thought in Britain during the Nineteenth Century, by John Tulloch, was published in London by Longmans, Green, & Co. in 1885. No subsequent edition or reprint of the work has ever been published. The present volume reprints photographically the whole of the 1885 text.

J. L. Madden

MOVEMENTS OF

RELIGIOUS THOUGHT IN BRITAIN

DURING THE NINETEENTH CENTURY

BEING THE FIFTH SERIES OF ST. GILES' LECTURES

BY

JOHN TULLOCH, D.D., LL.D.

SENIOR PRINCIPAL IN THE UNIVERSITY OF ST. ANDREWS

LONDON

LONGMANS, GREEN, & CO.

1885

TO

Mrs. OLIPHANT,

AUTHOR OF ' THE CHRONICLES OF CARLINGFORD,' ' A BELEAGUERED
CITY,' ' LIFE OF EDWARD IRVING,' ' THE LITERARY HISTORY OF
ENGLAND, 1790-1825,' ETC.

My dear Mrs. Oliphant,

It is a great pleasure to me to be allowed to associate your name with these Lectures. Slight as they are, I have been reminded more than once, during their preparation, of a large subject which used to engage our discussion many years ago, and in the treatment of which you were to bear what would have proved by far the most interesting part. This, like many other projects, is not now likely to be attempted; but the thought of it has brought you and our long friendship much to my mind.

If I were to express all the admiration I feel for your genius, and still more all the esteem I have learned to cherish for your character, I should use language which I know you would refuse to read; but I may at least be allowed to say thus publicly, that I know of no writer to whose large powers, spiritual insight, and purity of thought, and subtle discrimination of many of the best aspects of our social life and character, our generation owes so much as it does to you.

Always faithfully yours,

JOHN TULLOCH.

University, St. Andrews,
August 1885.

CONTENTS.

LECTURE I.

COLERIDGE AND HIS SCHOOL.

LECTURE II.

THE EARLY ORIEL SCHOOL AND ITS CONGENERS.

LECTURE III.

THE OXFORD OR ANGLO-CATHOLIC MOVEMENT.

Contents.

LECTURE IV.

MOVEMENT OF RELIGIOUS THOUGHT IN SCOTLAND.

LECTURE V.

THOMAS CARLYLE AS A RELIGIOUS TEACHER.

LECTURE VI.

JOHN STUART MILL AND HIS SCHOOL.

LECTURE VII.

F. D. MAURICE AND CHARLES KINGSLEY.

LECTURE VIII.

F. W. ROBERTSON AND BISHOP EWING.

Contents.

MOVEMENTS

OF

RELIGIOUS THOUGHT.

1820-60.

ST. GILES' LECTURES—FIFTH SERIES.

I.

COLERIDGE AND HIS SCHOOL.

I HAVE undertaken to give in a course of eight lectures some account of the Movements of Religious Thought in our country during the present century. As the subject is in any view a large one, and presents many aspects, it is important at the outset to indicate its exact character and the limits within which I propose to treat it.

Our subject then is the Movements of Religious Thought—not of Religion—within the century. Religion is a wide word, with some meanings of which we have nothing to do. The expression 'Religious Thought' may be also more or less widely interpreted; but on any interpretation it leaves outside much belonging to religion and its life and movement in the world. It leaves outside, for example, not only the large field of practical Christian action, but also that of ecclesiastical and politico-ecclesiastical parties. With these, properly speaking, we have nothing to do. It is only when their *motif* or spirit, as in the Oxford movement, is inextricably intertwined with impulses of new or revived thought, that we touch upon them.

A movement of religious thought implies the rise of some fresh life within the sphere of such thought—some new wave of opinion either within the Church, or deeply affecting it from without, modifying its past conceptions. It is a moulding influence, leaving behind it definite traces, and working its way more or less into the national consciousness, so that this consciousness remains affected even if the movement itself disappears. It is this character which gives significance to our subject, and will be found to lend to it interest for all who are really concerned with religious questions and the progress of higher civilisation.

Thus definite in subject, our lectures are limited locally. The movements of which I am to speak are movements within our country alone. The large field of Continental criticism and speculation in matters of religion is not before us, although it may be impossible at times to refrain from stretching our view towards it.

Further, our lectures run within definite chronological limits; and this claims particular notice. They have nothing to do with the last twenty-five years, or immediately preceding generation. They only reach to 1860 at the utmost, about which time a marked change took place in the current of philosophical and religious speculation, a change which may generally, and for our present purpose, be indicated by the word now so common—Evolution. New schools of thought have arisen in all directions, in philosophy, ethics, and theology, more or less affected by the idea which this word denotes. But all these schools in the meantime are beyond our scope. It was undesirable to attempt to embrace a more extended field within one course of lectures ; and my only fear is that the course will be found not too limited, but too diversified and ample. From Coleridge to John Stuart Mill, from Newman to Maurice, from Carlyle to Kingsley and Frederick Robertson, carries us so wide afield that we shall have to complain not of lack of material, but of an embarrassment of rich material.

The interest and importance of the subject can hardly be doubted by any who understand it. The movements of religious thought in our own country lie at least very close to us and the life and work of all our churches. We cannot escape the influence of those movements whatever be our own position. Even those who most disown all connection with modern Thought are sometimes found strongly reflecting its influences,—more frequently perhaps mistaking its real meaning. It seems to be the duty therefore of all intelligent persons to try in some degree to understand the impulses moving their time. Such and such opinions, it is often said, are 'in the air.' The thought of our own time, in its evolving phases or folds of varied hue, bathes us like an atmosphere. It wraps us round, penetrating often to our inmost sentiments. A certain class of minds remain indifferent,—secure within their well-worn armour of traditionary prejudgment. Another class is apt to be carried away altogether, and lose their old moorings. But religious thought is happily not at the

mercy of either of these classes.   Rightly viewed, it is
typified neither by tradition nor revolution.   It is a
continuous power in human life and history, moving
onwards with the ever accumulating growths of human
knowledge and of spiritual experience ; ever new yet
old ; linking age to age, it is to be hoped, in happier
and more benign intelligence.

Let me further say that I do not mean to charac-
terise what may be right or wrong in these movements.
I only venture to describe them, and set them fairly
before you as I myself understand them.   Particularly
my aim will be to show in a purely historical spirit
how naturally they connect themselves with one
another, and so far explain each other and themselves in the circumstances of their rise and course.
I do not myself believe in movements of thought
brought about by man's device, nor in the application of such commonplaces as 'orthodox' and
'heterodox' to the description of such movements.
I believe in the continuous movement of the Divine
Spirit enlarging, correcting, and modifying human
opinion.

We speak of the eighteenth and nineteenth centuries
as marking distinct phases of thought ; but we have
to remember that such classifications are conventional and so far inapplicable.   The intellectual revival
particularly identified with our century had begun
before the close of the last century, and it was not
till twenty years after our era commenced that any
new movement can be traced in the sphere of
religious thought.   The flush of new insight and
passion, arising from the larger and closer study of

Nature and Humanity born of the French Revolution, poured itself forth in poetry long before the larger and intenser spirit of the time showed itself in other directions. It may be said that Wordsworth gave voice to a higher thought not only about nature but about religion. The 'Solitary among the Mountains' is a preacher and not only a singer. He goes to the heart of religion and lays anew its foundation in the natural instincts of man. But while the poetry both of Wordsworth and Coleridge was instinct with a new life of religious feeling, and may be said to have given a new radiancy to its central principles,[1] it did not initiate any distinctive movement. In religious opinions Wordsworth soon fell back upon, if he ever consciously departed from, the old lines of Anglican tradition. The vague pantheism of the 'Excursion' implies rather a lack of distinctive dogma than any fresh insight into religious problems or capacity of co-ordinating them in a new manner. And so soon as the need of definite religious conceptions came to the poet, the Church in her customary theology became his satisfactory refuge. The 'Ecclesiastical Sonnets' mark this definite stage in his spiritual development. Wordsworth did for the religious thought of his time something more and better perhaps than giving it any definite impulse. While leaving it in the old channels he gave it a richer and deeper volume. He showed with what vital affinity religion cleaves to humanity in all its true and simple phases when uncontaminated by conceit or frivolity. Nature and man alike were to him essentially religious, or only conceivable as the out-

[1] 'Admiration, Hope, and Love.' See *The Excursion*, B. IV.

come of a Spirit of Life, 'the Soul of all the worlds.'[1]
Wordsworth in short remained, as he began, a poet.
He did not enter into the sphere of religious thought
or busy himself with its issues.

Coleridge's career presents a marked contrast to
that of his friend. He may be said to have abandoned poetry just when Wordsworth in his quiet settlement at Grasmere (1799) was consecrating his life to it.
Fellows in quickening the poetic revival of their time,
they were soon widely separated in life and pursuit.
Whether it be true, according to De Quincey, that
Coleridge's poetical power was killed by the habit of
opium-eating, it is certainly true that 'the harp of
Quantock'[2] was never again struck save for a brief
moment. The poet Coleridge passed into the lecturer, and political and literary critic, and then,
during the final period of his life, from 1816 to 1834,
into the philosopher and theologian. It is this latter
period of his life that alone concerns us.

I need not say how differently Coleridge has been
estimated as a religious thinker. Carlyle's caricature
of the Sage as he sat 'on the brow of Highgate
Hill' in those years,[3] is known to all ; and a severely

---

[1] *The Excursion*, B. IX.

[2] Not only the *Ancient Mariner* and the first part of *Christabel*, but
also *Kubla Khan* were composed at Nether Stowey among the Quantock
Hills in 1797. The second part of *Christabel* belongs to the year
1800, and was written at Keswick, although not published till 1816.
Nothing of the same quality was ever produced by Coleridge, although
he continued to write verses.

[3] The value of Carlyle's description may now be judged more fairly
in the light of his own Life and Letters, and the indiscriminate and
savage assaults which he has made on so many reputations. 'It may be
found,' said a reviewer of the *Life of John Sterling* in the *North British
Review*, Feb. 1852, with a prescient insight too unhappily realised by

critical, but, as we must judge, superficial estimate
has been lately given by Mr. Traill in the series
of ' English Men of Letters.' Our business is not
so much to attempt any criticism of the value of
Coleridge's thought as to describe it as a new power.
That it was such a power is beyond all question.
It is not merely the testimony of such men as Archdeacon Hare and John Sterling, of Newman and
of John Stuart Mill, but it is the fact that the
later streams of religious thought in England are
all more or less coloured by his influence. They
flow in deeper and different channels since he lived.
Not only are some of those streams directly traceable to him, and said to derive all their vitality
from his principles, but those which are most opposed
to him have been moulded more or less by the impress of his religious genius. There was much in
the man Coleridge himself to provoke animadver-
sion; there may have been aspects of his teaching
that lend themselves to ridicule ; but if a genius,
seminal as his has been in the world of thought and
of criticism as well as poetry, is not to excite our
reverence, there is little that remains for us to reverence in the intellectual world. And when literature
regains the higher tone of our earlier national life,
the tone of Hooker and of Milton, Samuel Taylor
Coleridge will be again acknowledged, in Julius

Mr. Froude's biographic labours, ' It may be found when the secrets of
another Sanctuary are unveiled, that if there was not much " pious "
or " partly courteous snuffle " in the discourse there, there was yet in
plenty " a confused unintelligible flood of utterance threatening to
swamp all known land-marks of thought and drown the world and us "
—a vast vituperative commotion which made noise in the ear without
bringing much light or life to the heart.'

Hare's words, as 'a true sovereign of English thought.' He will take rank in the same line of spiritual genius. He has the same elevation of feeling, the same profound grasp of moral and spiritual ideas, the same wide range of vision. He has in short the same love of wisdom, the same insight, the same largeness—never despising nature, or art, or literature for the sake of religion, still less ever despising religion for the sake of culture. In reading over Coleridge's prose works again, especially his *Aids to Reflection*, and his *Confessions of an Inquiring Spirit*,—returning to them after a long past familiarity, —I am particularly struck with their massive and large intellectuality, akin to our older Elizabethan literature. There is a constant play of great power, of imagination as well as reason, of spiritual insight as well as logical subtlety.

To speak of Coleridge as an eminently healthy writer in the higher regions of thought may seem absurd to some who think mainly of his life, and the fatal failure which characterised it. It is the shadow of this failure of manliness in his conduct, as in that of his lifelong friend Charles Lamb, which no doubt prompted the great genius who carried manliness, if little sweetness, from his Annandale home, to paint both the one and the other in such darkened colours. We have not a word to say on behalf of the failings of either. They were deplorable and unworthy ; but it is the fact notwithstanding that the minds of both retained a serenity and a certain touch of respectfulness which are lacking in their Scottish cotemporary. They were both finer-edged than Carlyle. They inherited a more delicate and polite personal culture ;

and delicacy can never be far distant from true manliness. Neither of them could have written of the treasures of old religion as Carlyle did in his Life of Sterling; whether they accepted for themselves these treasures or not, they would have spared the tender faith of others, and respected an ancient Ideal. And be sure, this is the higher attitude. Nothing which has ever deeply interested humanity, or profoundly moved it, is treated with contempt by a wise and good man. It may call for and deserve rejection, but never insult. Unhappily this attitude of mind, reserved as well as critical, reverent as well as bold, has been conspicuously absent in some of the most powerful and best-known writers of our era.

The *Aids to Reflection* summon us, both by title and contents, to thoughtfulness. It is a book which none but a thinker on Divine things will ever like. It is such a book as all such thinkers have prized. To many it has given a new force of religious insight, while for its time, beyond all doubt, it created a real epoch in Christian thought. It did this certainly not from any merits as a literary composition, for it is fragmentary throughout; and the thought of the volume is nowhere wrought into a complete system. But it had life in it; and the living seed, scattered and desultory as it was, brought forth fruit in many minds.

The Evangelical movement, which in the last century kindled so many hearts, and wrought such living Christian energy in many lives, survived into the present century under the vigorous guidance of Wilberforce and Simeon of Cambridge. It was still active, living, and powerful, although it had lost its first freshness. Nor was the Anglican tradition, as personified in men like Keble, so weak as has been sometimes assumed. There was more quiet and effective religion throughout the land than our generalisations sometimes allow ; witness, for example, among the Unitarians such a man as Frederick Maurice's father. There was, however, a lack of earnest movement save in the Evangelical direction. The testimony of Newman in England, the career of Chalmers in Scotland, may be held as evidence of this. From the Evangelical Succession—Wilberforce on the one side, and Romaine and Thomas Scott on the other—came the first impulses which in the second decade of our century moved these great minds. Evangelicalism was, in short, the only type of aggressive religion then, or for some time, prevailing, although its aggressiveness was more of a practical than of an intellectual kind. Intellectually there was little or no directing power in the sphere of religion. In the course of the next fifteen years, or onwards from 1810 to 1830, there sprang up a great variety of new influences : Whately and Arnold in England, Thomas Erskine in Scotland, Newman and the whole Anglo-Catholic host some years later. We shall have occasion to advert to all. But the movement which sprang from Coleridge claims our first attention. It stands upon the whole in advance of the others. It has been the most fertile and pervasive. All the other movements may be said to have borrowed more or less from Coleridge. Whatever he borrowed was from Germany, or from long-past sources of our own literature.

What, then, were the characteristics of the Coleridgian movement? In what respects is it true that Coleridge gave a definite impulse to the religious thought of his time? In three respects, as it appears to us: 1*st*, by a renovation of current Christian ideas; 2*dly*, by an advance in Biblical study; and, 3*dly*, by an enlarged conception of the Church.

(1.) Coleridge, we know, was a man of many ambitions never realised; but of all his ambitions, the most persistent was that of laying anew the foundations of spiritual philosophy. This was 'the great work' to which he frequently alluded as having given 'the preparation of more than twenty years of his life.'[1] Like other great tasks projected by him, it was very imperfectly accomplished; and there will always be those in consequence who fail to understand his influence as a leader of thought. We are certainly not bound to take Coleridge at his own value, nor to attach the same importance as he did to some of his speculations. He failed to do justice to them in more senses than one. Nor can Mr. Green's volumes, reverent and studious as they are, be taken in place of an adequate exposition by the author himself. His more abstract speculations, we confess, do not much interest us. It has indeed been said that Coleridge's speculative philosophy lies at the foundation of all his theology.[2] This may be so; to a large extent it is so; but no one knew better than Coleridge himself that there was nothing new in his Platonic

---

[1] *Spiritual Philosophy, founded on the Teaching of the late Samuel Taylor Coleridge.* By Jos. Henry Green, F.R.S., D.C.L. 1865.

[2] This idea is elaborated in a clever, but somewhat narrow book, *Modern Anglican Theology*, by the Rev. James H. Rigg. 1857.

realism. It was merely a restoration of the old religious metaphysic which had preceded 'the mechanical systems,'[1] which became dominant in the reign of Charles the Second. He himself constantly claims to do nothing more than re-assert the principles of Hooker, of Henry More, of John Smith, and Leighton, all of whom he speaks of as 'Platonizing divines!' But the religious teaching of Coleridge came upon his generation as a new breath, not merely or mainly because he revived these ancient principles, but because he vitalised anew their application to Christianity, so as to transform it from a mere creed, or collection of articles, into a living mode of thought, embracing all human activity.

Coleridge is misjudged when looked upon as a mere theosophic dreamer or ontologist. His Transcendentalism, borrowed from Kant and Schelling, his famous distinction of the Reason and the Understanding, his speculative analysis of the Trinitarian idea, are not without their significance ; but these were not the factors that made his teaching influential. Coleridge was no mere metaphysician. He was a great interpreter of spiritual facts—a student of spiritual life, quickened by a peculiarly vivid and painful experience ; and he saw in Christianity, rightly conceived, at once the true explanation of the facts of our spiritual being, and the true remedy for their disorder. He brought human nature, in all the breadth of its activities, once more near to Christianity, and found in the latter not merely a means of salvation in any limited evangelical sense, but the highest Truth and Health—a perfect Philosophy. His main power

[1] See particularly his own statement.

lay in this subjective direction, just as here it was
that his age was most needing stimulus and guidance.

The Evangelical School, with all its merits, had
conceived of Christianity rather as something super-
added to the highest life of humanity than as the
perfect development of that life ; as a scheme for
human salvation authenticated by miracles, and, so
to speak, interpolated into human history rather
than a divine philosophy, witnessing to itself from the
beginning in all the higher phases of that history. And
so Philosophy, and no less Literature, and Art, and
Science, were conceived apart from religion. The
world and the Church were not only antagonistic in
the biblical sense, as the embodiments of the Carnal
and the Divine Spirit—which they must ever be ; but
they were, so to speak, severed portions of life divided
by outward signs and badges ; and those who joined
the one or the other were supposed to be clearly
marked off. All who know the writings of the Evangelical School of the eighteenth and earlier part of
the nineteenth century, from the poetry of Cowper
and the letters of his friend Newton, to the writings
of Romaine, John Foster, and Wilberforce, and
even Chalmers, will know how such commonplaces
everywhere reappear in them. That they were
associated with the most devout and beautiful lives,
that they even served to foster a peculiar ardour
of Christian feeling and love of God, cannot be
disputed. But they were essentially narrow and
false. They destroyed the largeness and unity of
human experience. They not merely separated
religion from art and philosophy, but they tended to
separate it from morality.

Coleridge's most distinctive work was to restore the broken harmony between reason and religion, by enlarging the conception of both, but of the latter especially,—by showing how man is essentially a religious being having a definite spiritual constitution, apart from which the very idea of religion becomes impossible.   Religion is not therefore something brought to man ; it is his highest education. Religion, he says, was designed 'to improve the nature and faculties of man, in order to the right governing of our actions, to the securing the peace and progress, external and internal, of individuals and of communities.'[1]   Christianity is in the highest degree adapted to this end ; and nothing can be a part of it that is not duly proportioned thereto.

In thus vindicating the rationality of religion, Coleridge had a twofold task before him as every such thinker has.   He had to assert against the Epicurean and Empirical School the spiritual constitution of human nature, and against the fanatical or hyper-evangelical school the reasonable working of spiritual influence.   He had to maintain, on the one hand, the essential divinity of man, that 'there is more in him than can be rationally referred to the life of nature and the mechanism of organisation,' and on the other hand to show that this higher life of the spirit is throughout rational—that it is superstition and not true religion which professes to resolve 'men's faith and practice' into the illumination of such a spirit as they can give no account of,—such as does not enlighten their reason or enable them to render their doctrine intelligible to others.   He fights, in short,

[1] *Aids to Reflection* (ed. 1848), vol. i. p. 143.

alike against materialistic negation and credulous enthusiasm.

The former he meets with the assertion of 'a spirituality in man,'—a self-power or Will at the root of all his being. ' If there be ought spiritual in man, the will must be such. If there be a will, there must be a spirituality in man.' He assumes both positions, seeing clearly—what all who radically deal with such a question must see—that it becomes in the end an alternative postulate on one side and the other. The theologian cannot prove his case, because the very terms in which it must be proved are already denied *ab initio* by the materialist. But no more can the materialist, for the same reason, refute the spiritual thinker. There can be no argument where no common premiss is granted. Coleridge was quite alive to this, yet he validly appeals to common experience. ' I assume,' he says, 'a something the proof of which no man can give to another, yet every man may find for himself. If any man assert that he has no such experience, I am bound to disbelieve him, I cannot do otherwise without unsettling the foundation of my own moral nature. For I either find it as an essential of the humanity common to him and to me, or I have not found it at all. . . . All the significant objections of the materialist and necessitarian,' he adds, ' are contained in the term morality, and all the objections of the infidel in the term religion. These very terms imply something granted, which the objector in each case supposes not granted. A moral philosophy is only such because it assumes a principle of morality, a will, in man, and so a Christian philosophy or theology has its own assumptions resting on three ultimate facts, namely, the reality of the law of conscience; the existence of a responsible will as the subject of that law; and lastly, the existence of God.' . . . 'The first is a fact of consciousness; the second, a fact of reason necessarily concluded from the first; and the third, a fact of history interpreted by both.'

These were the radical data of the religious philosophy of Coleridge. They imply a general conception of religion which was revolutionary for his age, simple and ancient as the principles are. The evangelical tradition brought religion to man from the outside. It took no concern of man's spiritual constitution beyond the fact that he was a sinner and in danger of hell. Coleridge started from a similar but larger experience, including not only sin, but the whole spiritual basis on which sin rests. 'I profess a deep conviction,' he says, 'that man is a fallen creature,' 'not by accident of bodily constitution or any other cause, but as diseased in his will—in that will which is the true and only strict synonyme of the word I, or the intelligent Self.' This 'intelligent self' is a fundamental conception lying at the root of his system of thought. Sin is an attribute of it, and cannot be conceived apart from it, and conscience, or the original sense of right and wrong, governing the will. Apart from these internal realities there is no religion, and the function of the Christian Revelation is to build up the spiritual life out of these realities—to remedy the evil, to enlighten the conscience, to educate the will. This effective power of religion comes directly from God in Christ.

Here Coleridge joins the Evangelical School, as

indeed every school of living Christian Faith. This was the element of truth he found in the doctrine of Election as handled 'practically, morally, humanly,' by Leighton. Every true Christian, he argues, must attribute his distinction not in any degree to himself —'his own resolves and strivings,' 'his own will and understanding,' still less to 'his own comparative excellence,'—but to God, 'the Being in whom the promise of life originated, and on whom its fulfilment depends.' Election so far is a truth of experience. 'This the conscience requires; this the highest interests of morality demand.' So far it is a question of facts with which the speculative reason has nothing to do. But when the theological reasoner abandons the ground of fact and 'the safe circle of religion and practical reason for the shifting sandwastes and mirages of speculative theology'—then he uses words without meaning. He can have no insight into the workings or plans of a Being who is neither an object of his senses nor a part of his self-consciousness.

Nothing can show better than this brief exposition how closely Coleridge in his theology clung to a base of spiritual experience, and sought to measure even the most abstruse Christian mysteries by facts. The same thing may be shown by referring to his doctrine of the Trinity, which has been supposed the most transcendental and, so to speak, 'Neo-Platonist' of all his doctrines. But truly speaking his Trinitarianism like his doctrine of Election is a moral rather than a speculative truth. The Trinitarian idea was indeed **true** to him notionally. The full analysis of the notion 'God' seemed to him to involve it. 'I find a certain notion in my mind, and say that is what I understand by the term God. From books and conversation I find that the learned generally connect the same notion with the same word. I then apply the rules laid down by the masters of logic for the involution and evolution of terms, and prove (to as many as agree with my premisses) that the notion "God" involves the notion "Trinity."' So he argued, and many times recurred to the same Transcendental analysis. But the truer and more urgent spiritual basis of the doctrine of the Trinity, even to his own mind, was not its notional but its moral necessity. Christ could only be a Saviour as being Divine. Salvation is a Divine work. 'The idea of Redemption involves belief in the Divinity of our Lord. And our Lord's Divinity again involves the Trinitarian idea, because in and through this idea alone the Divinity of Christ can be received without breach of faith in the Unity of the Godhead.' In other words, the best evidence of the doctrine of the Trinity is the compulsion of the spiritual conscience which demands a Divine Saviour; and only in and through the great idea of Trinity in Unity does this demand become consistent with Christian Monotheism.[1]

These doctrines are merely used in illustration, as they are by Coleridge himself in his *Aids to Reflec-*

---

[1] This was a favourite thought with Coleridge, as, for example, in his *Literary Remains* (vol. i. pp. 393-4) :—' The Trinity of Persons in the Unity of the Godhead would have been a necessary idea of my speculative reason. God must have had co-eternally an adequate idea of Himself in and through which He created all things. But this would have been a mere speculative idea. *Solely in consequence of our redemption* does the Trinity become a doctrine, the belief of which as real is commanded by conscience.'

tion. We do not dwell upon them. But nothing can show in a stronger light the general character of the change which he wrought in the conception of Christianity. From being a mere traditional creed, with Anglican and Evangelical, and it may be added Unitarian, alike, it became a living expression of the spiritual consciousness. In a sense, of course, it had always been so. The Evangelical made much of its living power, but only in a practical and not in a rational sense. It is the distinction of Coleridge to have once more in his age made Christian doctrine alive to the Reason as well as the Conscience,— tenable as a philosophy as well as an evangel. And this he did by interpreting Christianity in the light of our moral and spiritual life. There are aspects of Christian truth beyond us. *Exeunt in mysteria.* But all Christian truth must have vital touch with our spiritual being, and be so far at least capable of being rendered in its terms, or, in other words, be conformable to reason.

There was nothing absolutely new in this luminous conception ; but it marked a revolution of religious thought in the earlier part of our century. The great principle of the Evangelical Theology was that theological dogmas were true or false without any reference to a subjective standard of judgment. They were true as pure data of Revelation, or as the propositions of an authorised creed settled long ago. Reason had, so far, nothing to do with them. Christian truth, it was supposed, lay at hand in the Bible, an appeal to which settled everything. Coleridge did not undervalue the Bible. He gave it an intelligent reverence. But he no less reverenced the spiritual consciousness or Divine light in man, and to put out this light, as the Evangelical had gone far to do, was to destroy all reasonable faith. This must rest not merely on objective data, but on internal experience. It must have not merely authority without, but rationale within. It must answer to the highest aspiration of human reason, as well as the most urgent necessities of human life. It must interpret reason and find expression in the voice of our higher humanity, and so enlarge itself as to meet all its needs.

If we turn for a moment to the special exposition of the doctrines of Sin and Redemption which Coleridge has given in the *Aids to Reflection*, it is still mainly with the view of bringing out more clearly his general conception of Christianity as a living movement of thought rather than a mere series of articles or a traditionary creed.

In dealing first with the question of sin he shows how its very idea is only tenable on the ground of such a spiritual constitution in man as he has already asserted. It is only the recognition of a true will in man—a spirit or supernatural in man, although 'not necessarily miraculous,'—which renders sin possible. ' These views of the spirit and of the will as spiritual,' he says more than once, ' are the groundwork of my scheme.' There was nothing more significant or fundamental in all his theology. If there is not always a supernatural element in man in the shape of spirit and will, no miracles or anything else can ever authenticate the supernatural to him. A mere formal orthodoxy, therefore, hanging upon the evidence of miracles, is a suspension bridge without any real support. So all questions between Infidelity and Christianity are questions here at the root, and not what are called 'critical' questions as to whether this or that view of the Bible be right, or this or that traditionary dogma be true. Such questions are truly speaking inter-Christian questions, the freest views of which all churches must learn to tolerate. The really vital question is whether there is a divine root in man at all—a spiritual centre answering to a higher spiritual centre in the universe. All controversies of any importance come back to this. Coleridge would have been a great Christian thinker if for no other reason than this, that he brought all theological problems back to this living centre, and showed how they diverged from it. Apart from this postulate, sin was inconceivable to him; and in the same manner all sin was to him sin of origin or 'original sin.' It is the essential property of the will that it can originate. The phrase original sin is therefore 'a pleonasm.' If sin was not original, or from within the will itself, it would not deserve the name. 'A state or act that has not its origin in the will may be a calamity, deformity, disease, or mischief; but a sin it cannot be.'

We may be pardoned for adducing a still longer illustration of his mode of argument. 'A moral evil is an evil that has its origin in a will. An evil common to all must have a ground common to all. But the actual existence of moral evil we are bound in conscience to admit; and that there is an evil common to all is a fact, and this evil must therefore have a common ground. Now this evil ground cannot originate in the Divine will; it must therefore be referred to the will of man. And this evil ground we call original sin. It is a mystery, that is a fact which we see but cannot explain, and the doctrine a truth which we apprehend, but can neither comprehend nor communicate. And such by the quality of the subject (namely, a responsible will) it must be, if it be truth at all.'

This inwardness is no less characteristic of Coleridge's treatment of the doctrine of Atonement or Redemption. It is intelligible so far as it comes within the range of spiritual experience, just as the doctrine of sin is. So far, its nature and effects are amply described or figured in the New Testament, especially by St. Paul. And the apostle's language, as might be expected, 'takes its predominant colours from his own experience, and the experience of those whom he addressed.' 'His figures, images, analogies, and references,' are all more or less borrowed from this source. He describes the Atonement of Christ under four principal metaphors :—1. Sin-offerings, sacrificial expiation. 2. Reconciliation, atonement, καταλλαγή. 3. Redemption, or ransom from slavery. 4. Satisfaction, payment of a debt. These phrases are not designed to convey to us all the Divine meaning of the Atonement, for no phrases or figures can do this; but they set forth its general aspects and design in so far as we, no less than the Jews and Greeks of the time, are interested in the doctrine. One and all they have an intelligible relation to our spiritual life, and so clothe the doctrine for us with a concrete living and practical meaning. But there are other relations and aspects of the doctrine of Atonement that transcend experience, and consequently our powers of understanding. And all that can be said here is, *Exit in mysteria.* The rationalism of Coleridge is at least a modest and self-limiting rationalism. It clears the ground within the range of spiritual experience, and floods this ground with the light of reason. There is no true doctrine that can contradict this light, or shelter itself from its penetration. But there are aspects of Christian doctrine that outreach all grasp of reason, and before which reason must simply be silent. For example, the Divine Act in Redemption is 'a Causative Act—a spiritual and transcendent mystery *that passeth all understanding.* " *Who knoweth the mind of the Lord, or being his counsellor hath instructed him ?" Factum est.*' This is all that can be said of the mystery of Redemption, or of the doctrine of Atonement, on its Divine side.

And here emerges another important principle of the Coleridgian Theology. While so great an advocate of the rights of reason in theology, of the necessity, in other words, of moulding all its facts in a synthesis intelligible to the higher reason, he recognises strongly that there is a province of Divine truth beyond all such construction. We can never understand the fulness of Divine mystery, and it is hopeless to attempt to do so. While no mind was less agnostic in the modern sense of the term, he was yet, with all his vivid and large intuition, a Christian agnostic. Just because Christianity was Divine, a revelation, and not a mere human tradition, all its higher doctrines ended in a region beyond our clear knowledge. As he himself said, ' If the doctrine is more than a hyperbolical phrase, it must do so.'

There was great pregnancy in this as in his other conceptions ; and probably no more significant change awaits the theology of the future than the recognition of this province of the unknown, and the cessation of controversy as to matters which come within it, and therefore admit of no dogmatic settlement.

(2.) But it is more than time to turn to the second aspect, in which Coleridge appears as a religious leader of the thought of the nineteenth century. The *Confessions of an Inquiring Spirit* were not published till six years after his death, in 1840; and it is curious to notice their accidental connection with the *Confessions of a Beautiful Soul*, which had been translated by Carlyle some years before.[1] These *Confessions*, in the shape of seven letters to a friend, gather together all that is valuable in the Biblical Criticism of the author scattered through his various writings ; and although it may be doubtful whether the volume has ever attained the circulation of the *Aids to Reflection*, it is eminently deserving—small as it is, nay, because of its very brevity—of a place beside the larger work. It is eminently readable, terse and nervous, as well as eloquent in style. In none of his writings does Coleridge appear to greater advantage, or touch a more elevating strain, rising at times into solemn music.

The *Confessions of an Inquiring Spirit* were of course merely one indication of the rise of a true spirit of criticism in English theology. Arnold, Whately, Thirlwall, and others, it will be seen were all astir in the same direction, even before the

---

[1] In his well-known translation of *Wilhelm Meister*.

Confessions were published. The notion of verbal inspiration, or the infallible dictation of Holy Scripture, could not possibly continue after the modern spirit of historical inquiry had begun. As soon as men plainly recognised the organic growth of all great facts, literary as well as others, it was inevitable that they should see the Scriptures in a new light, as a product of many phases of thought in course of more or less perfect development. A larger and more intelligent sense of the conditions attending the origin and progress of all civilisation, and of the immaturities through which religious as well as moral and social ideas advance, necessarily carried with it a changed perception of the characteristics of Scriptural revelation. The old Rabbinical notion of an infallible text was sure to disappear. The new critical method, besides, is in Coleridge's hands rather an idea—a happy and germinant thought—than a well-evolved system. Still to him belongs the honour of having first plainly and boldly announced that the Scriptures were to be read and studied, like any other literature, in the light of their continuous growth, and the adaptation of their parts to one another.

The divinity of Scripture appears all the more brightly when thus freely handled. 'I take up this work,' he says, 'with the purpose to read it for the first time as I should read any other work—as far at least as I can or dare. For I neither can, nor dare, throw off a strong and awful prepossession in its favour—certain as I am that a large part of the light and life, in and by which I see, love, and embrace the truths and the strengths co-organised into a living body of faith and knowledge has been directly or indirectly derived to me from this sacred volume.' All the more reason why we should not make a fetish of the Bible, as the Turk does of the Koran. Poor as reason may be in comparison with 'the power and splendour of the Scriptures,' yet it is and must be for him a true light. 'While there is a Light higher than all, even the *Word that was in the beginning ;*—the Light, of which light itself is but the shechinah and cloudy tabernacle ;'—there is also a 'Light that lighteth every man that cometh into the world ;' and the spirit of man is declared to be 'the candle of the Lord.' 'If between this Word,' he says, 'and the written Letter I shall anywhere seem to myself to find a discrepance, I will not conclude that such there actually is ; nor, on the other hand, will I fall under the condemnation of them that would *lie for God,* but seek as I may, be thankful for what I have—and wait.'

Such is the keynote of the volume. The supremacy of the Bible as a divinely inspired literature is plainly recognised from the first. Obviously it is a book above all other books in which deep answers to deep, and our inmost thoughts and most hidden griefs find not merely response, but guidance and assuagement. And whatever there *finds* us 'bears witness for itself that it has proceeded from the Holy Spirit.' 'In the Bible,' he says again, 'there is more that *finds* me than I have experienced in all other books put together ; the words of the Bible find me at greater depths of my being ; and whatever finds me brings with it an irresistible evidence of its having proceeded from the Holy Spirit.'

But there is much in the Bible that not only does

not find us in the Coleridgian sense, but that seems full of contradictions, both moral and historical ; the psalms in which Dàvid curses his enemies ; the obviously exaggerated ages attributed to the patriarchs ; and the incredible number of the armies said to be collected by Abijah and Jeroboam (2 Chron. xiii. 3), and other instances familiar to all students of Scripture. What is to be made of such features of the Bible ? According to the old notion of its infallibility such parts of Scripture, no less than its most elevating utterances of 'lovely hymn and choral song and accepted prayers of saint and prophet,' were to be received as dictated by the Holy Spirit. They were stamped with the same Divine authority. Coleridge rightly enough emphasises this view as that of the Fathers and Reformers alike ; but he no less rightly points out that not one of them is consistent in holding to their general doctrine. Their treatment of the Scriptures in detail constantly implies the fallacy of the Rabbinical tradition to which they yet clung. He no less forcibly points out that the Scriptures themselves make no such pretension to infallibility, 'explicitly or by implication.' 'On the contrary, they refer to older documents, and on all points express themselves as sober-minded and veracious writers under ordinary circumstances are known to do.' The usual texts quoted, such as 2 Tim. iii. 16, have no real bearing on the subject. The little we know as to the origin and history of many of the books of the Bible, of 'the time of the formation and closing of the canon,' of its selectors and compilers, is all opposed to such a theory. Moreover, the very nature of the claim stultifies itself when examined.

For 'how can infallible truth be infallibly conveyed in defective and fallible expression?'

But it may be asked, as it has been often asked, where is this selective process to stop? If the Bible as a whole is not infallibly inspired, how are we to know what is of Divine authority and what is not? The only answer to such a question is the answer of common sense given in all other cases. The higher thought and power of any writing is self-revealing. It is not to be mistaken. It takes captive the reason as well as the conscience. If I speak enthusiastically of Shakespeare, and of the well-nigh divine wisdom of many of his plays, do I thereby receive all that Shakespeare writes as elevating or good? Do I pronounce any opinion as to the question respecting Titus Andronicus, or the larger portion of the three parts of Henry VI.? Shakespeare in ordinary speech stands for the unity of genius which his works represent. In this is also to be found the true explanation of the words of our Lord in speaking of Moses and the prophets. In using such expressions our Lord does not mean to indicate any opinion of the authenticity of the books of Moses, or of the infallible authority of all contained in the Old Testament; but only to appeal to the unity of Divine light which the Jews themselves recognised in the Holy Scriptures. They owned a Divine authority contained in certain writings. Moses was *par excellence* their Divine teacher. If only they had understood their own Scriptures, they would have known that Moses spake of Him. The argument thus used by our Lord was conclusive. In the light of their own belief it left no escape to them, and this was beyond doubt all that our Lord meant by such an appeal. To suppose that he implied further that there can be no doubt that Moses is the author of the Pentateuch as a whole, or that every word of it was dictated by God to Moses, is to suppose something not only absurd in itself, but utterly irrelevant to the purpose in view. So in effect Coleridge argued and with a force as irresistible as it was new in his day.

But if the tenet of verbal inspiration has been so long received and acted on ' by Jew and Christian, Greek, Roman, and Protestant, why can it not now be received ?' ' For every reason,' answered Coleridge, ' that makes me prize and revere these Scriptures ;— prize them, love them, revere them beyond all other books.' Because such a tenet ' falsifies at once the whole body of holy writ, with all its harmonious and symmetrical gradations.' It turns ' the breathing organism into a colossal Memnon's head, a hollow passage for a voice,' which no man hath uttered, and no human heart hath conceived. It evacuates of all sense and efficacy the fact that the Bible is a Divine literature of many books ' composed in different and widely distant ages, under the greatest diversity of circumstances, and degrees of light and information.' So he argues in language I have partly quoted and partly summarised. And then he breaks forth into a magnificent passage about the song of Deborah, a passage of rare eloquence with all its desultoriness, but which will hardly bear separation from the context. The wail of the Jewish heroine's maternal and patriotic love is heard under all her cursing and individualism—mercy rejoicing against judg-

ment.   In the very intensity of her primary affections
is found the rare strength of her womanhood, and
sweetness lies near to fierceness.   Such passages probably give us a far better idea of the occasional glory
of the old man's talk as ' he sat on the brow of Highgate Hill,' than any poor fragments that have been
preserved.   Direct and to the point it may never
have been, but at times it rose into an organ swell
with snatches of unutterable melody and power.

The conclusion of the whole is that the divinity of
Scripture resides not in the letter but in the spirit,
in the unity of Divine impression which they convey.
And historical criticism has precisely the same task
in reference to the Bible as any other collection of
ancient and sacred writings.   An undevout criticism
will no doubt blunder and misinterpret, as an
ungenial and inappropriate criticism must always
do in every direction.   But a false can only be corrected
by a true criticism, and a narrow and meagre rationalism by a profound and enlightened sacred learning,
capable of understanding the depths of the spiritual
life, while rigorously testing all its conclusions and
processes of development, both moral and historical,
intellectual and ethical.

(3.) But Coleridge contributed still another factor to
the impulsion of religious thought in his time.   He
did much to revive the historic idea of the Church as
an intellectual as well as a spiritual commonwealth.
Like many other ideas of our older national life this
had been depressed and lost sight of during the
eighteenth century.   The evangelical party, deficient
in learning generally, was especially deficient in
breadth of historical knowledge.   Milner's History,

if nothing else, serves to point this conclusion. The idea of the Church as the mother of philosophy, and arts, and learning, as well as the nurse of faith and piety, was unknown. It was a part of the evangelical creed, moreover, to leave aside as far as possible mere political and intellectual interests. These belonged to the world, and the main business of the religious man was with religion as a personal affair, of vast moment, but outside all other affairs. Coleridge helped once more to bring the Church as he did the Gospel into larger room as a great spiritual power of manifold influence.

The volume *On the Constitution of Church and State according to the idea of each* was published in 1830, and was the last volume which the author himself published. The Catholic emancipation question had greatly excited the public mind, and some friend had appealed to Coleridge expressing astonishment that he should be in opposition to the proposed measure. He replied that he is by no means unfriendly to Catholic emancipation, while yet 'scrupling the means proposed for its attainment.' And in order to explain his difficulties he composed a long letter to his friend which is really an essay or treatise, beginning with the fundamental principles of his philosophy and ending with a description of antichrist. The essay is one of the least satisfactory of his compositions from a mere literary point of view, and is not even mentioned by Mr. Traill in his recent monograph. But amidst all its involutions and ramblings it is stimulating and full of thought on a subject which almost more than any other is liable to be degraded by unworthy and sectarian treatment. Here,

as everywhere in Coleridge's writings, we are brought
in contact with certain large conceptions which far
more than cover the immediate subject in hand.

It has been sometimes supposed that Coleridge's
theory of the church merely revived the old theory
of the Elizabethan age so powerfully advocated by
Hooker, and specially espoused by Dr. Arnold in
later times.   According to this theory the church and
state are really identical, the church being merely
the state in its educational and religious aspect
and organisation.   But Coleridge's special theory
is different from this, although allied to it.   He
distinguishes the Christian Church as such from any
national church.   The former is spiritual and catholic,
the latter institutional and local.   The former is
opposed to the 'world,' the latter is an estate of the
realm.   The former has nothing to do with states
and kingdoms.   It is in this respect identical with the
'spiritual and invisible church known only to the
Father of Spirits,' and the compensating counterpoise
of all that is of the world.   It is in short the Divine
aggregate of what is really divine in all Christian
communities and more or less ideally represented 'in
every true church.'   A national church again is the
incorporation of all the learning and knowledge—
intellectual and spiritual—in a country.   Every
nation, in order to its true health and civilisation,
requires not only a land-owning or permanent class
along with a commercial, industrial, and progressive
class, but moreover, an educative class to represent
all higher knowledge, 'to guard the treasures of past
civilisation,' to bind the national life together in its
past, present, and future, and to communicate to all

citizens a clear understanding of their rights and duties. This third estate of the realm Coleridge denominated the 'Clerisy,' and included not merely the clergy, but, in his own language, 'the learned of all denominations.' The knowledge which it was their function to cultivate and diffuse, embraced not only theology, although this pre-eminently as the head of all other knowledge, but law, music, mathematics, the physical sciences, 'all the so-called liberal arts and sciences, the possession and cultivation of which constitute the civilisation of a country.'

This is at any rate a large conception of a national church. It is put forth by its author with all earnestness, although he admitted that it had never been anywhere realised. But it was his object 'to present the *Idea* of a national church as the only safe criterion by which we can judge of existing things.' It is only when 'we are in full and clear possession of the ultimate aim of an institution' that we can ascertain how far 'this aim has ever been attained in other ways.'

These, very briefly explained, are the main lines along which Coleridge moved the national mind in the third decade of this century. They may seem to some rather impalpable lines, and hardly calculated to touch the general mind. But they were influential, as the course of Christian literature has since proved. Like his own genius, they were diffusive rather than concentrative. The Coleridgian ideas permeated the general intellectual atmosphere, modifying old conceptions in criticism as well as theology, deepening if not always clarifying the channels of thought in many directions, but especially in the direction of

Christian problems.   They acted in this way as a
new circulation of spiritual air all round, rather than
in conveying any new body of truth.   The very
ridicule of Carlyle testifies to the influence which
they exercised over aspiring and younger minds.
The very emphasis with which he repudiates the
Coleridgian metaphysic probably indicates that he
had felt some echo of it in his own heart.

Of the more immediate disciples of Coleridge,
there are only two that claim our attention here.
Others, such as Edward Irving, Maurice, and
Kingsley, will afterwards come under notice in their
special places.

Of all the disciples of Coleridge, Julius Charles
Hare may be reckoned the most direct and confessed.
He acknowledges his obligations to him everywhere.
' Of all recent English writers, the one whose sanction
I have chiefly desired is the great religious philosopher to whom the mind of our generation in England owes more than to any other man, and whose
aim it was,' he says, 'to spiritualise not only our
philosophy but our theology, to raise them both
above the empiricism into which they had fallen, and
to set them free from the technical trammels of logical
systems.'   It was in 1846 that Hare thus wrote,[1] and
in his *Life of John Sterling*, published two years
later, he was equally emphatic in his admiration and
enthusiasm for the ' great Christian philosopher,' on
Sterling's account as well as his own.   Sterling was
not content, he tells, to be a reverent student of
Coleridge's writings, but 'when an opportunity

[1] Preface to *Mission of the Comforter*.

occurred, he sought out the old man in his oracular shrine at Highgate, and often saw him in the last years of his life'—the fact, indeed, to which we owe the rival satiric description of the Highgate Sage and his pupils in Carlyle's better known life of the gifted friend of both these men.

To what extent Hare himself had any personal intercourse with Coleridge does not appear ; but we see readily the influences which moved him towards the same line of thought. Born twenty-three years after Coleridge, or in 1795, Hare passed, after a brilliant career at school, to Cambridge in 1812, where he numbered among his fellow-students such men as Whewell and Thirlwall. Here it was, at his 'entrance into intellectual life,' that he enjoyed, as he says, the singular felicity, along with his compeers, of having his thoughts stimulated and trained by Wordsworth and Coleridge, 'in whom practical judgment, and moral dignity, and a sacred love of truth, were so nobly wedded to the highest intellectual powers,'[1] as opposed to the noxious influence of Byron, with his 'sentimental and self-ogling misanthropy.' The young Cambridge intellect of that day delighted to look to these pure masters of thought and song. Coleridge, indeed, had not yet entered on his theological stage, and Wordsworth fortunately remained a poetic teacher all his life ; but early inclination towards the Lake, rather than the Byronic, school of poetry, naturally led to an admiration of Coleridge's later writings. Hare was also, along with his English master, a diligent student of German philosophy. He had

[1] *Mission of the Comforter.*

gone while quite a youth to Germany, and as, on the Wartburg, he saw the mark of Luther's ink-stand on the castle wall, he learned, as he after-wards said, 'to throw inkstands at the devil.' Again, in 1832, before he settled on his living at Hurstmonceaux,[1] he had gone abroad and made the friendship of Bunsen, and otherwise become further acquainted, not only with German philosophy, but with the new movement in German theology initiated by Schleiermacher. He was caught and greatly moved by all these fresh influences, and naturally turned to Coleridge as the chief leader in the fresh outburst of theological thought at home.

With all Hare's noble enthusiasm and captivating spirit of Christian culture, it cannot be said that he is much of a leader of thought himself. He is critical, didactic, philosophic in tone, always cul-tured. He writes at times with a fine, if desultory, eloquence; and his books, especially the *Guesses at Truth*, which he published along with his brother first in 1828, were much read, and felt to be highly stimulating, forty years ago. I can never forget my own obligation to some of them; yet it must be con-fessed that both author and writings are now some-what dim in the retrospect. They have not lived on, and this no doubt mainly because both reflected for the greater part the movement of his time rather than added any new and creative force to it. It was impossible for a mind so critical and scholarly as Hare's, with such a range of varied and interesting

[1] This seems the proper spelling of this name (See *Memorials of a Quiet Life*, c. III. p. 69), but it is often spelt, and even by Julius Hare himself, Herstmonceux.

knowledge, one of the best classical tutors in his day at Cambridge, the translator, along with Thirlwall, of Niebuhr's *History of Rome*, the student of Neander and Tholuck, as well as of Schleiermacher and Coleridge, not to own the breath of new life that was stirring everywhere the mental atmosphere around him, and to join in opening up new channels for it in which to circulate. It was his aim and ambition to lead, along with his master, the way to a more 'spiritual philosophy and theology;' and he has beyond doubt helped many on this way. But he has not made the way itself much clearer; and it may be questioned whether his purely controversial writings, such as his *Contest with Rome* against Dr. Newman, and his *Vindication of Luther* against Sir William Hamilton, have not more life in them than his more special contribution to thought. His undoubted learning and great fairness of temper, with (it must be admitted) keen severity of judgment when his spirit was roused, gave him great success as a controversialist; and whatever may be our legitimate admiration of our own Scottish philosopher, I do not think any impartial student can doubt that he fared badly indeed at the hands of the English archdeacon in his treatment of the great German Reformer. Here he met for once his own match in learning, and a far deeper insight than his own into the meaning of theological terms and conceptions.

In one, and that a very interesting manner, Julius Hare, his brothers, and kinsfolk, have been recalled to vivid life again in our day. The *Memorials of a Quiet Life*, the picture of devout and rational piety there presented to us, has touched many hearts notwithstanding its somewhat tedious and minute detail. Augustus William Hare, the joint author with his brother of the *Guesses at Truth*, and author of the well-known *Sermons to a Country Congregation* (1837), claims a niche beside his brother as a helper in the revival of a more direct religious teaching. A more devoted, self-sacrificing, and loving Christian minister, never lived; and his *Sermons* were a new awakening to many hearts. There are no more moving glimpses of spiritual life to be found in any literature than those which he and his widow, and the other inmates of the Rectory at Hurstmonceaux, present to a congenial reader. Whatever may be our estimate of the force of thought which emanated from this source, a more beautiful family life—a happier combination of 'beautiful souls' —was never brought together. The life of religion was never better exemplified; and in these days, when the veil has been lifted with such unhappy results on many interiors, it is well to be able to point to what religion may do for the most thoughtful and deeply-pondering minds, when its benign spirit has once possessed them.

Of John Sterling a few words must suffice. His name cannot be omitted, and yet we cannot dwell on it, nor are we called upon to do so. There must have been an infinite attractiveness in the man to have drawn out as he did such treasures of affection from teachers so different as Hare and Maurice on the one side and Carlyle on the other. Maurice hardly ever alludes to him without something of a sob, as if he might have done more for him than he did;

and the hardier spirit of Carlyle melts into tenderness as he writes of him. ' A man of perfect veracity,'
he says, 'in thought, word, and deed. Integrity
towards all men, nay, integrity had refined with
him into chivalrous generosity; there was no guile or
baseness anywhere found in him. A more perfectly
transparent soul I have never known.' His 'very
faults grew beautiful.' Again, 'I was struck with
the kindly but restless swift-glancing eyes, which
looked as if the spirits were all out coursing like a
pack of many beagles beating every bush.' It must
have been a loveable character which drew around
him so much love. There must also have seemed in
Sterling a marvellous potency as if, with due maturity,
he might have done great things in literature if not
in theology. But the brightness of his promise soon
spent itself. It may be doubted even whether if he
had lived he would have achieved much. ' Over
haste,' says Carlyle, ' was his continual fault. Over
haste and want of due strength.' His genius flashed
and coruscated like sheet-lightning round a subject
rather than went to the heart of it. He lacked depth
and the capacity of continuous thought. He was
moved, if not by 'every wind of doctrine,' by every
breath of speculation that braced his intellectual lungs
for a time. It was now Coleridge, and now Edward
Irving, and now Schleiermacher, and now Carlyle that
swept the strings of his mind and made them vibrate.
We have already seen all that Coleridge was to him.
He owed to him 'education,'—even 'himself.' The
Aids to Reflection was for many years his *vade mecum*.
Of Schleiermacher as late as 1836 he says, ' he was on
the whole the greatest spiritual teacher I have fallen

in with.' And at last, when Carlyle's teaching had long displaced any other, he doubted whether he had ever 'got any good of what he had heard or read of theology.' From his bright restless intellect all the bequests of Christian thinkers that once seemed to enrich him had been thrown off, and he went without theological help 'into the great darkness.' And yet not without help, yea with better help than any theological reading could give him, if the story told in Hare's life, but untold by Carlyle, be true. 'As it grew dark he appeared to be seeking for something, and on his sister asking him what he wanted, he said, "only the old Bible which I used so often at Hurstmonceaux in the cottages."'

Sterling was not destined to be any force of religious thought for his generation. With all his 'sleepless intellectual vivacity,' he was 'not a thinker at all.' The words are Carlyle's and not ours. Yet he deserves to be remembered, as he will continue to be associated with the great Teacher who first kindled both his intellectual and religious enthusiasm. Carlyle has embalmed his name and discipleship in beautiful form, and the picture will remain while English literature lasts. But students of religious opinion will always also think of him as a disciple of Coleridge, and the friend of Maurice and Hare.

II.

THE EARLY ORIEL SCHOOL AND ITS CONGENERS.

IN 1825, the same year in which the *Aids to Reflection* saw the light, appeared Whately's Essays *On Some of the Peculiarities of the Christian Religion.* Three years later, or in 1828, appeared a further series of essays by the same writer *On some of the Difficulties in the Writings of St. Paul.* But even before the earliest of these years Whately had been Bampton Lecturer, and published in the usual manner his lectures *On the Use and Abuse of Party Feeling in Religion* (1822).[1] In the third decade of the century, in short, Whately was something of a power in the theological world, as he had been long a power at Oxford. Entered at Oriel College as early as 1805 he became a Fellow in 1811, and finding a congenial soil there in such minds as Davison—still somewhat remembered in connection with *Discourses on Prophecy,*—and Copleston, afterwards Bishop of Llandaff, he may be said to have founded, or at least inspired with its most vigorous life the 'old' or 'early Oriel School,' which made a name for itself before Newman and his immediate

---

[1] His *Historic Doubts respecting Napoleon Buonaparte*—the most popular of all his books—was still earlier, 1819.

friends joined the society.   Keble, indeed, was a
fellow of the college at this early time, but it was
the spirit not of Keble but of Whately that then
ruled the place, and brought it fame.   Arnold came
as a youthful scholar from Corpus in 1815, and
Hampden, who had been trained at Oriel from the
first, had also entered it as a fellow the year before
(1814).

A more remarkable combination of able men has
seldom been brought together.   In addition to the
names already mentioned, that of Dr. Hawkins
deserves to be signalised.   Already significant as a
man of ability before 1825,[1] he succeeded Copleston
as head of Oriel in 1828, and survived to our own
time—a venerable figure, whose bright eyes and
vivacious expression, bespeaking the sharp and
kindly intelligence within, none can forget who ever
came in contact with him.   Through all changes he
maintained the liberal traditions of the place, even
when Newmanism was at its height.   His writings
are now forgotten, but his personal influence was
powerful for more than one generation.

It was Copleston, however, who was the original
master-mind of the movement.   His lectures and
converse had been 'like a new spring of life' to
Whately on his entrance to the College ; and long
afterwards (1845), Whately wrote to him from
Dublin :—' From you I have derived the main principles on which I have acted and speculated through

---

[1] His *Dissertation on Unauthoritative Tradition* appeared as early
as 1819.   Various publications followed, especially, in 1833, *Discourses
upon some of the principal objects and uses of the Historical Scriptures
of the Old Testament.*

life.'[1]   Another says of Copleston :—' Under a polished and somewhat artificial scholarlike exterior, and an appearance of even overstrained caution, there lurked not only much energy of mind and precision of judgment, but a strong tendency to liberalism in Church and State, and superiority to ordinary fears and prejudices.   It was in this direction that he especially trained Whately's character;'[2] and Whately in his turn diffused the liberal spirit which he drank at the fountain-head.   The new Oriel men were called ' Noetic.'   The School was the ' Noetic School ;'[3] and they seem to have rejoiced in the reputation of superior mental penetration and independence. ' Whether they were preaching from the University pulpit, or arguing in common rooms, or issuing pamphlets,' on passing occasions, they made a noise which arrested attention and filled with alarm many of the older University minds, who, Mr. Mozley says, ' felt the ground shaking under them.'   ' Whately especially was claimed by his admirers to have a spiritual as well as mental pre-eminence,' and his presence infused terror among all ' who wished things to remain as they were in their own lifetime.'

It is difficult now to realise the commotion once excited in the English theological mind by Whately and Arnold, and particularly by Hampden, now so little known ; but the alarm which they excited was very genuine at the time, as their influence upon the course of theological thought was very considerable.   It is necessary, therefore,

---

[1] *Memoir of Copleston*, p. 103.
[2] Herman Merivale, *Whately's Life*, vol. i. p. 13.
[3] Mozley's *Reminiscences*, vol. i. p. 18.

that we should review this influence and try to estimate it. No view of the course of religious thought in our century which omitted these names would be at all complete. They stand together also as a common group or School connected with Oriel College, widely separated as were their respective activities in life. By 1820 Arnold had finally left Oriel and his work as a fellow, although he afterwards returned to Oxford as Professor of History (1841). In 1831 Whately had become Archbishop of Dublin, and left Oxford permanently. Hampden alone remained in a succession of University posts till 1847, when he became Bishop of Hereford. An intimate correspondence, however, continued to unite the friends. It was Whately's ear into which Hampden poured his troubles when they arose in 1836 on his appointment as Professor of Divinity. It was Arnold who came to his assistance at the same crisis in his powerful article in the *Edinburgh Review,* in the same year, on 'The Oxford Malignants.' The bonds of intellectual and religious fellowship, therefore, continued to unite them long after Oriel had been left behind, and a new sect, so to speak, had become identified with it. The two sects, in fact, ran closely into one another, as we have already indicated. Keble was the friend of Arnold, for whom he always expressed a warm regard ; and Whately was 'the encouraging instructor' of Newman, who, according to the Cardinal's own record, opened his mind and taught him to 'use his reason.' In our next lecture we shall consider the band of Anglo-Catholics in the blaze of whose movement the 'Noetic' School disappeared. But to the members of this School **we** must first direct attention.

There are other names intimately associated with the school which also deserve notice, as representative of liberal theological opinion. Chevalier Bunsen appears in the background, intimately connected with the critical movement of the time, and with not a few of the men in England engaged in it. Blanco White is another associate of significance. Singularly he was an inmate of Oriel College from about 1826 to 1831. He then followed Whately to Dublin and lived in his house till the stirrings of his restless mind drove him to Liverpool and the Unitarianism in which he closed his strangely revolving career. Blanco White would make an interesting study by himself with all his spiritual vicissitudes and pathetic ways. But two masters of spiritual diagnosis, Neander[1] and Mr. Gladstone,[2] have already sketched him, and we cannot do more here than set him in his place and draw attention to him. Influence in some degree he must have been, for he was the most sensitive and radiating of mortals, either giving or receiving light every day of his life. But curious and touching as he is in himself, I have failed to trace any definite impulse communicated by him to the Oriel School, or even to the religious thought of his time. Like many other men who have been trained in close systems of thought, when the spirit of doubt was awakened in him, he merely fell out of one system into another — Romanism, Atheism, Anglicanism, Unitarianism. He had little conception of true inquiry, or of the patience of thought which works

[1] *Blanco White*, Berlin, 1848.   [2] *Gleanings*, vol. ii.

through all layers of systems to the core of truth beneath.

Two names, however, deserve, along with the Oriel men already mentioned, a special space in this lecture—names belonging in their full brilliancy to the later history of the Church of England—but which emerged into prominence in the days of Whately and Arnold. Already before 1830 both Milman and Thirlwall had acquired a distinctive reputation. They had entered on new fields of critical speculation in regard to Scripture, and ruffled even to violence the surface of the religious world. We must therefore, before closing our present lecture, glance at the historian of the Jews and the translator of Schleiermacher's Essay on the Gospel of St. Luke.

Richard Whately is the foremost name in our list. He was fifteen years younger than Coleridge, and eight years older than Arnold.[1] He was born, so to speak, into the Church, his father having been a vicar, and also Prebendary of Bristol. He was the youngest child of a large clerical family, as Coleridge was, and weak and somewhat ailing as a child—another point of coincidence between the poet and logician. In all other respects no two men could be conceived less alike in youth and manhood, although very notably in both cases the 'youth' was the father of the 'man.' The boyhood of Coleridge as all know was given to poetry and metaphysics. There may have been as youthful poets—there never was as youthful a metaphysician. The boyhood of Whately was

[1] Whately was born in 1787 ; Arnold in 1795 ; Coleridge in 1772.

given to arithmetic. There was something quite remarkable in his calculating faculty, which began to show itself between five and six. He could do the most difficult sums in his head before he knew anything of the names of the processes by which he worked them. He had his share also of castle-building, in the metaphysical line, as his powers matured ; and became at times so absorbed in self-reflection, or in mental calculation, 'as to run against people in the street.' The extraordinary thing is that all his arithmetical precocity came to nothing. His powers of calculation entirely left him as he grew up. ' The passion wore off,' he says ; 'I was a perfect dunce at cyphering, and so have continued ever since.' He went to a good school near Bristol at nine years of age, and to Oxford when he was eighteen. He early contracted a great fondness for out-of-door wanderings, and studies in natural history, which never left him. ' Of fishing he was particularly fond.' Throughout life he retained his love for exercise in the open air. It may be mentioned also that he retained through life, like many other men of concentrated habits of thought, the absence of mind which characterised him as a boy ; and to this feature in some degree is no doubt to be attributed such strange freaks as those with his climbing dog, in which he afterwards indulged even when a don at Oxford, to the consternation of all the more staid orderly behaved dons.

He very early developed real powers, not only of scholarship but of thought. As one of his friends said to him, ' From the beginning, and emphatically, Whately was a thinker. His favourite authors

were few—Aristotle, Thucydides, Bacon, Bishop
Butler, Warburton, Adam Smith.' Here, as in other
things, unlike Coleridge, whose reading was always
of an omnivorous character; yet strangely a like imputation of plagiarism was made against both—in
the case of Coleridge obviously because he forgot,
in the plenitude of his philosophical reading, what
was his own and what was others',—in the case of
Whately because he was often falling upon thoughts
which, if he had been more of a reader, he would have
known that others had produced long ago. He was
an Aristotelian in all the principles and methods of
his philosophy, and to no man was the adage which
he quotes in one of his early volumes more contemptible; 'Errare malo cum Platone quam cum
istis vera sentire.'

In theology, as in other things, Whately was an
active and fertile thinker, animated by an insatiable
love of finding the truth and plainly stating it. In
sheer grasp of faculty—in laying hold of 'some
notion' which he considered practically important—
and following it out in all its details,—beating it plain
till no one could fail to see it as he himself saw it,—
he was unrivalled. Clearness, common sense, honesty,
and strength of intellect were his great characteristics,
and it is in virtue of these rather than in any depth or
richness of new and living thought that he became
a power first at Oxford and then in the theological
world. Whereas Coleridge brought to the interpretation of Christianity the light of a fresh spiritual
philosophy, and sought some synthesis of thought by
which religion in its highest form should be seen not
only to be in harmony with human nature, but to be

its only perfect flower and development, its true philosophy;—Whately—taking the prevailing philosophy as he found it,—brought the daylight of ordinary reason and of historical fact to play upon the accumulated dogmas of traditionary religion, and to show how little they had, in many cases, to say for themselves. He was a subverter of prejudice and commonplace—of what he believed to be religious as well as irreligious mistake, more than anything else. The majority of people seemed to him,—as probably is always more or less the case,—to live in an atmosphere of theological delusion, mistaking their own conceits for essential religious principles,—making the New Testament writers responsible for notions that, to a just and intelligent criticism, had no existence there, and were indeed contrary to its spirit and teaching rightly interpreted. A whole cluster of beliefs came in this way under his destroying hand : for example, the belief of any priesthood under the Gospel other than the common priesthood of Christians alike ; the belief of verbal inspiration ; and again, of the Fourth Commandment as being the obligatory rule for the Christian Sunday. So also the common evangelical doctrines of Election, of Perseverance, of Assurance, and of Imputation, all drew upon them his incisive pen. He did not maintain that there were not truths in Scripture answering to these doctrines ; but the great aim of his volume *On the Difficulties of St. Paul's writings* was to show that the common evangelical ideas on these subjects were not Pauline. St. Paul's notion of election, he maintained, was entirely different from the common dogma which, in his view, virtually makes salvation

and election identical. Analysing at length the use
of the Pauline word, he comes to the conclusion that
it is to be interpreted always in a general sense of the
body of the Church, 'even as the whole nation of
Israel was of old the chosen.' It has no relation to
the final destiny of individuals. When 'the Apostles
address these converts universally as the " elect " or
" chosen" of God, this must be understood of their
being chosen out of the whole mass of the Gentiles to
certain peculiar privileges.' But the result in each
case depends upon the use of the privileges. 'We
are in his hands,' says the Predestinarian, 'as clay in
the potter's who hath power of the same lump to make
one vessel to honour and another to dishonour ;' but
this very passage, he argues, so far from favouring the
predestinarian doctrine makes against it, 'since the
potter never makes any vessel for the *express purpose*
of being broken and destroyed.' On the contrary,
the meaning of the statement is that he makes 'some
to nobler and some to meaner uses : but all for some
use, not with a design that it should be cast away and
dashed to pieces.' Even so, 'The Almighty, of his
own arbitrary choice, causes some to be born to wealth
or rank, others to poverty or obscurity, some in a
heathen and others in a Christian country ; the advantages and privileges are various, and so far as we
can see arbitrarily dispensed. But the final rewards
or punishments depend, as we are plainly taught, on
the use or abuse of those advantages.'

It would be interesting, if we had time, to com-
pare Coleridge's and Whately's modes of treating
this mysterious doctrine—the more inward, spiritual,
experiential treatment of the one,—the critical and

historical treatment of the other. No handling could well be more different in the two cases, and yet there is an affinity between them in end, if not in means. Both are alike opposed to the hyper-logical forms under which the doctrine has been chiefly transmitted to us. It was the aim of both, in this and other matters, to 'free theology from its logical trammels,' to bring it in the one case to the test of spiritual experience, in the other to the test of historical criticism.

Logician as Whately was, no man more strongly repudiated the application of logical forms to Scriptural truth. One of the chief hurts of religion in his opinion had arisen from this very cause, and the consequent multiplication of 'foolish and unlearned questions' in the theological world. Questions however 'interesting and sublime,' which plainly 'surpass the limits of our faculties,' should be left alone. There was in him as in Coleridge a strong vein of Christian agnosticism. All such questions gender strife and hopeless controversy, for how can men agree in bold theories respecting points on which they can have no correct knowledge, which are in fact unintelligible to them? To this cause he attributes the heresies on the subject of the Trinity in the early Church, and especially denounces certain rash attempts made in his own day,—by Hervey, for example, the once well-known author of *Meditations among the Tombs*,—'to explain on the abstract principle of justice' the counsels of the Most High, on the equally incomprehensible mystery of the Atonement.[1]

We might give many illustrations of Whately's

[1] *Bampton Lectures* (1822), p. 179.

mode of theological thought. It must suffice to emphasise its general character. Whately was undoubtedly for his day a strong man, who believed that he had a reforming mission to accomplish in the Church,—to make men think more simply and sincerely about religion,—to teach them to look at Scripture with their own eyes,—and to destroy, as he conceived, grave errors both on the side of Puritanism and of Sacerdotalism. He had no fear of any man or of any party. The very limits of his theological as of his philosophical reading gave an intensity to his own principles, and a confidence in ventilating them, which a larger acquaintance with the history of theology, and of human nature in connection therewith, would probably have abated. Certain it is that the special forms of opinion against which he strove were not killed in his day, and that some of them are as vigorous as ever. But this does not detract from the real force that he was, nor from the respect that is due to his constant courage and love of the truth. No man ever loved truth more, or more boldly followed it as he found it. No one more fully acted on his own principle that 'fairness and candour' are the best allies of truth, and that religion can never suffer from any theory on any subject that is really well founded and sound.[1] He loved with all his heart what he held to be the verities of religion, and defended them with all his might ; but he hated superstition in every form. The excesses of Anglo-Catholic Theology and of German Rationalism were alike obnoxious to him. He closed equally with Newman and Strauss, and beat them with the pitiless and persistent force of his argument

[1] *Essays* (1823), p. 27.

and ridicule.[1]   One reason, no doubt, of the comparative neglect which has overtaken his works is that
they had all in this way a more or less immediate
and temporary purpose.   They were called forth by
the exigencies of circumstance or opinion in which
his life was passed.   Many of them, moreover, are
neither more nor less than tracts, such as his once
well-known and highly popular *Cautions for the
Times.*   And no such writings, however lively, suggestive, and successful for the moment, have any future
life before them.   They perish in their use, and a
second generation cannot find any interest in what
may have even violently agitated or amused their
predecessors.

Dr. Arnold was Whately's great friend and frequent
correspondent.   The old days at Oriel, from 1815 to
1820, had bound them closely together, and the bond
was only severed by Arnold's sudden death in 1842.
To Arnold as to Newman, in their first Oriel connection, Whately had been something of a master.
Even after both had left Oriel,[2] Arnold tells us that a
visit to Whately was 'a marked era in the formation
of his opinions.'   Again, in the preface to his first
volume of sermons, published in 1828, Arnold expresses his special obligation to the author of the
Essays on the writings of St. Paul, and his apprehension that some of his sentences were so like passages
in the *Essays* that he might be accused of plagiarism.
The truth was that his own views, while excogitated
independently and before he had seen Dr. Whately's

---

[1] See his *Cautions for the Times*, as well as his *Historic Doubts*.

[2] In 1822, when Whately was temporarily resident at Halesworth,
in Suffolk, a living to which he had been presented by his uncle.

volume, had yet been greatly helped, 'confirmed, and extended,' by communication with his friend. When Whately was promoted to the Archbishopric of Dublin three years later, Arnold bears the warmest testimony to his fitness for that high office. He is 'a man so good and so great that no folly or wickedness will move him from his purpose,' and 'in point of real essential holiness there does not live a truer Christian than Whately.'

In this and other inward qualities most people would probably now-a-days reckon Arnold as the superior. The head-master of Rugby was certainly a good and holy man, if ever man was. We may dispute his breadth and calmness of temper, his knowledge of the world and of the history of human thought and character,—historian as he was; we may even doubt the results of his teaching (they could hardly fail, in some respects, to have been deeply disappointing to himself if he had lived); but we cannot doubt the deep devotion and piety of his nature. There have been few more thoroughly Christian minds in our century, and it gives one a shock like a personal wound when we read a statement of Newman's, made in the fit of petulant zeal that seized him when abroad, before his mission at Oxford began. Some one, he tells us, said in his hearing that a certain interpretation of Scripture must be Christian 'because Dr. Arnold took it.' He interposed, 'But is *he* a Christian?' Arnold had his doubts in his youth; he was never all his life a Christian after the pattern of Dr. Newman and his school; but we can hardly think of a mind in recent times—unless it be Maurice's—more habitually under the influence of the Divine than that of Arnold. From the time that he took orders and settled at Laleham (1819-28), there was with him 'a deep consciousness of the invisible world.' All his being was interpenetrated with religion. All the acts of his life were coloured by it.[1] 'No one could know him even a little,' said a friend, 'and not be struck by his absolute wrestling with evil, and, with the feeling of God's help on his side, scorning as well as hating it.' As he strove with evil, so he loved Christ, and clung to Him as the one supreme Object of thought, imagination, and affection. He was Christian to the core, and it was the very ardency of his Christian interest that kindled his fierceness alike against 'Oxford malignancy' and school-boy dishonour. He could not bear that men should profess the Christian faith and yet act, whether for a party purpose or school-boy gratification, in the face of Christian principle and precept.

It was the same evident devotion to religion and its verities, as he felt them, that gave his liberal opinions so much weight. Men in general felt, when they heard of his free thoughts about Scripture and the Church, that here at least was the speech of a man who did not undervalue any religious obligation. It was known to be the aim of his life to make a public school Christian, and a more self-denying or devoted task could hardly be imagined than this. Whatever he wrote or said, there were those, and they were an increasing number, who said that it was a genuine religious impulse, and nothing else, that inspired him.

If we ask more particularly what were the elements

---

[1] See *Life*, vol. i. p. 30 *et seq.*

of Arnold's power in quickening religious thought, the answer must be first of all that he too vitalised as Coleridge did the Christian conceptions of his time. He did so, not by carrying them as the former did into a higher region of thought, or fitting them anew to the inner constitution of humanity, but in an equally real and important manner by showing how Christian ideas extend into every aspect of conduct and duty, transfusing and elevating the whole round of life. This was the key-note of his first volume of sermons,[1] and it was more or less the key-note of all. Arnold's studies and tastes, much as he prized Coleridge, did not lead him towards the Coleridgian metaphysics. His views were objective and practical. Christianity, whether or not complete as a philosophy, was to him plainly perfect as an ethic or discipline. It took up the whole man, and there was no part of life beyond its inspiration and control. It was no affair of sects, or mere rule of the 'religious life' specially so called. All idea of isolating religion and keeping it select,—the employment, whether of evangelical or of Anglo-Catholic votary—was hateful to him. It was a life-blood permeating all human activity— school, college, politics, literature,—no less than what is commonly meant by the Church. So it was when he went into the pulpit; he did not put on any clerical tone or separate himself from his other occupations as scholar, historian, inquirer. He was *himself* there as everywhere else, and sought to speak in simple unconventional words, as he would 'in real life,' in

[1] Published in 1828. The last edition was issued by his daughter, Mrs. Forster, in 1878.

serious conversation with a friend, or with those who asked his advice.

There was of course nothing absolutely new in this way of conceiving and applying Christianity, no more than there was anything original in Coleridge's realistic philosophy. It had been a commonplace from the beginning that Christianity was a 'religion of common life.' But not less certainly had it become in many quarters an esoteric or sectarian rather than a common religion; a religion of the cathedral or the conventicle; of 'the fathers' or 'reformers;' of the evangelical tea-circle or the Anglo-Catholic coterie. It bore a note of segregation and exclusion in many forms, and spoke in artificial and 'pious' phraseology. It required, therefore, if not originality, yet something of vital force to bring it back to its primitive energy as not only 'the light of all our seeing,' but the inspiration of all our doing. Arnold and Augustus William Hare did more by their sermons to break down the old technicalities of the pulpit, and to spread a homely vital 'common interest in Christian truths' than any other preachers of their time. Men were made to feel in all ranks how much religion concerned them,—how closely it had to do with their everyday work,—and was designed to be the very breath of their being not merely on Sunday,— or at service and sacrament,—but in every form and expression of public and private activity.

It was this vital and broad grasp of Christian truth that lay at the root of Arnold's well-known idea of the Church as only another name for the State in its perfect development. This seems now an astounding proposition, fitted to take the breath away from some

accepted public teachers. But, as we saw in our last
lecture, large ideas of the Church had a charm for the
highest intelligence of the opening century. The
reign of sectarian commonplace had not yet begun,
and thoughts which the genius of Hooker and of
Burke has consecrated by their exposition were
still deemed worthy of discussion. Neither these
thinkers nor Arnold of course sought to identify the
activities of the Church and the State. They knew
very well that these were two bodies with distinct
spheres of action. They knew also well that, as
things are, they cannot be identical. What they
meant was that the ideal of each of these bodies
merges in that of the other. The State can only
attain its true object, the highest welfare of man,
when it acts 'with the wisdom and goodness of the
Church.' The Church can only attain the same object when 'invested with the sovereign power of the
State.' On the one hand Arnold repudiated strongly
the merely secular view of the State 'as providing
only for physical ends ; ' on the other hand he hated
if possible still more what he regarded as an anti-
Christian view of the Church, that it should be
'ruled by a divinely appointed succession of priests
or governors,' rather than 'by national laws.' The
national commonwealth as represented by Parliament—which in this connection is the *bête noire* of
modern ritualist and dissenter alike—was to him the
fit sphere for the realisation of Christianity.

In speaking of the Church as clothed with the
powers of the State Arnold did not of course mean,
as Anglican and Puritan had both meant in the
seventeenth century, that the Church should enforce

legal penalties, or enact by its authority any uniform plan of church-government and discipline. This was quite inconsistent with his whole mode of thought, and with his special ideal of the Church. He would have the Church 'a sovereign society,' not as exercising separate powers, but because its powers were merged in those of a Christian State, all the public officers of which should feel themselves to be also 'necessarily officers of the Church.' So it seemed to him that the superstitious distinction between clergy and laity would vanish, and so also their consequent jealousy of one another—their spheres being in fact the same, nothing being 'too secular to claim exemption from the enforcement of Christian duty, nothing too spiritual to claim exemption from the control of the government of a Christian State.' Then, as Dean Stanley explains his position, 'the whole nation, amidst much variety of form, ceremonial, and opinion, would at last feel that the great ends of Christian and national society now for the first time realised to their view were a far stronger bond of union between Christians, and a far deeper division from those who were not Christians, than any subordinate principle either of agreement or separation.'

With such general views of the Church it may be imagined that Arnold's ecclesiastical outlook was by no means a happy one in the disturbed years that followed the passing of the Reform Bill. On the one hand he saw, as the liberal politicians of the day did, the urgency of Church reform. It did not appear to him that the Anglican establishment could live unless greatly modified, so as to make an open door for dissenters; on the other hand, he prized the Church

of England as one of the most precious institutions
of the country; and nowhere is there a more eloquent
defence of the blessings of a parochial ministry than
in the pamphlet which he published at that time.
None of his writings made more noise, or gave more
offence, than the *Principles of Church Reform.* It
offended equally churchmen and dissenters. Its
latitudinarianism was obnoxious to the one ; its
defence of an Established Church, and its assaults
upon sectarianism, obnoxious to the other. Its
advocacy of large and liberal changes repelled the
Conservatives ; its severe religious tone displeased
the Liberals. One proposal which it contained
raised a special outcry, namely, that the parish
churches should be open to different forms of worship at different hours, with a view to the comprehension of the dissenters. The plan has been long
acted upon on the Continent ; but to the average
English Churchman there is something peculiarly
exasperating in this suggestion. It stirs his wildest
feelings as well as his most foolish prejudices. And
the storm which descended on Arnold for this and
other suggestions was of the most violent kind. It
even penetrated Rugby, and for a time painfully
interfered with the serenity of his school work.

Yet, as it has been remarked, not a few of the
changes which Arnold then advocated for the increased efficiency of the Church of England have
been since carried out with advantage ; such changes
as the multiplication of bishoprics, the creation of
subordinate or suffragan bishops, the revival of an
inferior order of ministers or deacons, the use of
churches on week-days,' and a more simple order of

service than is enjoined at morning and evening prayer. So it is for the most part. The abuse of the reformer, as well as the blood of the martyr, becomes the seed of the Church, and when the evil day is past the good seed springs up to life.

But we have still to notice the chief service of Arnold to the Christian intelligence of his time. He was not only a profoundly Christian man, breathing the vital atmosphere of Christian truth in all his teaching; nor was he only a church reformer; but he was perhaps more eminently a critical and historical student of Scripture. Here, too, he followed the wake of Coleridge after his own way. He did not borrow from this great teacher. There is hardly any evidence of Coleridge's direct influence upon him; and the *Confessions of an Inquiring Spirit* were not made public till 1840. But his own tastes and studies led him independently in the same direction. He was from the first an earnest student of Niebuhr's great *History of Rome*, and delighted in its critical method. He learned German, so as to be able to read it in the original. He corresponded both with Bunsen and Julius Hare as to its merits. He made, moreover, Bunsen's personal acquaintance in 1827, and derived much stimulus from him in this and other respects. Yet withal Arnold remained, as did also Whately, and their common friend Hampden, entirely English in their spirit of theological inquiry; and of German theology as a whole Arnold seems to have known almost nothing. So far he is different, not only from his friend Hare and Hare's collaborator Thirlwall, but also from Milman, as we shall see, who were well versed in German theological research. If ever, indeed, there was a mind intensely English in the practical ethical bent underlying all his studies and all his work, it was Arnold's.

His powers as an interpreter of Scripture therefore sprang from his own native instincts of inquiry and the clear moral sense which made him hate confusion of thought in all directions. He saw that the whole method of scriptural interpretation, as represented by the Evangelical and High Church Schools alike, was untenable. Scripture was made to mean anything, according to the preconceptions of each. Particularly, it may be said, he had no respect for patristic interpretation. The whole patristic superstition which once more rose to prominence in his day was strongly repelled by him. He recognised no special intelligence in the Ante-Nicene Church, still less in the Church of the fourth and fifth centuries. The interpretation of prophecy more than other parts of Scripture appeared to him a chaos, and to this, therefore, he devoted his main attention. His two sermons, with preface and notes, on this subject, published in 1841, remain the most complete and systematic of any of his fragments on Exegetical Theology. Ten years before, he had drawn attention to the general subject in an essay affixed to his second volume of sermons. Then he was in the more aggressive mood that characterised his earlier years, and expressed himself so as to excite violent commotion in various quarters. In point of fact, there was nothing alarming in Arnold's essay 'on the Right Interpretation of the Scripture.' The only exception to it that would be taken to it now-a-days, as to certain recent interpretations of 'Ruling Ideas of Early Ages'[1] in connection with the Old Testament, is that it does not grasp all the difficulties of the subject or set them in the full light of the historical method. It deals too much in ingenious explanation.

Arnold's principle and method of interpretation are both in the right direction. He recognised clearly that Scripture is not to be regarded as a Koran or infallible code composed at one time, but as a literature of many fragments and times, and of divers authority. Its commands and teaching alike are to be judged according to the occasion and circumstances in which they were given. In other words, they are to be interpreted not absolutely but relatively. The Bible, as to its text, structure, the authorship of its several parts, and its literary and didactic form, is to be read and understood like all other ancient literature ; and if this may seem to render Scriptural interpretation a difficult and somewhat hopeless task, save for the scholarly and trained intelligence, the difficulty is no more than is to be found elsewhere. We cannot fully understand any ancient writings except in this manner. And the Bible has this advantage over all ancient writings, that while it can only be interpreted by the same processes, and is liable to similar uncertainties, there is more than enough in its pages for practical guidance to the simplest reader. In this sense, and in no other, is it true that 'he that runneth may read' and profit by it.

In short, the divine side of Scripture, the side on

---

[1] *Ruling Ideas of Early Ages and their relation to Old Testament Faith*, by J. B. Mozley, D.D., late Professor of Divinity at Oxford.

which it appeals to our spiritual life and *finds* us, as Coleridge said—is legible by every devout reader. But the human or literary side of it presents everywhere difficulties of a similar character to those found in all literature of the remote past. These difficulties must be faced in the same manner and by the very same processes as we must face similar difficulties in the works of Plato or Aristotle. It proves nothing against the truth to be found in these writings, that scholiasts and commentators have given véry different versions of parts of them or of the principles they are supposed to teach. Nor is the perplexity of commentators, in the case of the Bible or any other writing, a necessary index of the obscurity of the writers. Misreading of Scripture, no less than misreading of Plato, may come, and in point of fact does come, more frequently from reading into them ideas of our own than from any real obscurity in the texts themselves.

How much this has been the case with Scripture it is needless to say. Dogmas have been brought to Scripture, and Scripture been made to square with them, instead of truth being sought carefully in its pages, or by comparison of Scripture with Scripture. To the true interpreter dogma is the end and never the beginning of Scriptural interpretation. In the strict sense, indeed, dogma is not found in Scripture at all. It is deduced from it ; but it is the product of much more than Scripture. There it only appears, in a limited 'concrete' sense, as bearing on religious feeling and character.

We cannot too highly estimate the services of Arnold as a Biblical student in his time. His friend

Bonamy Price [1] has perhaps spoken of his work in this direction in somewhat extravagant terms, and with too little regard to the work of others. For the spirit of genuine historical criticism was in fact largely at work in the years that preceded the Oxford movement, not only in Coleridge, but in Hare and Thirlwall at Cambridge, and again in Whately and Milman. Yet more than any of these men, perhaps, Arnold combined with critical acumen and breadth of historical perception a devout, inspiring, and solemn appreciation of the spiritual side of Scripture. In exegesis he was certainly richer, if not stronger or clearer, than his friend Whately. The two sermons 'On the Interpretation of Prophecy' speak a deeper and more evangelical language than the essays 'On the peculiar difficulties of St. Paul's writings.' There, as everywhere, Arnold is not only Christian, but delicately, pervasively, and in the right sense, if not in the commonplace sense of the word, evangelically Christian. To the impartial student of these, as indeed of all Arnold's sermons, it must remain a saddening thought that the religious world, both Anglo-Catholic and Puritan, should have once denounced such a teacher and called for his condemnation.

But it was neither Whately nor Arnold, but the third of the friends, since comparatively forgotten, who called forth the loudest denunciations of the time. To the historian of religious opinion there is something highly significant in the successive agitations which were excited in the Church of England by Dr. Hampden. According to all unbiassed testimony, he was a particularly gentle and peace-

[1] In a Letter, *Life of Arnold*, vol. i. p. 213.

loving man. Of all the contentions associated with his name, 'his only part in them,' it has been said, 'was the pain they could not fail to occasion him.' He was, however, Mr. Mozley says, 'one of the most unprepossessing of men.' There was a certain stolidity about him that contrasted strongly with the bright, vivacious, and singularly loveable figures with whom the eyes of Oriel men were then familiarised. Even the less agreeable men had life, candour, and not a little humour. Hampden's face was inexpressive, his head was set deep on his broad shoulders, and his voice was harsh and unmodulated. Some one said of him that he 'stood before you like a milestone and brayed at you like a jackass.'[1] We have quoted these words, certainly not for any value they have, but as a piquant expression of old Oxford humour—I suppose. In Mr. Mozley's volumes there are not a few such sketches, but none more animated or inspired with more bitterness. The book, as a whole, is a readable collection of old stories and recollections of the famous men who then adorned Oriel; but it is almost absolutely worthless for any other purpose. Its judgments of men and things are neither candid nor intelligent. It fills one with astonishment that the author of such a book should at any time have had influence in connection with a theological or religious movement. Hampden was probably what is called a 'heavy man;' his books are certainly not light reading; but so far from being unloveable, he seems to have been a singularly amiable and tender-hearted man.

But what then was his special offence? And why should he, more than any of the early Oriel School,

---

[1] *Reminiscences,* vol. i. p. 380.

have been the victim of persecution and annoyance? The real reasons are not far to seek. His success, first in being appointed to the Chair of Divinity in 1836, and then, eleven years later, in being made Bishop of Hereford, was unacceptable to many.[1] His pamphlet, in 1834, advocating the admission of Dissenters to the University, was not only unacceptable but deeply offensive.[2] The man who, at that date, wrote in Oxford as follows, could only be regarded equally by Anglicans and Puritans with much dislike. ' I do not scruple,' he says, ' to avow myself favourable to a removal of all tests, so far as they are employed as securities of Orthodoxy. Tests are no part of religious education.' But further, Hampden in his very earliest work on *The Philosophical Evidence of Christianity* (1827),[3] and again, in his famous Bampton Lectures (1832), assailed what has long been and continues to be the very apple of the traditional theologian's eye—the vast fabric of ' logical theology.' The whole aim of his Bampton Lectures was to explain how such a theology had grown up under the influence of the scholastic philosophy. It was, in

[1] Was there not something also in his having snatched the Chair of Moral Philosophy from Newman in 1834?

[2] H.R.H. the Duke of Sussex wrote (June 1837) to Dr. Hampden : ' The unfair and unjust attacks on your " Bampton Lectures " were all the more disreputable, because unheard of until a public testimony of the approval of a liberal government had been conferred on you. I fear that jealousy, not justice, was the prompter to such acts.' Lord Radnor, in the House of Lords, said, ' He had no doubt that all the hostility to him (Dr. H.) arose from his advocating the admission of dissenters to the University.'

[3] *Essay on the Philosophical Evidence of Christianity ; or the credibility obtained to a Scriptural Revelation, from its coincidence with the facts of nature.* 1827.

his view, no Divine product nor even any directly derivative product of Divine revelation. It was largely a purely human compound, based on the logical terminology of the Patristic and Mediæval schools, and instead of being a blessing to the Church it had, as he supposed and said, been in many ways a curse, 'the principal obstacle to the union and peace of the Church.' 'The combination and analyses of words which the logical theology has produced have given occasion,' in his own words, 'to the passions of men to arm themselves in behalf of the phantoms thus called into being.'

The wonder is not that such sentiments raised a commotion when they came to be understood, but that they should not have excited more attention when they were delivered. There was nothing essentially untrue or dangerous in them, but they touched to the very core the dogmatic spirit. Whately had assailed many popular theological errors, dogmas which he considered to be mistakenly identified with the teaching of St. Paul. Arnold had proclaimed his dislike of theological technicalities by divesting his own preaching of them entirely, and setting forth in ordinary language and direct and simple forms for his parishioners, and afterwards for his schoolboys, what he believed to be the truth as it is in Jesus. Both had, by their broader interpretations of Scripture, emphasised the distinction between the simple apostolic doctrine and later elaborate theologies. But Hampden did more than this. He explained, or endeavoured to explain, how the earlier Scriptural faith had passed into later creeds and theologies. And it is strange, but true, that to the polemical Theologian *explanation* is often more exasperating than *contradiction*.[1] Not only so, but the principle of explanation with which Hampden worked, not merely threatened this or that traditional dogma, but was a solvent of all. The whole fabric of patristic, mediæval, and Anglo-Catholic theology seemed to go down before it, and to be converted into nothing but a phantasmal terminology. The dogma of the Trinity, in its Athanasian form, vanished into a mere series of scholastic propositions. This, and nothing less than this, was the contention of his opponents afterwards. The famous pamphlet, *Elucidation of Dr. Hampden's Theological Statements*, attributed to Dr. Newman and denounced by Dr. Arnold, as containing a series of deliberate misrepresentations ('falsehoods' is Arnold's word, but we shrink from using it), took up this ground. Dr. Pusey took the same ground. Samuel Wilberforce, Mr. Gladstone, and many others happily forgotten, virtually took the same ground; and this in face of Hampden's own statement in his lectures that the Trinitarian doctrine itself, in its scriptural simplicity, ' emerged from the mists of human speculation, like the bold naked land on which an atmosphere of fog had for a while rested and then been dispersed.'

The wonder, then, truly is, in the light of all that was afterwards said and written of the Bampton Lectures, that they passed at the time without hostile criticism. Not only did they do so, but, according to

[1] Such a sentence as the following may be supposed to have been particularly exasperating : ' Whilst theologians of the schools have thought they were establishing religious truths by elaborate argumentation, they have been only multiplying and rearranging theological language.'

Dr. Hampden's friends, they were received by large and approving audiences. Even Mr. Mozley admits that 'a considerable number went to hear the first lecture.'[1]   Afterwards he says they were neither

---

[1] It is hardly necessary to say that all that Mr. Mozley says as to Dr. Hampden is to be received with suspicion. A writer who still virtually asserts that the Bampton Lectures were inspired, if not composed, in great part by Blanco White, notwithstanding the testimony of Dr. Hampden's family to the contrary (his children having often played in his study while he was writing them), and the absolute discrepancy between such a style as that of the Lectures and Blanco White's writings, is really unworthy of credence. The story was a silly and false scandal at the time, which could only have sprung up in the atmosphere of ridiculous gossip often found at a University seat. It is not made any better by Mr. Mozley's new statements as to his being a witness to the great intimacy which prevailed between Hampden and Blanco White in 1831 and 1832, while Hampden was preparing the Lectures. Be it so. Because two men are friends, and take constant walks together, and even give and receive 'material assistance in the way of information,' is one to be accused of having given lectures, and published them as his own, while they were in reality those of his friend? For if the plagiarism does not come to this, it comes to nothing. In gathering information, and even getting 'material assistance,' surely any author is not only entitled, but bound to utilise his friends—if they are willing to be so utilised. But the whole charge was a silly one, hurtful to those who made it, and despicable in those who repeat it. It shows, moreover, a singular lack of intelligence in an Oxford *littérateur* or theologian. To any real insight or knowledge it is no more doubtful that the same mind which conceived and produced the Essay on 'The Philosophical Evidence of Christianity,' when in London in 1829, conceived and produced the Bampton Lectures—with whatever assistance—in Oxford in 1832, than it is that these two books were published at their respective dates. An injurious and unworthy note in S. Wilberforce's Life, vol. i. pp. 468-9, has contributed to revive this scandal about the composition of Dr. Hampden's Lectures; but it contains nothing new. The fact of the prevalence of the scandal—its 'being spoken of,'—seems to a certain class of ecclesiastical critics evidence that it was true. Really this is only evidence of the facility with which the same class of minds propagate what they wish to be true.

' listened to nor read.' But the fact remains, that they were delivered with some degree of approval three years before, and published two years before, they were found to contain the dangerous heresies afterwards attributed to them. Both Whately and Arnold dwell upon this fact, in evidence of the personal rancour that animated many of Dr. Hampden's opponents, and of ' the folly and cruelty and baseness' of the calumnious agitation with which he was assailed.

There have been successive agitations of a similar kind in Oxford since 1836 ; Hampden himself, eleven years later (1847), when made Bishop of Hereford, was for a second time the victim of the same persecuting and unworthy spirit. But none of these attacks exceeded in noise and malignity the famous or infamous outburst which in 1836 assailed the Bampton Lectures of 1832. There have been, as Whately said, ' other persecutions as unjust and as cruel (for burning of heretics was happily not in the power of the Hampden persecutors) ; but for impudence I never knew the like.' The exhibition of riotous and hostile feeling was ' startling even to those who had not anticipated much greatness or goodness from human nature.'[1] ' Was there ever,' says Arnold, ' an accusation involving its unhappy promoters in such a dilemma of infamy, compromisers of mischievous principles in 1832, 1833, 1834, and 1835 ; or slanderers of a good and most Christian man in 1836?'

As soon as Hampden's appointment to the Divinity professorship was announced the outbreak began, under the stimulus and leadership of the High Church party. Representations were addressed to

[1] Whately.

Government, to the Archbishop, to the Bishops.   A
committee, which met in the common room of Corpus
Christi College, was nominated to conduct the prosecution against one who had asserted principles not
only subversive of the authority of the Church, but of
the whole fabric and reality of Christian truth.   Newman and Pusey vied with each other in setting forth
Dr. Hampden's errors.   A Convocation was sum-
moned [1] to consider a Statute to be passed by the
University depriving the author of his voice in the
nomination of Select Preachers.   The 'non-placet' of
the Proctors at the first meeting interposed to prevent
the passing of the Statute.   'Instantly,' writes Mr.
Nassau Senior, who is not likely to have exaggerated
the scene, 'there arose shouts, screams, and groans
from the galleries and the area, such as no deliberative
Assembly probably ever heard before.'   A second
Convocation was called for May, when a change of
proctors had taken place, and the obnoxious and, it
is believed, 'illegal' Statute was then passed.   The
press, of course, from different sides, whipped up the
excitement ; and a debate in the House of Lords in
the following year brought it to a height, and possibly
helped in some degree to allay it.   The fever heat,
however, may be said to have continued for two years,
and even when it calmed down, left embers still burning and ready to flame forth again—as it did in 1847.
Great names of statesmen as well as ecclesiastics were
prominent in the fray, and came out of it with a somewhat damaged reputation.   The Archbishop (Howley)
makes a poor figure throughout.   The Duke of
Wellington did not add to his glory.   His attitude

[1] March 22, 1836.

in the House of Lords in reference to Dr. Hampden's explanations was neither magnanimous nor intelligent. Mr. Gladstone, long afterwards, in 1856, had the grace to write to Dr. Hampden, expressing regret for his concurrence in the vote of the University. He had not taken actual part in it, but was only prevented from doing so ' by an accident.' The letter is alike honourable to the writer, and to the Bishop, all whose ' heretical ' troubles were by this time past. There is one other famous name in the renewed persecution of 1847 that bore to the last the unhappy dint of encounter with Dr. Hampden. It is one of the melancholy lessons of the history of religious opinion that the interests, or supposed interests, of Christian Faith should too often overcome the interests of righteousness and fair dealing. And it is sad, but true, that the names of Samuel Wilberforce and John Henry Newman should both bear the scar of ' unfairness ' in dealing with this matter, which the most ingenious defences of their friends have wholly failed to remove.[1]

[1] In vindication of what is said in the text as to Dr. Newman, it is enough to quote a single sentence from a letter of Bishop Wilberforce to the Bishop of Exeter, when the movement against Dr. Hampden so entirely collapsed in 1848. He is defending himself to his friend for his having withdrawn the prosecution against Dr. Hampden :—' I can only account for my words seeming to mean more by my writing in some indignation at the *unfairness of the Extracts* [by which Dr Newman sought to condemn Dr. Hampden], *an unfairness I had pointed out to Newman in* 1836.' This is the statement not of an enemy, or of Dr. Arnold, but of a friend, and in 1836 a co-operator. Further, as to Dr. Wilberforce himself, and the eclipse which his name suffered in connection with the second prosecution of Dr. Hampden, I would refer readers to vol. i. c. vi., of the well-known *Life*. It is one of the saddest chapters in an entertaining, but by no means edifying, book. The dislike of Dr. Hampden by High Church writers to this day is quite 'phenomenal,' as the newspapers say. Witness a review of Dr. Mozley's

In comparison with his host of persecutors, the character of Hampden himself, uninteresting as he may have been, shines forth with consistent lustre. I will venture on a further statement, which is true at least to my own experience, astounding as it may be to conventional theologians on one side and the other, that there are seeds of thought in Dr. Hampden's writings far more fertile and enduring than any to be found in the writings of his chief opponents. There is hardly one of the principles for which he contended —the supremacy of Scripture over tradition—the independence of spiritual religion both of theological nomenclature and Sacramental usage—above all the great distinction of the truth as it is in Scripture from the later dogmatic forms in which it has been embodied, that have not since more or less commended themselves to all rational theologians. Forgotten as they now are, and never in any sense popular, the student of Christian thought will always turn to the Bampton Lectures of 1832 with interest and profit.

A few words must suffice for the two other names which, although not belonging to the Oriel school, were so far animated by the same spirit at the same time. These names in their full significance belong, we have already said, to a later period in the history of religious opinion. They are rightly noticed here, however, because both struck, in the years of the ' noetic' school, a note of theological advance which

Letters, in the *Spectator* of 15th Nov. 1884, where he is roundly abused not only as ' a dull writer and confused thinker—but an intolerant bigot till he became a bishop ' ! How strangely inextinguishable is the fire of old ecclesiastical feuds !

resounded widely amid the so-called 'heretical' noises of the time. Thirlwall's translation of Schleiermacher's Essay on St. Luke, with a lengthened introduction, appeared in 1825. The translator was not then even a clergyman. He was a student at Lincoln's Inn, in preparation for the career of the barrister. Connop Thirlwall, however, had from his early Cambridge days been almost as much interested in theology as in literature and history. Pascal's *Thoughts* was one of his choicest studies. He contemplated learning Hebrew while still at school. His visit to Germany and acquaintance with Bunsen before 1820, not to speak of his 'inseparable' friendship with Julius Charles Hare, strengthened his interest in sacred and critical studies ; and shortly after the publication of the *Essay on St. Luke,* he abandoned the legal for a clerical career. The publication of this essay, according to Dean Perowne, the editor of Thirlwall's very interesting letters, 'was an epoch in the history of English theology,' as well as in Thirlwall's own life.[1] The volume is entirely critical in its

---

[1] The latter statement is made specially in allusion to the fact that the publication of the essay may be said to have procured for him his bishopric. Lord Melbourne, who had taken an interest in his career from the first, read the Essay, with the Introduction, and was much struck by both. He had wished, therefore, to promote Thirlwall even earlier to the Episcopal bench, but the bishops whom he consulted 'expressed a want of confidence' in the orthodoxy of the volume ! In 1840, however, when the See of St. David's fell vacant, he appointed him at once to the vacancy, and a graphic account has been preserved (see Torrens's *Memoirs of Viscount Melbourne,* vol. ii. pp. 330-332) of the interview which took place between the Premier and the Bishop-designate. When Thirlwall waited upon him, Melbourne was in bed, surrounded with letters and newspapers, but immediately opened the conversation. ' Very glad to see you ; sit down, sit down ; hope you are come to say you accept ; I only wish

character, and could hardly have been read beyond the circle of the learned. The explanation of the interest which it created is to be found in the prevalent stagnation of the theological atmosphere at the time, and the current notions that any critical inquiry into the composition of the books of Scripture, and of the Gospels in particular, was inimical to the full acceptance of their sacred character. Biblical criticism, notwithstanding the labours of Bishop Marsh in the beginning of the century, was so dead in England that even Christian scholars shrank from any real sifting into sources or text. The inquiries of German theologians, so far as known, were looked upon with suspicion. The Bampton Lecturer of 1824, Mr. Conybeare, had sounded a note of alarm regarding them, which was taken up, as we shall see in our next lecture, by Hugh James Rose and others. The sacerdotal influences which were beginning to move Oxford were equally hostile with Puritanism to all German criticism and divinity. Then as always, even to our own time, German theologians

you to understand that I don't intend, if I know it, to make a heterodox bishop. I don't like heterodox bishops. As men they may be very good anywhere else, but I don't think they have any business on the bench. I take great interest,' he continued, 'in theological questions,' pointing to a pile of folio editions of the Fathers. 'They are excellent reading, and very amusing ; some time or other we must have a talk about them. I sent your edition of Schleiermacher to Lambeth, and asked the Primate to tell me candidly what he thought of it ; and, look, here are his notes on the margin ; pretty copious too. He does not concur in all your opinions, but he says there is nothing heterodox in your book.' It is a fact deserving notice that it was to Lord Melbourne also that Hampden's appointment as Regius Professor of Divinity was owing, and expressly on the ground ' of profound theological knowledge,' combined with ' a liberal spirit of inquiry tempered by due caution ' !

of the most varying tendency were slumped together as equally heterodox. As Thirlwall himself wrote, 'It would almost seem as if at Oxford the knowledge of German subjected a Divine to the same suspicion of heterodoxy which was attached some centuries back to the knowledge of Greek.' Particularly the hypotheses which had then begun in Germany, and which were destined to run in such endless series, as to the composition of the Gospels, and their relation to one another, were viewed with jealousy as being, in the words of a once well-known book,[1] 'not only detrimental to the character of the sacred writers, but also as diminishing the value and importance of their testimony, and further, as tending to sap the inspiration of the New Testament.' The mere fact that the Biblical studies of the age were mainly pursued under the guidance of this book—not without value in its day, but entirely uncritical in its spirit and method—is the best evidence of how low these studies had sunk, and how little the theological mind of the time was prepared to welcome such an Essay as Thirlwall introduced to it.

His 'Introduction' is a singularly enlightened, closely reasoned, and wise piece of writing, like all the theological disquisitions in the shape of 'Charges,' that long afterwards came from his pen. He admits at once the inconsistency of such inquiries as those of Schleiermacher and his forerunner Eichhorn and others with the long prevailing doctrine of verbal inspiration—a doctrine, however, which, although still generally received, he esteems so entirely abandoned

[1] Horne's *Introduction to the Critical Study and Knowledge of the Holy Scriptures* (1818).

by the learned as not to require refutation. Nor does he think the more flexible theories of inspiration as divided into 'inspiration of suggestion' and 'inspiration of superintendency' any more tenable in the face of the facts which the text of Scripture brings before us. He turns rather with approval to the 'old opinion' that Scripture is indeed inspired, but only in its substance and spirit,—'in the continual presence and action of what is most vital and essential in Christianity itself.' And this, the only true and tenable view consistent with the actual character of the Biblical Literature, has no need, he says, to fear 'any investigation into the mutual relation and origin of the Gospels.'

This was a strong and bold attitude in 1825, before Coleridge's *Confessions of an Inquiring Spirit* had seen the light. It shows plainly how the critical spirit was working in many minds. There is no evidence of Coleridge having exercised any special influence over Thirlwall, notwithstanding the latter's close friendship with Hare, and participation in many of his sympathies. The connection of the two friends was on the side of philology and history rather than of philosophy. Thirlwall's mind, moreover, was cast in a quite different mould. Its highest attribute was a dry light without any mystic depths or philosophic aspirations. Changing his career after mature deliberation, he carried with him into the Church the same compass and balance of judicial faculty which would have made him one of the greatest lawyers, as they made him, intellectually, the greatest bishop of his time. No one on the contemporary bench can be named with him in mere intellectual magnanimity and power.

There were other non-Episcopal names greater in theological insight and in the sustained contributions which they made to sacred literature. But there were none who brought a more massive learning or more rational lucidity to the discussion of theological questions. He was a true Christian sage, fitted to take his place in the innermost circle of the sages of all time. And it was well, as Dean Stanley says, that this was so, and that a bishop of such massive intellectuality and large wisdom should have been one of the ruling spirits of our time.

The name of Milman does not pale beside that of Thirlwall. There are those indeed who esteem it a still more brilliant name in sacred literature. So far both were alike. They never acquired the sort of popular distinction that waits on the leaders of great ecclesiastical parties,—men of the stamp of the late Dr. Wilberforce or Dr. Pusey. Distinction of this kind was alien to their nature. Just because they were men of large intellectual vision, and bore the crown of literary as well as theological genius, they were unfitted to be party men, or to soil their garments in the mire of ecclesiastical contention. Both spent their lives more or less in their study, rather than in the religious world. And so there has not come to either the kind of fame which resounds in this world, and which is apt to be the reverberation of a common noise, rather than the intelligent appreciation of intelligent minds. Milman is probably less known than even Thirlwall. I have met with people of education, and some degree of culture, who were, if not ignorant of his name, ignorant of all he has done. They were astonished to hear him spoken of as a great historian. They had never read a word of his *History of Latin Christianity*, nor even of his *History of the Jews*. They had never heard of him as one of the greatest names that the Church of England has ever produced. In combination of pure genius with learning, of sweep of thought with picturesque and powerful variety of literary culture and expression, he has always seemed to me by far the first of modern English churchmen.

Henry Hart Milman was educated at Oxford, and was a conspicuous man there during both the earlier and later Oriel movements. He was distinguished as a poet as early as 1820; and although his poetry has failed to live, save in a few hymns, it remains an interesting monument of the early glow and splendour of his genius. *The Fall of Jerusalem* and *The Martyr of Antioch* contain passages of great power and beauty; but, like the poetic efforts of a great female genius of our times, they are lacking in creative art and movement. They are poetical essays, rather than poems springing spontaneously and irresistibly out of the heart and imagination of the writer. Poems of this secondary class, however fine in part, never survive. Already, in 1827, Milman was Bampton Lecturer as well as Poet; and his genius seems to have been recognised by the different schools of thought that had risen or were rising within the University. The *élève* of Brazenose College, and Professor of Poetry, did not however join himself to any of these schools. Before the date of his Bampton Lectures he had already diverged into paths of inquiry entirely separating him from traditional Anglicanism. An

Anglo-Catholic of the Keble or Newman type he could never have been with all his poetic and concrete tastes. But he did not any more connect himself with the 'Noetic' school. Whately and Hampden could hardly have been congenial to him. From the first, however, he belonged to the school of inquiry and not of tradition. He had imbibed the same critical spirit and love of original historic research that we find in Arnold, and Hare, and Thirlwall. He had made himself, as they had done, familiar with German learning, and entered as early they had done upon the application of its principles to history. Not only so, but he had chosen for this purpose the most difficult of all departments, the history of the Jews, which, as he himself said, had been looked upon as forbidden ground. He resolved that there was nothing in so-called sacred history, any more than in the history of Greece or Rome, to exempt it from the laws of criticism. The same principles which proved so fertile in the one case would yield no less rich results in the other. This was the key-note to the great work to which he had consecrated his life, while Whately was still busy with his Essays, and Arnold was writing his Sermons. The *History of the Jews*, in three small volumes of the Family Library, was published in 1829.

No sooner were the volumes made public than they raised a wild commotion, not only in England, but in Scotland. All the current religious magazines assailed them as subversive of the supernatural in Scripture, and generally tending to minimise or degrade the idea of Divine Revelation. The *Christian*

Instructor, the once well-known organ of the evangelical party in the Church of Scotland, while ac-
knowledging the 'captivating style of the book, and
the felicity and attractiveness of its historical pictures,
is forced deeply to lament that it should ever have
seen the light, especially as part of the Family
Library, intended for domestic use.' So violent
proved the noise against the book, and so persistent
the prejudices with which it was assailed, that the
publisher was forced to stop the series of which it
formed a part.

What then is the real character of the book? It is
a charming and attractive narrative. Forty years
ago it charmed me more than I can well recall and
express. For the first time one felt the heroes of the
Old Testament, and the institutions and usages of
the Hebrew people described with a vividness and
reality that made them live before the mind's eye and
brought them within the sphere of fact, rather than
of pulpit convention. Strange, this was one of the
very accusations against the History. It spoke of
Abraham as an 'Eastern Sheik' or 'Emir,' of the
'quiet and easy Isaac,' of the 'cautious, observant,
subtle, and kind Jacob.' It pointed to the undoubted
fact that we do not find even in Abraham 'that nice
and lofty sense of veracity which came with a later
civilisation.' It explained the overthrow of the
cities of Sodom by the inflammable character of the
soil on which, and of the materials with which, they
were built. It made nothing of the then received
chronology of the Bible, which has really no higher
authority than Archbishop Ussher in the seventeenth
century. It recognised the exaggeration of the

Scriptural numbers so obvious to every intelligent reader, and naturally arising out of the circumstances. 'All kinds of numbers,' as the author afterwards explained,[1] 'are uncertain in ancient MSS., and have been subject to much greater corruption than any other part of the text.' And so long ago as the time of Bishop Burnet, the matter was left to the free judgment of the clergy of the Church of England. It explained naturally the passage of the Red Sea, and generally brought the light of criticism to bear upon 'the Eastern veil of Allegory' in which much of the narrative of the Old Testament is invested. Doubtless at the time these were startling features in a 'History of the Jews,' and those who are familiar with the state of the religious world then and long afterwards will not wonder at the violent excitement which it raised. In truth, however, Milman, in the light of such Old Testament criticism as we are now familiar with, must be pronounced a highly conservative historian. Our modern schools would, I fear, judge him 'unscientific.' He repudiated in good faith any antisupernatural bias, and deliberately separated himself from the extreme school of modern criticism. Its spirit of endless analysis and love for turning everything upside down was thoroughly uncongenial to his mind. He had too much imagination as well as faith and sobriety of temper for such work; and he remained to the end what he was plainly from the first, an historical genius who, while urged by his critical powers to sift everything to the bottom and to take nothing for granted merely because it was connected with traditional theology, was yet no less urged

[1] New Edition, Preface, 1863.

by his poetic and concrete tastes to paint a picture
rather than give a mere tableau of critical processes.
Erudite as any German, and familiar to the time of
his death (1868) with the latest results of German
critical speculation, he was yet, in the moulding power
of his great intellect and his large knowledge of life
and literature—in short, in his gifts as an historic
artist,—as unlike as possible to the common type of
German theologian.   He was thoroughly English in
his tastes ;   and his main distinction, like that of
Whately and Arnold and Hampden, was his clear
recognition of the difference between a simple and
traditional Christianity, between what is essential
to religion, and what is temporary and extraneous
to it.   This thought pervades his earlier History ;
it is emphasised in the Preface to the new and
enlarged edition of 1863.   It is the closing thought
of his great *History of Latin Christianity.*   Whatever part of our ancient dogmatic systems, he says,
may fall into disuse 'as beyond the proper range of
human thought and language,' and however far the
'Semitic portions' of the sacred records may have
to submit to 'wider interpretation' 'in order to
harmonise them with the irrefutable conclusions of
science,' the 'unshadowed essence' of Divine Truth
as enshrined in the words of Christ, 'the primal and
indefeasible truths of Christianity,' will live for ever.
All else is transient and mutable—dogmatic form—
sacramental usage—ecclesiastical rite.   That which in
its very nature is changing, and which the history
of the Church shows to have already changed many
times, cannot be enduring.   But the 'truth as it is in
Jesus' 'shall not pass away,' 'clearer, fuller, more

comprehensive and balanced' as may become our view of it. Here the very note of the 'Noetic' School is struck, and Milman therefore deserves a place by the side of it. He is greater than most if not all of the School, but it is the same liberal spirit which speaks in it and in him.

III.

OXFORD OR ANGLO CATHOLIC MOVEMENT.

WHAT is known as the Oxford Movement had its first beginnings in the same centre of intellectual life as the early Oriel School. It sprang as a secondary crop from the same soil. The early Oriel men had all attained to maturity by the year 1825. Hampden, the youngest, was then thirty-two years of age.[1] Keble was the oldest of the new Oxford group,[2] and chronologically, as we before remarked, may be said to blend the schools. He was a fellow of Oriel before either Arnold or Hampden.[3] The same 'Oriel Common Room' where so many 'learned and able, not rarely subtle and disputatious conversations took place,' found those men frequently together in the later years of the second decade of the century.[4] Who can tell whether the seeds of the great reaction against liberalism, which Keble formally commenced, may not have been sown as far back as those discussions? But the author of the *Christian Year* did not need any

[1] Born 1793.

[2] Born 1792. Pusey was born 1800; J. H. Newman 1801.

[3] Keble was elected Probationer Fellow in 1811. Hampden became fellow in 1814; Arnold in 1815.

[4] Keble fancied that he had quitted Oxford officially in 1817, but he became College tutor in the end of the year, and remained more or less closely connected with the College till 1823.

provocation to the course on which he entered. He was from the first an Anglican of the Anglicans. Unlike Newman, he had no evangelical or liberal preconceptions to get rid of. He was a Tory of the old school, to whom the Church of England was not only dear, but to whom there was no other Church.[1] The *Christian Year* had already appeared in 1827, and when the strain of the liberal storm came in 1832, and all the spirit of the young Oxford Churchmen was stirred within them, it was only natural that he, quiet but intensely dogmatic as he was, should have taken a temporary lead. Dr. Newman has expressly signalised his famous Assize Sermon in the summer[2] of 1833, and published under the title of *National Apostasy*, as the formal beginning of the movement.[3]

The same master hand has sketched the general influences under which the movement arose. The new literary spirit of the time, the poetry of the Lake School, the mediæval romanticism of Sir Walter Scott, the philosophy of Coleridge, all bore their share in deepening men's thoughts and awakening the thirst after nobler ideas in religion as in other things. It is a special tribute to the far-reaching genius of our countryman that his romances should have not only been the delight of thousands, but should have stimulated the enthusiasm for a richer culture, and prepared the mental soil everywhere for

[1] Yet he says in one of his letters to his biographer, Sir J. T. Coleridge, 'I was myself inclined to Eclecticism at one time.' A very mild inclination of this sort may have marked his earliest Oriel days, but no trace of it remains in any of his writings.

[2] 14th July.   [3] *Apologia*, p. 100.

larger conceptions of society and of the Church. As
may be supposed, the opinion expressed by Newman
of Coleridge is a modified, while a highly significant
one. 'While history in prose and verse,' he says,
'was thus made the instrument of church feelings
and opinions, a philosophical basis for the same was
laid in England by a very original thinker, who, while
he indulged a liberty of speculation which no Christian can tolerate, yet after all instilled a higher philosophy into inquiring minds than they had hitherto
been accustomed to accept. In this way he made
trial of his age, and succeeded in interesting its genius
in the cause of Catholic truth.' [1]

During the crisis which followed the Reform Bill
of 1832, there were evidently two currents of religious
opinion running strongly—the one more or less in
sympathy with the prevailing liberalism, and the
other strongly against it. This latter current was
reactionary; but it was something more. It was
negative—opposed to liberalism in Church and State
—but it also contained within itself a new and creative conservatism, one of the chief principles of which
was a fresh organisation of the Church.[2] This is
apparent to all in the sequel of events. But what is
less understood is the extent to which these two
currents crossed one another and intermingled before
they took their respective directions. They not only
for a time lay side by side in the bosom of Oriel

---

[1] *Apologia*, p. 185, quoted from an Article by himself in the
British Critic, 1839.

[2] This is true of Scotland as well as England. The parallelism
between the rise of High Churchism in England and Scotland during
the decade 1832-42 has yet to be intelligently described.

College, but both the men who in the end led the conservative reaction for a time inclined to liberalism.

Dr. Newman has told us this of himself. He says, indeed, that whatever may have been Whately's influence over him, he was never inclined to his theology. Yet in the very same breath he tells us that there was a time in his Oriel experience when he was beginning 'to prefer intellectual excellence to moral.' He 'was drifting in the direction of liberalism,' and commonly understood, as we shall see, to be a follower of Whately. The case of Dr. Pusey is a more remarkable one. This great theologian and leader, so identified with the highest development of the dogmatic spirit in England, was, in the beginning of his career, supposed to be and vigorously denounced as a theological liberal. And there was good ground for the supposition. From the time that he obtained his Oriel fellowship in 1822, to the date of his first publication in 1828, the line of his main inquiry and thought ran in an eminently rational direction. He had been abroad—attracted, like other young minds of the time, by the phenomena of German theology,— and he gave the result of his studies to the world in a brief 'Historical inquiry into the probable causes of the Rationalist character of German Theology.' A second and larger part was added in 1830, after the author had become Regius Professor of Hebrew— an office retained by him during his long life.

The *motif* of Dr. Pusey's book was not indeed a vindication of German Theology in its rationalistic developments. It was, however, a defence of it from the indiscriminate assaults contained in 'Discourses preached before the University of Cambridge, by

Hugh James Rose,' and published by him in 1825,
under the title of *The State of Protestantism in
Germany*. Rose has been panegyrised by Dr. Newman. He was, so to speak, a Tractarian before the
Tractarians, a man of warmth and energy, with fine
sensibilities, and an enthusiastic love of what he
believed to be divine truth. He must have had
many high qualities to have left such an impression
as he has done, not only on Dr. Newman's mind, but
on many minds of a different order. But he had
also many of the vices of his school, invincible
prejudice, incapacity of discrimination, ignorance of
historic method, lack of tolerance and sympathy
beyond the range of the Church of England.[1] In
contrast to Rose's book, Pusey's is an eminently fair,
reasonable, and candid inquiry, liberal, in the best
sense of the word, as recognising what is good no less
than what is bad in German theology, and especially
as setting the worst phases of German rationalism in
the light of the causes which have operated in pro-
ducing them. The author was no more in love with
rationalism than Mr. Rose, but he understood, as the

---

[1] The spirit of Rose's book may be judged from the following
sentence :—' If it be essential to a Protestant Church to possess a constant power of varying her belief' (by which he means revising her
standards of belief), 'let us remember that ours is assuredly no
Protestant Church.' We can, of course, only judge of Rose from his
book, which is not in any sense a good or worthy book ; but a man is
so often much better than his books, especially if they are polemical,
that the feeling entertained by some of Hugh James Rose that he was
the most intelligent and high-minded of the theologians who set the
Anglo-Catholic movement agoing, and that its course would have been
different if he had been spared, may be well founded. Bishop Wordsworth of St. Andrews has expressed this opinion strongly to the
writer.

former did not do, all the phenomena which went under that name, what varying shades of truth and falsehood they presented, and by what intelligible links they were connected with one another. Nothing, indeed, is more remarkable in Dr. Pusey's work than the breadth and power of historical analysis it displays, its extreme fairness ; and even to this day, when so many accounts have been given of the historical development of German theology from different points of view, it still deserves perusal.

The result, as may be supposed, was that Pusey was denounced as a defender of Rationalism. The liberal spirit which he had shown in the study of strange opinions could only proceed from a theological liberal. He was accused, among other things, of 'an intemperate opposition to all articles'— a 'hatred of all systems'—of impugning 'the inspiration of the historical parts of Scripture'—of speaking of 'a new era of theology' (as if there could be such a thing), 'of scattering doubts on the truth of the genuineness of Scripture.' This was the reward of his dealing fairly with a difficult subject. It is pathetic to think of his early and his later career, and how little his experience of the poisoned weapons with which he had been assailed in his youthful and more intelligent enthusiasm, should have taught him the Christian duty of always understanding what he opposed, and of fairly construing the motives of those who differed from him. Doubtless the dogmatic temper was strong in him from the first, notwithstanding his large knowledge, and the higher historical temper which he everywhere shows. His place in the new movement will appear definitely as we advance. In the meantime we must turn to the true soul of the first stage of the movement—Newman himself, and his friend Richard Hurrell Froude. The *Apologia pro vita suâ* is still our best text-book on the subject. Mr. Mozley's *Reminiscences* have added hardly anything of substantive importance to its history.

John Henry Newman is almost as old as the century, having been born in the beginning of 1801. The son of a London banker, who had married the daughter 'of a well-known Huguenot family,' he was surrounded by religious influences from his youth, and at the age of fifteen became, under Calvinistic guidance, and the study especially of a work of Romaine's, the subject of 'an inward conversion,' of which he says (1864), 'I am still more certain than that I have hands and feet.' Five years before, Dr. Chalmers, very much under the same influences, but at a more mature age, became the subject of a similar change. Newman retained his Calvinistic impressions till the age of twenty-one, although never accepting certain conclusions supposed to be identified with Calvinism—the doctrine of reprobation, for example. A well-known evangelical writer—greatly studied and admired in the beginning of this century— Thomas Scott, now chiefly remembered for his Scripture Commentary, 'made a deeper impression on his mind than any other.' To him ('humanly speaking'), he says, 'I almost owe my soul. His death in 1821 'came upon me as a disappointment as well as a sorrow. I hung upon the lips of Daniel Wilson, afterwards Bishop of Calcutta, as in two sermons at St. John's Chapel he gave the history of Scott's life and death. I had been possessed of his Essays from a boy; his commentary I bought when I was an under-graduate.'

Newman early showed a dogmatic as well as a religious turn. He made a collection of Scripture texts in proof of the doctrine of the Trinity before he was sixteen, and a few months later he drew up a series of texts in support of each verse of the Athanasian Creed. Two other books, he says, greatly delighted him—Joseph Milner's *Church History*, and Newton on the *Prophecies*. There are, I dare say, some here who remember how common these books were in all religious households fifty years ago. They recall the fragrance of a home piety from the tender thought of which no good mind would willingly part. Newman tells us how much he was enamoured of the long extracts from St. Augustine and the other Fathers in Milner's History, and how he learned from Newton to identify the Pope with Antichrist, a doctrine by which, he adds, his imagination 'was stained up to the year 1843,' or till he was forty-two years of age.

At the age of twenty-one (1822), nearly two years after he had taken his degree, 'he came,' as he tells us, 'under very different influences.' He passed from Trinity College, where he had graduated, into Oriel as a fellow, and joined the band of liberal thinkers who had been so long working there. How far he was repelled by the atmosphere of the place at first— and how far for a time he came to sympathise with its intellectual spirit—it is difficult to say beyond what he has himself told us. During his first year of residence he says that, 'though proud of his College,' he 'was not at home there.' He was very much alone, and used to walk by himself. Again, we have seen, he describes himself as, some years later, leaning to Intellectualism, and even as 'drifting in the direction of liberalism.' With all the apparent frankness of the *Apologia*, there is no doubt much still to learn as to those years, and the full history of Newman's religious opinions will only be known when we know more of the steps of his transition from Evangelicalism to High Churchism, and how far he took liberalism on his way. During much of the time at Oriel that followed his appointment as a fellow, or from 1823 to the end of 1827, he was, according to his brother-in-law,[1] identified with Whately. 'It would not have been easy,' he says, 'to state the difference between their respective views.' Newman's religiousness, however, was always 'conspicuous,' and his instinct to conserve and build the fabric of Divine Truth, as well as to analyse and expose any part that seemed unsound. He hated from the first any movement of destruction. 'He used to talk of the men who lash the waters to frighten the fish, when they have made no preparation to catch them.' Probably no one who then knew Newman could have told which way he would go in the end. With a keenly inquisitive mind disposed to search to the root of religious problems, he was too logical, too dogmatic, to be satisfied with Whately's position ; and the latter soon discovered that Newman's was a spirit beyond his leading. He may have been wrong in saying that Newman was looking 'to be the head of a party' himself; and yet there is a side of his character that suggests this view. He had a great love of personal influence. From the first he

---

[1] Mr. Mozley married in 1836 Newman's elder sister.

attracted by his personality rather than by his intelligence—by the authority rather than the rationality of his opinions. He never seems to have understood any other kind of influence. In this kind he was supreme. He did not require to go in search of friends or followers. They gathered spontaneously around him, and there almost necessarily sprang out of this feature of his character a high ambition. Copleston seems dimly to have seen such a future in him, and all to have recognised beneath his shyness the growth of a new power.

The same year (1827) which saw the publication of Keble's wonderful volume is marked by a decisive advance in Newman's views. Illness and bereavement, he says, came to him with awakening effect. He had made the acquaintance of Hurrell Froude the year before, and began to feel the sway of his impetuous genius. In 1828 Hurrell Froude brought him and Keble together. Keble had previously been rather shy of him, he says, 'in consequence of the marks which I bore upon me of the evangelical and liberal schools;' but their conjunction, under the guidance of Froude, laid the springs of the movement which burst forth five years later. Henceforth Newman bore no more traces either of Evangelicalism or Liberalism. All fell away from him in the rush of new thoughts which were to carry him forward in his destined path.

Of Richard Hurrell Froude it is difficult to speak with confidence. He was, no doubt, as his brother tells us, 'gifted, brilliant, enthusiastic — an intellectual autocrat,' with the dashing, audacious characteristics of such a nature. Newman's estimate is more detailed. ' He was a man,' he says, ' of the highest gifts—so truly many-sided that it would be presumptuous in me to attempt to describe him, except under those aspects in which he came before me. Nor have I here to speak of the gentleness and tenderness of nature, the playfulness, the free elastic force and graceful versatility of mind, and the patient, winning considerateness in discussion, which endeared him to those to whom he opened his heart.' Again, he says, he was 'a man of high genius, brimful and overflowing with ideas and views, in him original, and which were too many and too strong even for his bodily strength, and which crowded and jostled against each other in their effort after distinct shape and expression. His opinions arrested and influenced me even when they did not gain my assent.' The two volumes of *Remains* published after his death, in 1836, so far bear out this impression, of a lively and versatile genius, warm-hearted and dashing. But the faults of such a genius are still more conspicuous than the merits. The volumes are full of violent misjudgments, riotous prejudice, silly introspection, and here and there of downright nonsense. It fills one with amazement, I confess, that men like Keble and Newman should have sanctioned, even taken a pleasure in their publication. Many of the sayings are more like those of a foolish, clever boy than anything else. Bred in ecclesiastical toryism, with ' the contempt of an intellectual aristocrat for private judgment and the rights of man,' Hurrell Froude's Oxford learning seems not only to have fostered his essentially narrow spirit, but to have added to it a species of intellectual petulance which would be offensive, if it were not ludicrous in absurdity.[1]

It is impossible to estimate highly the promise of such a genius ; and the *Remains* are now, with all their crude jauntiness, very dull reading.   They have none of the bright vivacity of Sterling's essays, or the spontaneous humour that might redeem their petulance.   There are no seeds of thought in them— nothing, for happy suggestiveness or rich if imma- ture power, fitted to live in any mortal memory.   The extravagance is often little more than ignorance, and the audacity, impudence.   Probably the author would have become wiser if he had lived.   He seems to have had ample knowledge on such subjects as Church Architecture and Ancient Liturgies.   Confessedly his ' religious views never reached their ultimate conclu- sion.'   It must remain doubtful, however, whether a man, so lacking in sense at the age of thirty-two, would have ever grown into wise activity.   The combination which he presents of formal deference to authority with essential irreverence is especially to be noted. Episcopacy is sacred to him, but the individual bishop contemptible.   All is right which he thinks right—nothing good which does not commend itself to his uninformed and headstrong judgment.   To what this spirit has come in ecclesiastical England it is needless to say.   The strange thing is that a

---

[1] Witness the following :—' Really I hate the Reformation and the Reformers more and more.   How beautifully the *Edinburgh Review* [1835] has shown up Luther, Melanchthon, and Co.'   ' Your trumpery principle about Scripture being the sole rule of Faith,' etc.   Again, of a different kind : ' Looked with greediness to see if there was goose on the table.   Meant to have kept a fast, and did abstain from dinner, but at tea, ate buttered toast.'

temper like this, so conspicuously typified in Froude, and so largely represented in the party which he helped to form, should have believed that it was destined to regenerate English Christianity, and to make it once more a living national power.

Newman evidently saw the weak points of his friend, if not exactly in the same light as we have presented them. He confesses that Froude had no turn for theology as such, and 'no appreciation of the writings of the Fathers, or of the detail and development of doctrine.' His great qualities were personal rather than intellectual. He was the knight-errant of the party—eager, courageous, opposed to what he thought shams or sophistries, all unconscious, like knight-errants in general, that his enemies were those of his own disordered brain mainly. His impetuosity, however, gave him a sort of influence. With a singular and sad simplicity Newman says : ' It is difficult to enumerate the precise addition to my theological creed, which I derived from a friend to whom I owe so much. He made me look with admiration towards the Church of Rome, and in the same degree to dislike the Reformation. He fixed deep in me the idea of devotion to the Blessed Virgin, and he led me gradually to believe in the Real Presence.' Froude could hardly communicate what he did not possess. If he had no turn for theology, he could hardly make any worthy addition to anybody's creed ; but his insatiable eagerness made a deep impression upon his friend, and helped to incline him towards Rome. Probably the road thither might have been found earlier if he had lived. ' Subtleties and nice distinctions would not have stood in his

way. His course would have been direct and straight-
forward.'[1]   This does not tell us much, but it may be
held as indicating the conclusion to which we point.
Hurrell Froude would have needed no 'nice distinctions,' because his mind was not of a distinguishing
order.   He had none of the scruples of wide knowledge, or of the rational habit that looks on both sides
of a question.   He had no occasion to ' minimise
doctrines,' or make a wry face over principles, many
of which he had already swallowed in all their enor-
mity.   The only question that can remain is whether,
had he lived, he would not have carried his friend to
Rome faster than he travelled.   That he should ever
have taken the lead, or competed with Newman as
' the master spirit of the movement,'[2] is hardly to be
imagined ; but his more downright and unhesitating
impulses would almost certainly have driven the movement more rapidly towards its predestined goal.

We have seen how Froude brought Newman and
Keble together in 1828.   And if he had never done
anything else, this was something, as he supposed, to
boast of.   ' If I was ever asked,' he said, ' what good
deed I had ever done, I should say that I had
brought Keble and Newman to understand each
other.'   Keble had been Hurrell Froude's tutor, both
at Oxford and at his curacy of Southrop.   He was
eleven years older, and no doubt greatly influenced
Froude, as Froude in turn, according to Newman,
acted upon him.   Both were Tories of the old Cava-
lier or Anglo-Catholic stamp.   They believed in the
Church not merely as national, but exclusive.   There

---

[1] The Oxford *Counter-Reformation*, p. 176. Froude's *Short Studies*,
etc., vol. iii.   [2] Mozley's *Reminiscences*, i. 125.

was no other Church unless the Oriental or Roman Catholic. They were men of high and honourable spirit, and yet neither their reason nor their religion had taught them to acknowledge in men differing from them the same honourable and Christian motives they claimed for themselves. Froude, with outspoken impetuosity, did not hesitate to clothe his judgments in the harsh language which naturally became them. Keble's was a wiser and higher mind. He saw around him with a somewhat larger vision. In all personal relations he was one of the most tender and affectionate of men. Among his friends at Oxford he was not only admired but revered. Newman relates with unconscious humour the estimate in which he was held. 'There's Keble,' said a friend to him one day walking in High Street, 'and with what awe did I look at him!'

Keble's personal character deserves all that can be said of it. It is of the type beautiful, and few could have known him without being the better for converse with such a high and gentle nature. His poetic and gracious gifts are embalmed in the *Christian Year*, which has touched so many hearts. There is an ineffable sweetness in its verse. Christian experience may outgrow the savour, but it lingers like a delightful fragrance in the memory. To Keble, as we have already said, more than to any other leader, the Oxford Movement was the natural outcome of a course of training and thought inbred in him from the first. There was no crisis or struggle in his life, only a deepening sense that Liberalism was evil and Anglo-Catholicism the only Christian power in the land. As a fellow and tutor at Oriel for about twelve

years (1811-1823), he had known the earlier Oriel
spirit in its full power. If it attracted him at all, as
he seems in one of his letters to imply,[1] it must have
been for a very brief period, and the reaction must
have soon followed. There was a gentle but immove-
able obstinacy in his Anglican convictions. I have
never seen in any one a more steadfast and unmoved
faith—faith not only in the Christian but in the
Anglican verities. And this is the secret of what
must be called, even with his higher temper and
range of intelligence, his intolerance. It has a sort
of innocence. It is a Christian virtue. He has no
idea how essentially offensive it is. Half cradled as
the Church of England was in Puritanism, it is to
him simply evil. He can see nothing great or good
in it. Political opinions differing from his own are
not merely mistaken—they are wrong, sinful. In his
correspondence with his friend and biographer, Sir
John Coleridge, he rebuts,—in a sort of playful way,
but with no doubt as to his real meaning,—all idea
that there may be good men on both sides of a
question. He and his friends, he says, call this the
Coleridgian heresy. By way of apology his biographer says that his convictions were very deep-
seated. They were ' stuff of the conscience.' No
doubt. It is impossible not to feel that they were
essential parts of his spiritual and intellectual nature ;
but while this makes them intelligible and respectable, it does not make them the less bigotries. A
man is responsible for the culture of his reason, as
well as of his sentiments. Keble seems never to have
conceived of any religious truth beyond the Church

[1] See preceding note, p. 87.

of England. All was false and wrong outside of it. He loved some who differed from him, among others, Arnold and Milman, who loved and admired him in turn, but it was with a sort of pity he gave them his affection, as if they were hopelessly in error. He delighted to see his little nephew under his teaching snapping at all the Round-heads, and kissing all the Cavaliers. You cannot be angry at bigotry like this, which smiles upon you, while it frowns on your opinions. But it is not admirable in itself. It is mournful. It is only its powerlessness that renders it innocuous. It is the child of ignorance, quite as much as of faith.[1]

Keble did much to encourage Newman in his career. The *Christian Year* strengthened in him 'the two main intellectual truths' which he had already learned from Butler—the sacramental or typical character of all material phenomena, and the influence of probability as the guide of life. All who know the volume will remember how constantly, and with what felicity of touch the sights and sounds of Nature are made to minister to spiritual instruction and discipline ; how rich the natural symbolism of the hymns is everywhere ; so that Nature becomes the mere veil of the higher life, the vesture of Divine communion, the parable of Divine mystery. All this met a deeply responsive chord in Newman, whose own poetry, with a deeper and more tragic vein, is full of the same symbolism. The principle

[1] Even Mozley admits that Keble's 'sympathies were very one-sided ;' and he mentions a curious instance of his intolerance, not otherwise recorded, so far as I know : 'that he induced a number of his neighbours and friends to sign a protest against Her Majesty choosing a Lutheran Prince for one of her sons' godfathers.'

of probability again played a powerful part in the spiritual life of both. Accepted by faith and love, this principle became a source of religious certitude. Transmuted by trust it was turned into a ground of conviction. The same idea pervades many of Keble's sermons, and it was ultimately worked by Newman into the shape of a cardinal doctrine in his *Grammar of Assent*. It would be far too long to discuss it here. I have elsewhere carefully examined it,[1] and found it at the root—as I think all who probe it critically must find it—to be little more than a process of make-belief. Only assent strongly enough to anything, and it will imbed itself in your mental constitution as a verity of the first order. But the further question always arises : What is the value of a principle of certitude which is, at bottom, planted neither in reason nor in evidence, but in the mere force of the grip which you yourself take of the thing believed ? Faith is good, but a faith that is neither enlightened nor determined by facts in the shape of evidence, but simply by the blind assent with which the mind sets itself upon its object, may be as much a basis of superstition as of religion. The argument springing out of such faith is admitted by Dr. Newman himself to be merely 'one form of the argument from authority.'

Such is a brief sketch of the chief figures engaged in the 'Oxford movement,' and, so far, of the principles which they represented. We must note, however, more clearly than we have yet done, the several stages of the movement, the causes which led to it, and the objects at which it aimed. We cannot within our limits do more, or extend our view much beyond

[1] *Edinburgh Review*, October 1870.

the time which may be said to be measured by the
Tracts for the Times, or Tractarianism as it has
been specially called.

Some years before, or from 1828 to 1833, Keble,
Newman, and Froude were all converging towards
some definite action.   Newman's spirit was warm-
ing within him as the dogmatic principle took a
firmer hold of his mind, and the Church seemed more
and more threatened by the political agitation sur-
rounding it.   Meantime, however, he was busy with his
studies on the *Arians of the Fourth Century,* as Keble
was busy in the preparation of his edition of Hooker's
Ecclesiastical Polity.   These studies deepened the
Catholic tendencies of both, as they braced and furnished them for the struggle before them.

All this time the political course of events was
fretting them intolerably.   Liberalism was not only
'in the air,' but had proved its ascendency everywhere.   Sir Robert Peel, at the time member for
Oxford, had been forced to give way and introduce
his Bill for the Emancipation of the Catholics.   This
led, as may be imagined, to a violent commotion at
Oxford ; heads of Houses divided against heads of
Houses, and the Dogmatic party, with Keble and
Newman in front, violently on the Orthodox side.   In
1831 and 1832 the political atmosphere became still
more agitated.   There was revolution in France; direct
assaults upon the Church at home.   'The Whigs had
come into power ; Lord Grey had told the Bishops
to set their house in order, and some of the Prelates
had been insulted and threatened in the streets of
London.'[1]   All these things made a deep impres-

[1] *Apologia,* p. 93.

sion upon the Oxford group, whom sympathy of feeling and opinion had by this time more or less banded together. Newman's mind was excited in the highest degree. 'The vital question,' he says, 'was, How were we to keep the Church from being liberalised;' 'the true principles of churchmanship seemed so radically decayed, and there was such distraction in the councils of the clergy.' Keble was less passionately, but hardly less deeply, moved. Froude required no kindling against the Whigs. He was violent against them from the first. He could have forgiven the Reform Bill, if it had not been for his personal hatred of the Whigs.[1] Here were the abundant materials of an outburst not merely ecclesiastical but political. It is impossible to ignore the political as well as the intellectual or theological side of the Oxford movement. It was a new Toryism, or designed to be such, as well as a new Sacerdotalism.

Newman's and Froude's journey abroad in the end of 1832 and spring of 1833, seems strangely to have acted as a stimulus to their ecclesiastical and political excitement rather than as a distraction. In the Mediterranean, in Sicily, in Paris, 'England was in my thoughts solely,' Newman says. 'The Bill for the suppression of the Irish Sees was in progress, and filled my mind. I had fierce thoughts against the Liberals. A French vessel was at Algiers; I would not even look at the Tricolour,' and so hateful was revolutionary Paris, with all its beauty, that he 'kept indoors the whole time' he was there. It was at this time that he so far forgot his Christian charity as to speak of Arnold in the manner we related in our

[1] *Remains*, vol. i. p. 250.

last lecture. Such a remark could only have come out of very harsh thoughts. Yet we know that he also had softer and tenderer thoughts. For it was then, as he lay becalmed in the Straits of Bonifacio, that he composed the wonderful lines, ' Lead, kindly Light, amidst the encircling gloom,' which have touched so many hearts, and brought the tears of spiritual tenderness to so many eyes.

Keble's Assize Sermon was preached the very Sunday after Newman's return to Oxford. This was as the match applied to a long smouldering excitement. Action followed at once. A conference was held at Hadleigh; but not much came directly of this. It brought together congenial minds, in addition to those already mentioned ; among others, Mr. William Palmer,[1] of Dublin University, afterwards of Worcester College, who, Newman says, was the only really learned man among them, and 'understood theology as a science.' But it was soon felt that there must be personal action, if anything effective was to be done. Mr. Palmer and others were for a committee— 'a board of safe and sensible men.' But no great movement was ever begun or carried forward by a committee, or by a system, Newman says ; and he points with strange audacity to Luther and the Reformation as an example!

Thus impelled to do something, he hit upon the idea of the *Tracts for the Times.* He is careful to point out that the idea was his own, and to take all the credit or discredit of the Tractarianism which became the great feature of the movement. He wrote or re-wrote and revised all the earliest of the

---

[1] Author of the well-known *Origines Liturgicæ.*

famous series. As Mozley truly enough says, no
one could write a *Tract* but himself. 'Others wrote
sermons or treatises,' but Newman from first to last
was *the Tractarian par excellence;* and, remarkably
with the cessation of the *Tracts,* eight years later he
may be said to disappear from the movement.

No one but Newman himself—not even he—saw
all the significance of the Tractarian movement.
Keble mentions the publications, almost accidentally,
in a letter.[1] They are ' a paper or two,' drawn up by
some friends at Oxford, in reference to the present
state of the Church of England. They are intended
'to circulate right notions on the apostolical succession, and also for a defence of the Prayer-book
against any sort of profane innovation.' In Dr.
Mozley's recent Letters the project is spoken of in the
same accidental way,[2] with some pointed criticism on
the peculiarities of Newman's style as a Tract-writer.
But there is reason to think that Newman saw, if
not all the consequences of the *Tracts* (that was impossible), something of their real import and moment.
He had the penetration of genius here as elsewhere,
and he did not hesitate to give from the first ' strong
teaching,' as he calls it. He was full of the exultation
of health and self-confidence. The depression under
which he had lived abroad had passed away—yielded
to ' such a rebound' that his friends at Oxford
hardly knew him. No wonder. He had stripped
himself clear of all the older integuments which had
bound his religious thought and action. He was for
the time a reformer or restorer of the ancient ways.

---

[1] Letter to Dyson ; *Life,* vol. i. p. 220.
[2] Mozley's *Letters,* p. 34.

He had taken the 'ancient religion of England under his protection and defence. He says of himself, 'As to the High Church and the Low Church, I thought that the one had not much more of a logical basis than the other. I had a thorough contempt for the Evangelical.'

It is not to be supposed, however, that with all Newman's energy and genius the Tracts were at once successful. For some time they were only 'as seed cast on the waters.' As we read them now, or try to read them, it seems strange that they should have ever moved any number of minds. If some were found to be 'heavy reading' at the time, they are now mainly interesting to the theological antiquarian. But this only shows the more how inflammable the clerical and lay-clerical mind was at the time. There was a need for movement. The Evangelical wave had reached its height, and was on the ebb everywhere. The old Anglicanism was not dead, but inert, beautiful, but still, or stiffened to hardness in many a country parish, but with no life or aggression in it. The liberalism of the Whately school had never penetrated deeply or possessed attraction for the average clergyman. The limits of religious thought are easily reached in any age. The Tracts, therefore, backed as they were by higher teaching from the pulpit, met a want in the religious aspiration of the time. The *Christian Year* had done not a little to awaken this want. The assaults upon the Church from many quarters had, by a natural reaction, strengthened it. The genius of Newman—his writing and preaching —did more than all else to satisfy it, and in doing so, to create an era in the Church of England.

Yet it is his own confession that the new impulse would never have become 'a power' 'if it had remained in his hands.' It required the accession of another master spirit to consolidate the movement and give it adequate momentum. And this idea of the original leader is borne out strongly by the popular name which the movement ultimately took—the popular instinct having often in such matters a wonderful insight. Of Dr. Pusey we have already spoken. He had seemed at first to move on what we must judge a higher platform of thought than mere Church-of-Englandism. He had not only studied German theology, but he had understood and appreciated it. He had shown a certain liberality and largeness of mind rare in Anglican Divines. He had the power of entering into other theologies than his own. But the evils of the times had also come home to him, or the wave of High Churchism had gradually submerged all his more rational tendencies (I do not pretend to explain) ;[1] but when the Tractarian movement had been in existence for about two years he came to its assistance. Hitherto he had stood, if not aloof—for a tract of his on Fasting was printed in the series as early as the close of 1833 —yet in some degree apart. He had not given to the movement his name or influence. But in the end of 1835 there appeared his memorable Tract on Baptism, which marked an epoch in more senses than one. It drove Frederick Denison Maurice away, frightened at the company he had been keeping. It

---

[1] Dr. Liddon, in his forthcoming Life, will probably throw light on this comparatively obscure period of Dr. Pusey's life from 1828 to 1835.

raised the party to a position which it had not hitherto attained. No one can describe the effect so well as Dr. Newman himself. ' At once,' he says, ' Dr. Pusey gave to us a position and a name. Without him we should have had no chance of making any serious resistance to the Liberal aggression. But Dr. Pusey was a Professor and Canon of Christ Church; he had a vast influence in consequence of his deep religious seriousness, the munificence of his charities, his professorship, his family connections, and his easy relations with the University authorities. He was to the movement all that Mr. Rose might have been, with that indispensable addition which was wanting to Mr. Rose, the intimate friendship and the familiar daily society of the persons who had commenced it. And he had that special claim on their attachment which lies in the living presence of a faithful and loyal affectionateness. There was henceforth a man who could be the head and centre of the zealous people in every part of the country who were adopting the new opinions ; and not only so, but there was one who furnished the movement with a front to the world, and gained for it a recognition from other parties in the University. Dr. Pusey was, to use the common expression, a host in himself; he was able to give a name, a force, and a personality to what was without him a sort of mob.' It is in the light of such words that we can understand how the Tractarian movement came to be characterised as Puseyism—an epithet at first felt to be a vulgarism,[1]

---

[1] Dr. Mozley's *Letters*, p. 129, where we have a curious illustration of the manner in which this name came to be used instead of Tractarianism.

but which soon acquired such notoriety as to supersede for a time all other names.

As the movement advanced it gathered not only strength, but a clearer logical basis. Newman had to clear more and more to his own mind the principles on which he was acting. What the principles of the movement were at the outset he has plainly expressed under three heads. First, the assertion of the principle of Dogma—'my battle,' he says, 'was with Liberalism ; by Liberalism I meant the anti-dogmatic principle and its developments ;'—secondly, the assertion of a Visible Church with sacraments, and rites, and definite religious teaching, on the foundation of dogma ; and thirdly, the assertion that the Anglican Church was *the* Church as opposed to the Church of Rome. The dogmatic principle lay at the root of the movement. All else followed from this; and this principle Newman brought with him from the Evangelicals among whom he had been trained. 'From the age of fifteen,' he says, 'dogma had been the fundamental principle of my religion. I know no other religion—I cannot enter into the idea of any other sort of religion.' Here was the exactly opposite note to the 'Noetic' school of Whately and Arnold and Hampden, whose great aim in all their theological writings had been more or less to discriminate between dogma and religion— to show that dogma is a later growth from religion, and not religion itself. Not at all that the Noetic School looked upon religion 'as a mere sentiment ;' but it was its work more or less to show that the primitive ideas of Christianity as presented in the New Testament are distinct from later dogmatic developments; that Paulinism, in short, is not Athanasianism, nor even the theology of St. John quite the theology of the Nicene creed. All this was at variance with the dogmatic principle. It struck it at the base; and with Newman's convictions, it struck Christianity at the base. He afterwards, indeed, expounded the principle of development in his own way; but the true historical conception of it has always been unintelligible to him. And no less the idea of the Church as a Spiritual community of diverse forms of expression and government—of varying nationality. This idea was, if possible, still more repellent to him. Nothing was conceivable or of Divine right but a Visible Church with definite rites and prerogatives—his own Church of course being this Church. Romanism, therefore, at the outset necessarily incurred his hostility. Anglicanism was the only Divine system. 'My own Bishop was my Pope,' as he says.

This was his logical position. He and Keble and Pusey set themselves to vindicate it. Theological argument remained in the main in his own hands. It was the stress of his logic, we shall see—piercing sophism after sophism—that at length drove him out of the movement, and finally to Rome. Keble and Pusey were much less polemical, less at the mercy of a spirit of argumentative restlessness. They busied themselves with the historical aspects of the question. They engaged by translations and otherwise to prove that Anglicanism was identical with Patristic Christianity. While Newman laboured in an elaborate work[1] to show that Catholicism, as

[1] *The Prophetical Office of the Church viewed relatively to Romanism and Popular Protestantism.*

embodied in the Church of England, was the only
Divine System in relation to Romanism on the one
hand, and Popular Protestantism on the other hand ;
Dr. Pusey began the well-known Library of the
Fathers, which remains the most elaborate literary
monument of the movement. It is curious, in looking back upon these patristic labours, especially in
view of Dr. Pusey's large-minded dealing with
the phenomena of German theology, to notice how
entirely uncritical they are. The Fathers were taken
without question. Neither chronological order nor
historical method regulated their selection. A heap
of documents of varying authority, or of no authority, were cast before the reader. The Ignatian
Epistles passed unchallenged, and in one way and another play a significant part in the controversy. If a
writing contained the assertion of what was called
Church principles, this was ample guarantee of its
excellence and genuineness. The very thing that was
suspicious, became the index of authority—so dead
was the historic spirit in the members of the school.
No movement ever started with a larger *petitio
principii*, and the premiss only swelled as it advanced.
There was endless building up out of old stones.
This was confessedly Newman's idea of what the
Church needed.[1] But what the stones themselves
were really worth was never asked. The translation
of Fleury's Church History and the series of the
Lives of English Saints all came from the same
pure appetite for tradition. Whatever had the note
of antiquity was to be brought to the light, and the
lineaments of the Ancient Church were sought among

[1] *Apologia*, pp. 144-5.

the debris of mediæval and patristic times rather than in the living pages of the New Testament. The Patristic Church, or anything of its true lineaments, came as a refreshing picture to many minds accustomed to the disguises of popular Protestantism; but the picture certainly no more corresponded to the original reality than any ultra-Protestant representation.

The Hampden episode already described proved the fighting power of the party, and as the years passed on they became more emboldened and aggressive. Newman grew vastly in personal influence. His afternoon sermons at St. Mary's became a spiritual power. They deserved to be so. Here he is at his best, away from the field of history and of controversy, searching the heart with the light of his spiritual genius, or melting it to tenderness with the music of his exquisite language. All his strength and little of his weakness, his insight, his subtlety, his pathos, his love of souls, his marvellous play of dramatic as well as spiritual faculty, his fervour without excitement, his audacity without offence or sophistical aggression, appear in his sermons. He was a preacher as other men are poets or orators. In these years, 1838-1839, his position was at its height, and the movement was reaching its climax. As the decade closed the Anglo-Catholic party had become a power in the Church, and 'an object of alarm to her rulers and friends.'

The first check came in the moment of its power, when the Bishop of Oxford in 1838 animadverted upon the Tracts. Newman professed his willingness to stop them, and even to withdraw such as his Lordship objected to. His Lordship did not insist on this step, and the Tracts went on. But the pressure both of logic and of circumstances soon developed grave results. Newman's own line of thought rapidly ran out in the only way in which it could run. From Antiquity as the note of the Church and the *via media*, he passed to Catholicity as a surer note. Then trains of thought based on his Patristic studies came to shatter the idea of Catholicity as applied to the Church of England. He was driven forward from one point to another. He stood on the *via media* as long as he could. The Church of England was a true branch of the Catholic Church, he argued. It is ancient and apostolical. It has the true order of succession. Rome has yielded to modern errors. But about 1839 he began to have doubts as to the Anglican order of succession. The 'Catholicity' of Rome began to overshadow in his mind the 'Apostolicity' of Anglicanism. The Church was One, *quod semper quod ubique quod ab omnibus.* The Roman argument became more powerful, the Anglican more doubtful. The great Donatist controversy deepened the shadow on his mind. The Roman communion as a matter of fact represented 'the main body of the Church Catholic.' Were not the Donatists by their schism cut off *ipso facto* from the heritage of Christ? How should it fare better with the Church of England? It might have *antiquity* in its favour; but was not the true apostolic descent in the main body? The pressure of this argument was irresistible, if the true and only church be an external institution with certain recognisable notes or features. *Apostolical succession* is an outward and traceable fact, or it is nothing at all. It cannot belong to two churches. If sacramental grace be the exclusive property of an external order, this order must be visible, and it must also be exclusive. It must be in the Roman communion, or the Anglican communion, or the Presbyterian communion ; it cannot be in all three. To Newman it had existed beyond doubt in the Church of England, because this church was, as he and his friends supposed, 'Catholic' in England in the sense of displacing all others. Romanism had no logical footing where Catholicism already existed. So long as one can hold to this ground the position is good. But then of course the converse is equally logical, that where Catholicism in the Roman or Oriental form exists, Anglicanism has no footing. The Roman or Oriental form may be corrupted, but no High Churchman can doubt that they represent the true Church however corrupted, wherever they prevail.

Various consequences follow inevitably from this doctrine. If Anglicanism represent the Catholic Church in England, it must speak with a Catholic voice. If the Church of England be in England that One church of which in old times Athanasius and Augustine were members—as the Church of Rome is in France or Spain — then the doctrine must be the same. The Anglican formularies cannot be at variance with the authoritative teaching of the old Church. And then again, wherever the Christian Church exists in the direct or original line of descent, Anglicanism and still less Protestantism can have no right of interference.

Dr. Newman's *via media* was destined to break

against both these rocks. The 39 Articles were the monument of Church of England Protestantism. They must be minimised; their meaning sophisticated; their language explained. In other words, they must be brought into accord with mediæval doctrine, against which in many points they were a protest. Hence Tract 90, which at length brought the series to an end in the explosion which it caused. It was his own bishop[1] who said that in this Tract the author had made the Articles *mean anything or nothing*. The words cut him to the quick. Nor can an impartial judgment say that they were too strong. Both Keble and Pusey, as well as the author himself, have indeed written in defence of the mode of argument employed in Tract 90.[2] The sum of this defence may be said to be that Newman sought to give the 'literal grammatical sense' of the Articles, apart from later meanings attributed to them; and that this principle of interpretation had already been recognised on behalf of the liberal Theologians, and in the common saying that the Articles 'admitted both Arminians and Calvinists.' This is ingenious, but nothing more. Because Articles admit of a certain latitude of interpretation which all historical statements of doctrine must do, it by no means follows that any given interpretation of them

[1] Dr. Bagot, of whom Dr. Newman speaks highly in the *Apologia*— 'a man,' he says, 'whom, had I had a choice, I should have preferred' (as his ecclesiastical superior) 'to any other bishop on the bench, and for whose memory I have a special affection.'—P. 123.

[2] A new edition of Tract 90 was issued, with 'a historical preface' by Dr. Pusey, in 1861. Keble's defence is embodied in a letter to Mr. Justice Coleridge, privately printed in 1841, and afterwards published along with the new edition of the Tract.

is warrantable, still less that doctrines against which they appear to every unsophisticated mind to have been directed are not really condemned in them, but something quite different—having an obscure relation to the doctrines in question. To read the Articles themselves, and then to turn to Dr. Newman's explanations, is a painful process for most minds, even minds accustomed to theological subtleties. And this of itself may be held to settle the question.

Four tutors, including the late Archbishop of Canterbury, published a protest against the Tract, and a formal censure was passed upon it by the heads of Houses a few days later. The Tract was finally withdrawn at the request of the Bishop of Oxford. Then immediately following, and while all the pain that arose from these proceedings was still sharp in his heart, came the establishment of the Jerusalem Bishopric. As the Catholic continuity of the Church had snapped in his hands on the side of doctrine, so it had broken as well on the historical side. The Jerusalem Bishopric was not only an invasion of Catholicity, but an invasion which carried with it (as he believed) the express sanction of Lutheran and Calvinist heresy. His famous protest against it bears that ' Lutheranism and Calvinism are heresies repugnant to Scripture and anathematised by east as well as west.' It is very instructive that the Jerusalem Bishopric—which has proved practically of no consequence in the Christian world—should have divided enthusiastically the two forces of Liberalism and Anglo-Catholicism now running with such force against one another. To Bunsen and his friends the bishopric was a pet project, designed as a symbol of Christian union in the broadest sense : to Newman and his friends it was as the 'abomination of desolation,' tending to the 'disorganisation of the Church of England, and the denial of its claim to be considered a branch of the Catholic Church.' It is hardly possible to say whether the hopes of the one or the fears of the other have been more completely falsified by the event.

It was now evident to Newman's own mind that his place of leadership in the Oxford movement was gone. From this date—the spring of 1841—he says he was 'on his deathbed' as regards the Church of England. He formally gave up his place in the movement, and retired to Littlemore. As yet, however, he did not contemplate leaving the Church of England. Littlemore was his *Torres Vedras* from which again he thought he might advance within the Anglican Church. There were still points as in reference to the 'honours paid to the Blessed Virgin and the saints,' on which he differed from the Church of Rome. It is unnecessary for us, however, to follow the 'history of his religious opinions' further. Everybody may read their further course in his own interesting narrative. It need only be added that in the autumn of 1843 he resigned the parochial charge of St. Mary at Oxford ; that by the end of 1845 he had become a Roman Catholic, and that in the beginning of 1846 he left Oxford and passed formally within the pale of the Roman Church.

The retirement of Newman from the scene of action virtually closes the movement, so far as it can be embraced within this course of lectures. Much,

however, remains to be described in a full history of
the Modern Anglo-Catholicism ; the agitation at Oxford in 1844 and 1845 in connection with Mr. Ward's
book *The True Ideal of a Christian Church;* the
secession of Mr. Ward, Mr. Oakley, and others to the
Church of Rome ; Dr. Pusey's suspension, and then his
continued labours in connection with the movement ;
the rise of a younger Anglo-Catholic party, represented
by such men as Samuel Wilberforce, Mr. Gladstone,
James B. Mozley, Mr., now Dean Church, and
others.   Mr. Gladstone's once well-known volume on
The State in its Relations with the Church appeared
in 1838 ; and his book on *Church Principles* in
1840.   These publications, more distinctly perhaps
than any others, mark the rise of the younger Anglican school to which Keble warmly attached himself, and of which Pusey, after a time of irresolution,
became again the animating head.   It is only justice
to this school to say that it has been from the first
and continues to be genuinely Anglican.   Whether
its avowed principles may or may not imply the
conclusions to which Newman felt himself irresistibly
driven, is a polemical question with which we have no
need to meddle here.   The fact is that the school of
doctrine, of which both Samuel Wilberforce and Mr.
Gladstone have been conspicuous ornaments, and of
which the late Dr. Mozley (younger brother of the
author of the *Reminiscences*) was the chief theologian,
is a definite product of Anglican Christianity.   It is
native to the Church of England ; and all its writers
and thinkers have a stamp which it may be doubted
whether John Henry Newman ever had.   His Anglo-
Catholicism was after all only a state of transition

from Evangelicalism, or something like Liberalism, to Romanism.[1] In 1826 he was drifting in the direction

[1] There is an interesting paper by Dr. Mozley in the *Christian Remembrancer*, January 1846, on Dr. Newman's secession, in which a line of thought as to Dr. Newman's relations to Anglo-Catholicism or the *via media* is suggested not unlike that in the text. Founding on a remarkable passage in the Introduction to Newman's lectures on *Romanism and Popular Protestantism* to the following effect :—' Protestantism and Popery are real religions ; they have furnished the mould in which nations have been cast ; but the *via media* has never existed except on paper ; it has never been reduced to practice ;'— Dr. Mozley observes that with all Newman's great power as a preacher and writer within the Church of England, it seems to be doubtful whether he ever realised himself as identified with its life and work. 'He did not energise as a parish priest, but as an author. His sermons were addressed to a University audience. He had weekly communion and daily prayers, and he had the church at Littlemore with its daily duties. But all this was a thing attached to his great position as a religious mover, and not that position to it. He had one line, that of a spreader of opinions ; and this line, however appropriate a one, was still one which kept the Church distant, as it were, to his mind, and did not bring her near him.' All this is something like saying in another way that Dr. Newman had never breathed the true air of Anglo-Catholicism, or felt himself quite at home in it. It was always to him, in some degree, a mere ' book-religion ' into which he had argued himself, and out of which he again argued himself. No one could know Dr. Newman—not even Hurrell Froude —better than Dr. Mozley, who was not only his pupil, but lived on terms of the closest intimacy with him from 1833 onwards till he left Oxford.

Mozley himself would make an interesting study, if we were able to treat of the secondary phenomena of the Oxford movement. He is a very different man from his brother—the author of the *Reminiscences*—and as a theologian is really great, although somewhat hard and polemical, not only in his *Bampton Lectures*, but in his earlier volume on *Predestination and Original Sin*. He had a good deal of the same literary power as his brother—the same facility and copiousness of pen ; but in his earlier essays also not a little of the same literary persiflage and intellectual insolence. His paper on *Arnold*, one of his earliest (1844), is a striking specimen of what I mean. He speaks of the great teacher at Rugby as ' a man who, without a vestige of internal scruple or misgiving, of liberalism ;[1] in 1836—certainly in 1839—he was drifting in the direction of Rome. He had never imbibed, as Keble and the Mozleys and others had done, the pure air of Anglicanism as a distinct religious life. To those who understand this, and how much more vital in religion as in other things affinity of feeling is than similarity of logical principle, it can be no wonder that Dr. Pusey and Mr. Keble remained firm in their adherence to the Church of England while Newman left it. The latter says[2] of Dr. Pusey, that all the time he knew him he was never 'in his reason and judgment' near to Rome. On the contrary, in Newman himself there was something from the first in his whole mode of thought and love of personal rather than rational supremacy, which had a tinge of popery,[3] and which carried him irresistibly forward, although by slow degrees, to his appointed end.

The Oxford movement remains a great, if not the very greatest, fact in the recent history of Anglican Christianity. Its principles in their polemical aspect suggest many further thoughts as to how far they are capable of rational vindication, and how far they shade off into Romanism. We could find no better

unchristianised the whole development of the Christian Church from the days of the Apostles, who made the very friends and successors of the Apostles teachers of corruption.' . . . Again, he says, 'We had much rather not think him as a religionist at all.' J. B. Mozley was a very young theological lion when he roared in this way, but the whole article is a bad specimen of a bad school, and of that strange and even coarse arrogance which is sometimes near to the best gifts.

[1] *Apologia*, p. 72.   [2] *Apologia*, p. 138.

[3] See a remarkable passage in his brother's *Phases of Faith*, referring to as early a period as 1823-6, p. 7. 9th Ed.

text-book for such a discussion than Mr. Gladstone's *Church Principles*, which treats in succession the great Anglo-Catholic doctrines, all, according to him, more or less involved in the idea of the church as 'one, holy, catholic, and apostolic.' In this and his earlier volume is undoubtedly preserved much of the pith of Mr. Gladstone's thought. I doubt if any one can understand the deeper impulses of a mind which has been and continues to be such a potent factor in our modern political life, who has not studied its workings and favourite modes of conception as embodied in these books. But our lectures here are designed not for discussion but for description; and the general character of the movement is already apparent in all that we have said. The great idea of the Church in its visibility and authority—in its notes of succession, dogma, and sacrament,—sums up its meaning. Many will dispute the very possibility of any such Church or embodiment of spiritual power ; but there are few who will not acknowledge that the Oxford movement has done more than all other movements in our time to revive 'the grandeur and force of historical communion and Church life,' and no less 'the true place of beauty and art in worship.' It is much to have brought home to the hearts of Christian people the reality of a great spiritual society extending through all Christian ages, living by its own truth and life, having its own laws, and rights, and usages. In a time when the 'dissidence of dissent,' and the canker of sectarianism have spread to the very heart of our national existence, with so many unhappy results, the idea of the Church as a great Unity—and no less the idea of Christian art—

of the necessity of order and beauty in Christian worship—are ideas to be thankful for. That both these ideas are capable, as history proves, of rapid abuse, unless interpenetrated by the light of reason, and used with purity of heart, is no ground for rejecting either. It is the very function of Christian sense to hold the balance of truth, and by 'proving all things,' to 'hold fast that which is good.'

IV

MOVEMENT OF RELIGIOUS THOUGHT IN SCOTLAND.

WE have seen how varied and full of interest was the movement of religious thought in England during the third decade of this century. What was Scotland doing at this time? She had not only joined in the intellectual revival of the century—but she had contributed some of its most powerful agents. In 1802 the first number of the *Edinburgh Review* was published; in 1805 Scott began his career as a poet. Of all the names that adorn the opening of our century Scott's must be pronounced upon the whole the greatest—at once the manliest and the most original and creative. He may rank below Wordsworth and Coleridge as a poet, although he is great in poetic qualities as old as Homer, in which both are entirely wanting; but take him all in all there is no intellectual figure comparable to him in breadth and richness. He strikes the new note of the century—its larger intelligence both for nature and life—its deeper insight into the past, as well as its freer, fuller, and clearer eye for the present, with a wider, a more extended and powerful sweep than any other.

Scotland was then well advanced in the intellectual

race which opened the century.   Is there any corresponding movement of religious thought such as
followed the intellectual revival in England, and
charged it with a deeper life ?   It is often assumed
that, keen as the intellectual activity of Scotland is,
this activity has not extended itself to theology.
The Calvinistic creed of the country is supposed
to have remained unshaken under all its mental
progress.   There is a certain measure of truth in this ;
and yet it is really a superficial judgment.   It is
true that Calvinism remains the common creed of
the country, and that the Scottish Churches have
not been disturbed in the same degree as the
Church of England by divers novelties of doctrine.
But it is far from true that Scotland has been
quiescent in religious thought.   It has not moved
with the same bulk or mass of movement ; in the
nature of things this was impossible ; but it has contributed new and powerful influences to the onward
current of religious opinion often reaching England
—and originating there new impulses, or adding
momentum to those already in operation.

In the very same decade which gave to England
the religious philosophy of Coleridge and the early
Oriel School, Scotland is seen full of religious as
well as intellectual activity.   Carlyle was elaborating
his new Gospel of Work ; George Combe was pro-
pounding a new philosophy of life ; and Thomas
Erskine, Macleod Campbell, and Edward Irving
were all supposed to be assailing the old theology
of the country.   There was vehement agitation, both
philosophical and religious.   Quick as was the pace
of thought in England between the years 1820 and

1830, it was hardly less so in Scotland. Thomas Erskine began his career as a religious writer in 1820; and the more his writings are studied the more remarkable will be found to have been their influence. The present lecture will be devoted in the main to trace this influence and what is known as the 'Row heresy.' Thomas Carlyle and his creed will afterwards claim attention in a separate lecture. To George Combe and his philosophy we can only give a paragraph as we pass onwards.

There has always from the days of Hume survived in Scotland a vein of naturalistic speculation. Men like Sir John Leslie and Thomas Brown, both Professors in Edinburgh, may be pointed to as representing this turn of mind in the earlier part of the century. It was the enemy of course of the prevailing theology; and the Church had signalised its opposition to it on the appointment of Leslie to the Chair of Mathematics in 1805. The Edinburgh Reviewers, a certain class of Intellectualists in the capital, were more or less identified with the naturalistic spirit. There was always, in short, a fitting soil in Edinburgh, if nowhere else, for the culture of what we now call Naturalism, or a theory of life and duty resting on Nature, rather than on Revelation; and George Combe became the apostle of such a theory in the years 1825 and 1828. In the former year appeared his *System of Phrenology,*[1] and at the later date his well-known volume on *The Constitution of Man.* The *Scotsman* newspaper, then in the first phase of its intellectual activity, and William and Robert Chambers, both exercising even then a well-established

[1] Originally published in 1819 as *Essays on Phrenology.*

influence on the popular literature of the day, were somewhat in the same line of thought. There was no combination or definite party, but many shared in a movement in which George Combe in every way deserves the pre-eminence. He was a man of spotless character and the most sincere enthusiasm, combining an earnest Christian theism with the most unhesitating belief in views of man's constitution and responsibility which seem constantly shading off into Materialism. Many of his special dogmas have vanished with the progress of knowledge, especially of that natural knowledge on which his system was based ; but there are also important aspects of his teaching, in its bearing on education, which survive, and have entered with enlightening force into our modern educational theories. Not only so. But, imperfect as we must judge, both from a philosophical and religious point of view, many of Combe's generalisations, in which he reposed implicit confidence, we feel that there was a healthy element in his speculations. They were as a salt in the intellectual and religious atmosphere, and at a time when there was much to harden and sometimes darken religious feeling, they helped to nourish a broader and freer opinion not without its beneficent bearing on religion.

It is, however, in other directions that we must look for the chief influences which at this time affected religious opinion in Scotland. Never, perhaps hardly even in our own time, when the note of unsettlement in belief is so common, has there been more excitement and novelty in Scottish religion than in those years. The pages of the *Christian Instructor*, then the organ of Evangelicalism in Scotland, bear everywhere testimony to this state of things. The age is spoken of as one of 'modern heresies,' and a single volume of that once well-known organ in 1830 recounts no fewer than three allied heretical movements.

It is strange that a quiet country gentleman, Mr. Thomas Erskine of Linlathen, should have been the prominent figure in these movements, and that his books, now hardly remembered, should have been so widely circulated and caused so much alarm. They were not merely assailed in the *Christian Instructor ;* but Dr. Andrew Thomson devoted a volume of sermons in 1830 to their refutation. A tract or part of a tract in the Oxford series was occupied with an elaborate analysis of one of them as illustrative of the rationalistic spirit of the time. On the other hand, Mr. Maurice is found constantly expressing his indebtedness to Mr. Erskine's books. Of one of the least known he says, 'It has been unspeakably comfortable to me,'[1] and generally he testifies again and again that they have helped him much in finding an answer to the question, 'What a Gospel to mankind must be.'

Of Thomas Erskine we might say much as a man. It was our privilege to enjoy his intimate friendship during the closing years of his life, when he was a veteran in the field of spiritual experience and theological thought, while we were only looking over the field with raw and inexperienced eyes. As the lifelong friend of Maurice and of Carlyle—spirits so apart,—he was naturally regarded by younger men,

[1] *Life*, vol. i. p. 121.

who knew anything of his beautiful, Christian nature, with affectionate feelings of respect.

It was impossible to know him, and still more to come near him in religious intercourse, without feeling one's-self in a spiritual presence of rare delicacy and power. Religious conversation of the ordinary sort is proverbially difficult. It is but too seldom a savour of life unto life, being apt to hide as much as express the heart. But with Mr. Erskine it was a natural effluence. It came from him as the expression of the abiding atmosphere in which he dwelt, and if one may have shrunk even with him sometimes from the awe of the topics on which he dwelt, yet his deeply meditative words were seldom without light. They lifted the soul towards Divine mystery, even when they failed to give meaning to it. One felt the deep sincerity of the man, and that *he* himself had laid hold of the Divine in his own heart whether he understood it rightly or not. Like his friend Maurice, he was an intense Realist in religion. Abstract theological questions had little interest for him ; religious controversy no interest whatever. Polemics of every kind he disliked ; and he was often playful over their folly. I remember once of his saying of an old acquaintance, whose polemical faculty much outran his powers of insight and reason, ' He is a great reasoner ; but I do not find any *light* in him at all. The thing itself he does not see, but he can give many powerful arguments for it. The Schoolmen were men of this stamp—endless writing and argument, but no light.'

His own nature, as may be supposed, was meditative, introspective, quietly brooding. He reached

the truth, or what he believed to be the truth,
not so much by enlarging his knowledge, or by
exercising any critical and argumentative powers,
as by patient thoughtfulness and generalisation
from his own experience. It was an unhappy conjunction that pitted him against Dr. Andrew Thomson, or rather Dr. Andrew Thomson against him.
They were utterly incapable of understanding one
another—Thomson being forensic, argumentative, systematic, rhetorical in the highest degree, and Erskine
the very opposite of all this,—yet with depths of
spiritual feeling and glimpses of insight of which
Thomson knew nothing. And so the well-aimed
shafts of the latter flew over his opponent's head ;
they failed of their mark altogether. It was of no
use exposing obscurities or inconsistencies in a writer
who did not aim to be systematic or to argue out a
thesis so much as to tell merely what he himself felt
as to the Gospel, the difficulties of its acceptance by
many minds, and the higher form in which it presented
itself to his own spiritual experience. Dr. Thomson's
polemics, it must be confessed, were not of a high
order ; occasionally they show a bad spirit. He had
noble gifts, we know ; there was a fine Christian
manliness in his character ; but there was also a
certain coarseness of fibre, and he does not shine in
encounter with Mr. Erskine. It is not to be denied
that the latter, with the school to which he belonged,
was highly provocative. Never retaliating, they yet
looked with ineffable pity on their assailants and the
countless arguments they directed against them. And
there is nothing perhaps harder to bear than the pity
which entrenches itself in silence, and looks down as

from a serener height on the wordy warfare.   It must be said also that while Erskine never personally attacked the dogmas of the Church, he yet, in all his writings, tended quietly to subvert them.   He spoke with disapproval of the prevalent religion taught from the pulpits and received by the people. This was a trying tone for men like Dr. Andrew Thomson, proud of the popular religion, and who, long since done with their theological education, had no idea of beginning it again in Mr. Erskine's school.

As for himself, Thomas Erskine was never all his life done with his spiritual education.   He was always learning, and, his opponents said, 'never coming to the knowledge of the truth.'   He had no belief in finality of any kind.   He was always seeking for more light.   If the truth had been offered him with the one hand, and the pursuit of it with the other, he would have chosen, with Lessing, the chase rather than the game.   'If we only could have an infallible church—an unerring guide!' it was once said in his hearing.   The remark raised all such combative energy as he had.   'O no!' he said, 'such a thing, if it could be, would destroy all God's real purpose with man, *which is to educate him,* and to make him feel that he is being educated—to awaken perception in the man himself—a growing perception of what is true and right, which is of the very essence of all spiritual discipline.   Any infallible authority would destroy this, and so take away the meaning of a church altogether.'

These few traits may serve to give some image of Mr. Erskine.   They are but feeble strokes of little value to any who knew him; but they are characteristic. He lived so far into our own time, and was so well known to some of our generation, that we are apt to forget how far back his activity as a writer and his religious influence commenced. He passed for the Scottish bar in 1810, and in his early years, as indeed through life, was the familiar friend of Jeffrey, Cockburn, and Rutherfurd. With Leslie, the well-known mathematician, he also lived in intimacy, and had a great liking for him and many stories of his eccentricities. His life-long friendship with Thomas Carlyle is known to all; and while many characters have been scorched beneath that dreadful pen, from which epithets fell like cannon shot, leaving an ineffaceable impression, there is no word but what is gentle and kind of his friend at Linlathen. Carlyle, indeed, might well love him, for he had a warm place always in Thomas Erskine's heart, who mourned for his unhappiness as if he had been a brother.

Erskine's first book appeared in 1820, and in the following year had reached a third edition. It was entitled *Remarks on the Internal Evidence for the Truth of Revealed Religion.* This work is not only interesting in itself, but especially interesting as marking a crisis in his own history, and what we may call a crisis in the theological thought of Scotland. The author had shared in the prevalent scepticism which marked the period of his youth and the Edinburgh society in which he had mingled. 'The patient study of the gospel narrative,' he says, ' and of its place in the history of the world, and *the perception of a light in it which entirely satisfied his reason and conscience,*' overcame his doubts and left him in the assured possession of divine truth. The death of his brother, whom he succeeded in the property of Linlathen, deepened his religious impressions. The current of his faith swelled strongly under God's dealing with him, and he was so moved that he committed his thoughts to paper with a view 'of putting them into the hands of his companions at the bar when he parted from them.' He does not seem to have carried out this intention, but the paper he then composed was afterwards used, with his sanction, as an 'Introductory Essay' to Samuel Rutherfurd's Letters.[1]

Mr. Erskine's first volume is in some respects his most characteristic. It is mainly the result of his own thought—as all his books were—but it may also in some degree have been suggested by a controversy of the day. Dr. Chalmers had published, ten years before, his well-known paper on Christianity in the *Edinburgh Encyclopædia*. In this paper he had, with the first fervour of his new-born faith, denounced the total insufficiency of natural religion to judge the contents of revelation or the character and conduct of God as given in revelation. Reason might judge, he argued, of the validity of the external evidences of Christianity, but 'its intrinsic merits' or internal evidences were quite beyond the competency of our natural judgment. If the authority of the Christian revelation is once established on the ground of its historical evidence, it is not our business to scrutinise its reasonableness, but 'to submit our minds to the fair interpretation of Scripture.' This was the natural but rash conclusion of an intense and absorbing

[1] Collins, Glasgow, 1825.

faith. It was a rash conclusion certainly—afterwards abandoned by Chalmers himself—for how can the divine authorship of anything be known apart from its character? The weakness of Dr. Chalmers's position was well exposed in an acute and able volume by Dr. Mearns of Aberdeen, in which it was shown how impossible it is to judge of the divine origin of Christianity apart from a consideration of its real nature, both as revealing the character of God, and as bearing on the character of man. Religion in other words must prove itself reasonable, worthy of God, and fitted to do good to man, before it can be accepted as divine. Dr. Mearns's volume was published in 1818.

Erskine can hardly fail to have been interested in this polemic, touching as it does so closely the line of his own thought. With him there could be no question as to the necessary connection between the Divine origin of Christianity and its Divine character, nor of the competency of our moral instincts to judge this character. No man could be less of a rationalist in the obnoxious sense of the word. He was steeped to the heart in the essential flavour of Christian truth. But all divine truth must find its echo within himself—must have a definite relation to his own spiritual experience, and, as he believed, to all Christian experience. In this consisted its reasonableness. A religion of mere authority, coming to man from the outside and compelling faith and obedience, was unintelligible to him. It was not even of the nature of religion, which must be always self-evidencing, showing itself by its own light ; proving itself what it professes to be by the

essential relation between its doctrines and the
spiritual elevation, the moral culture of those who
receive it. 'The reasonableness of a religion,' he
says, 'seems to me to consist in there being a direct
and natural connection between a believing of the
doctrines which it inculcates, and a being formed by
these to the character which it recommends. If the
belief of the doctrines has no tendency to train a
disciple in a more exact and more willing discharge
of its moral obligations, there is evidently a very
strong probability against the truth of that religion.
. . . What is the history of another world to me,
unless it have some intelligible relation to my duties
or happiness?'[1]

All this is simply to assert that religion, to be
accepted as true, must be real. Its doctrines must
be of such a nature that we cannot believe them
without being the better of believing them. They
are self-evidencing in the light of conscience. They
are self-transforming in the very act of reception.
This seems almost a truism, and yet this very
passage was one which was specially quoted to
indicate the rationalistic character of Erskine's
teaching.[2] It was pronounced presumptuous thus
to judge of Divine Revelation. Erskine's great
principle that the object of Christianity was ' to bring
the character of man into harmony with that of God,'
was supposed to minimise Revelation, to make man
its arbiter—as if we could judge of God's works
which 'look many ways,' and have 'objects innumer-
able.' But surely if we are to have any thoughts
about God and religion at all, such thoughts are

[1] P. 58.   [2] No. 73 of the Oxford Tracts.

the most worthy and reverent we can have. There is no true reverence in bowing before a mere authority, and taking for truth that which has neither light in itself, nor seems fitted to give us light, or to make us like to God.

Erskine no doubt in his first book as in all his books, and in the uniform strain of his thought, was inclined to dwell somewhat exclusively on the *internal* aspect of Religion. Religion was so great a reality to him, that he never dissociated it from its bearing on human character. He could barely imagine it in mere conventional or historical forms— as a formal revelation, or an external institution. By his own pure thinking,—out of the workings of his own heart,—he seemed to himself to have got beyond such critical questions as the veracity of the evangelical narratives and other historical difficulties, which in his earlier life had perplexed him. He had cut his way out of these difficulties, rather than solved them by patient and adequate inquiry. He had said to himself as many others have done, I cannot reach any clear settlement of such questions ; they are far too intricate and involve too many probabilities to be determined by me—perhaps to be determined by any one. He had none of the logical confidence of the old school of Paley, to whom the external evidences of Christianity presented themselves as a problem to be solved in a series of propositions, which they believed themselves to have satisfactorily proved. Even Chalmers, with all the splendour of his natural powers, was in the main a man of an eighteenth century turn of mind, who put the apostles—as witnesses of the Christian

miracles—into court, so to speak ; and, after interro-
gation, summed up in their favour. Erskine's intellectual mood was quite different. He had no argumentative or historical turn. His genius was purely
spiritual. If he was to receive Christianity at all,
therefore, it must come to him as an internal light,
flooding his soul—conditioning his whole life. He
saw that men believed in 'external evidences,' and
were attached to the Church as an institution,
without being any better men, or being inspired by
a divine spirit. But Christianity must be all or
nothing to him. He must see it as a divine truth.
' I must discern,' he said, ' in the history itself, a light
and truth which will meet the demands both of my
reason and conscience. In fact, however true the
history may be, it cannot be of any moral and
spiritual benefit to me, until I apprehend its truth
and meaning. This, and nothing less than this, is
what I require, not only in this great concern, but
in all others.'

Erskine, in short, without any indebtedness either
to Schleiermacher or Coleridge, and almost as early
as either, was in Scotland an apostle of the ' Christian consciousness.' He led in the great reaction
against mere formal orthodoxy, and, for that part of
the matter, formal rationalism, which set in with the
opening of the third decade of the century. Those
who called him a rationalist judged him from a wrong
point of view. He was rational certainly in comparison with all who saw in Christianity a body of mere
formal doctrines or observances, to be accepted on
authority. But he was the very opposite of rationalistic in the sense in which rationalism had prevailed

in Germany and England in the eighteenth century. This bastard form of reason had cut the heart out of all religion and reduced it to a *caput mortuum.* Erskine's religion was *all heart.* He did not understand religion without the living fire of faith and love and obedience animating it all through. It must be a light in his reason, a guide in his conscience—a life within his life,—a spiritual power glowing in his whole conduct. This was 'internal evidence,'—the revelation of Love to love, of Life to life,—of God to man, raising him to divine communion, and reflecting upon him the divine likeness. ' The first faint outline of Christianity,' he says, ' presents to us a view of God operating on the character of men through a manifestation of His own character, in order that, by leading them to participate in some measure in His moral likeness, they may also in some measure participate in His happiness.'

The same subjective tendency pervades all his special views of Christian doctrine. As with Coleridge, for example, the abstract doctrine of the Trinity had little interest for him. He recognised it indeed as speculatively true—as the necessary outcome of real thought on the subject of God. I heard him in later years discourse much on this subject, and endeavour to explain how the very idea of God as Love implied an object of love or divine Son from the beginning, and no less a divine Spirit. But so far the doctrine lay to him in obscurity. It was only in *the light of redemption* that it planted itself as a living truth in his Christian intelligence. ' The obscurity of the doctrine vanishes,' he says, ' when it comes in such a form as this, " God so loved the world, that he gave his only begotten Son, that whosoever believeth in him should have eternal life."' Again, while speaking of the dogma, in its article or creed form, as presenting difficulties to the mind—as being in fact of such an 'unintelligible nature' as to suggest the idea 'that Christianity holds out a premium for believing improbabilities'—he thinks that when taken in its Biblical connection,—as all doctrines should be taken,—it becomes an illuminating belief. In his own language—'it stands indissolubly united with an act of divine holiness and compassion which radiates to the heart an appeal of tenderness most intelligible in its nature and object, and most constraining in its influence.'

But Mr. Erskine's teaching gradually assumed a more definite and significant form. He passed from consideration of the general character and evidence of religion to that of the essential character of the Gospel as a Revelation of Divine Love. It was his later rather than his earlier teaching that may be said to have formed a school of which Maurice was an offshoot and of which Dr. Macleod Campbell became the chief theological representative in Scotland.

This more essential Christian teaching was embodied in a series of volumes,[1] but especially in a volume on *The Unconditional Freeness of the Gospel*, prepared by Mr. Erskine while on the Continent in 1827, and published on his return early in 1828. In this volume he explained how the current theolo-

---

[1] (1.) *An Essay on Faith,* 1822.
 (2.) *The Unconditional Freeness of the Gospel,* 1828.
 (3.) *The Brazen Serpent,* 1831.
 (4.) *The Doctrine of Election,* 1837.

gical terms such as Pardon, Salvation, Eternal Life, were, as he supposed, misinterpreted. Pardon was conceived as offered now to every sinner on condition of faith, Salvation as equivalent to justification by faith, and Eternal Life as a life in the future, locally represented under the name of heaven. According to him Pardon was *already* made for every sinner in the mission and death of Christ. ' The pardon of the gospel,' in his own words, ' is in effect a declaration on the part of God to every individual sinner in the whole world that his holy compassion embraces him, and the blood of Jesus Christ has atoned for his sins.' Salvation, again, is ' the healing of the spiritual diseases of the soul,' and Eternal Life ' the communication of the life of God to the soul.' Heaven is not necessarily associated with the idea of locality, but is ' properly the name for a state conformed to the will of God,' and hell the opposite of that state.

It is easy to see in all this the operation of the same subjective tendency—his desire to translate the gospel out of the formal conceptions in which it had become systematised in the doctrines of the Westminster Assembly, into experience and life.[1] These doctrines appeared to him to limit the gospel and keep it aloof from man till applied to him by the twofold act of divine election and justifying faith. On the contrary, he held that it is already the por-

[1] In one of his letters, Nov. 1833, addressed to Lady Elgin, he says in words exactly agreeing with those in the text, ' I believe all *notions* of Religion [the italics are his own], however true, to be absolutely useless or worse than useless.' Christ ' is far above all doctrines about Him, however true. He is the truth. A doctrine that can be separated from Himself is a vanity and deception.'

tion of every sinner. 'Christ,' as he said, 'is laid down at every door.' 'Salvation by faith does not mean that mankind are pardoned on account of their faith or by their faith. No, its meaning is far different. It means that they are pardoned already before they thought of it,' and that they *have only to realise what is already theirs* to enjoy all the blessings of salvation. Pardon, in other words, is *universal.* The gospel is a great scheme of universal restoration through Christ, which meets and remedies all the loss of the Fall. Men no longer need forgiveness, for they already have forgiveness in Christ. What they need is a *consciousness* of this—a subjective experience of the objective divine fact accomplished for them in Christ. Through God's great mercy, if they only knew it, pardon is theirs already.

All who are familiar with the theology of Mr. Maurice, in his books and in his remarkable letters recently published, will find there the expanded echo of this teaching. Mr. Maurice himself frankly owns this (1852) in dedicating one of his volumes[1] to Mr. Erskine. The general character of this theology therefore will again come before us, and we need only now fix its place in the development of Mr. Erskine's thought.

His volumes on *The Unconditional Freeness of the Gospel,* and *The Brazen Serpent* (1831), may be said to sum up his teaching. He continued to publish, but it cannot be said that he added anything further to the characteristics of his religious thought. *The Brazen Serpent* is the most theological of his writings, and particularly attracted Mr. Maurice, but it did not

[1] *The Prophets and Kings of the Old Testament,* 1852.

reach the same circulation as his preceding treatises.[1]
It contains in germ much of the same thinking which
afterwards, in the more powerful reflective mind of
Dr. Macleod Campbell, expanded into his well-known
treatise on *The Nature of the Atonement.*

Whatever we may think of Mr. Erskine's views,
and we are in a far better position now to judge of
their merits and defects than his own generation was,
there can hardly be any question of their variance
with the popular theology of Scotland. Dr. Chalmers
is said[2] to have cordially approved of 'the leading
principles of his essay on *The Freeness of the Gospel,*'
though dissenting from 'one of its positions,' and to
have expressed over and over again to his friends
his pleasure in the volume as one of 'the most
delightful books that ever had been written.' There
was a large-heartedness in Chalmers that responded
to its free and generous views, and in that and
some other matters he did not care for logical
consistency. But Dr. Andrew Thomson was the
truer interpreter of the mind of Scotland as well as
of the differences between the new and the old
theology. Whatever we may think of the spirit of
many of his criticisms, he saw clearly, and with logical
acumen, within his own sphere of vision, and there is
an argumentative as well as vindictive force in some
of his replies. What is most remarkable to a student
now-a-days in both is the lack of historical knowledge in dealing with Christian dogma. Mr. Erskine

[1] All Mr. Erskine's first books, *On the Internal Evidence for the
Truth of Revealed Religion* (1820), his *Essay on Faith* (1822), and *The
Unconditional Freeness of the Gospel,* went through many editions,
were translated into French, and the first also into German.

[2] Dr. Hanna's edition of *Mr. Erskine's Letters,* vol. i. p. 127.

is perhaps more deficient in this respect than his opponent. He has no consciousness of the real relation of his views to the older theology, or again to Arminianism, or again how far he was merely reviving or bringing forth anew, aspects of ancient doctrine. He was consequently astonished at the condemnation which his book called forth. A larger acquaintance with the history of theological opinion would have enabled him to see that a good deal of his distinctive teaching was not new in the thought of the Church, and on the other hand that it touched so very different a pole of thought from that of the theology of the Westminster Divines, that it was sure to evoke violent offence and discussion.

His mind was at once questioning and meditative —but he had never been a student of theology in any scientific sense, nor indeed in any large traditionary sense. So it was that the result of his own meditation upon Scripture came to him with a surprised delight, and seemed a Gospel unknown before, or at least unknown in Scotland. Constantly in his letters he deplores the darkness of the general Christian teaching ; and there was ground for much that he says ; but it was also true that the universal aspect of the Gospel had never been lost sight of in the Scottish Church in its most Calvinistic moods. No Calvinist, however rigidly he clung to his system, would have allowed that he limited the offer of Divine Love in the Gospel, or that any who chose to accept the offer was excluded from the pale of salvation.[1] Here,

---

[1] It must be conceded that Mr. Erskine at times somewhat wilfully misinterprets the current Theology, as in saying that it held that man is justified ' on account of his faith or by his faith,' whereas it is a well-

as everywhere, we are noting facts, and not dealing with theological difficulties or refinements. And it admits of no question that Scottish theologians, from Knox and Samuel Rutherfurd to Chalmers, have ever enforced with pathetic power the claim of the Divine Love upon sinners. Their technical theology may seem to have been inconsistent with this ; it was so in Mr. Erskine's eyes ; but no technical theology can alter facts, nor, indeed, resist the impulses of Divine affection in Christian hearts. There were many, therefore, in Mr. Erskine's day, who, while refusing to accept his way of putting the matter, or the form of the Gospel as set forth by him, would yet have maintained that they held all that was true and scriptural in his teaching.

It is melancholy, indeed, to reflect how at this critical period in the history of the Scottish Church, as in similar periods of Church history, men—on both sides—became excited over modes of language, and sought to emphasise the difference rather than the identity of their Christian conceptions. This is sufficiently conspicuous in the polemic which gathered around Mr. Erskine and his books ; but it is still more evident, as it had far more serious consequences, in the new phase of the movement which meets us on the shores of the Gareloch, and in which Mr. Macleod Campbell was the chief figure.

Mr. Campbell was settled in the parish of Row, lying on the Dumbarton shore of the beautiful Gareloch, in 1825—the year, it will be remembered, in which the *Aids to Reflection* saw the light. He had

known commonplace of Calvinism that faith is in no sense the *operative*, but only the *instrumental* cause of salvation.

grown up, if possible, in a still more sequestered parish, Kilninver, where his father had ministered for a lifetime, and where the savour of his honoured name still lingers. After a career of promise at Glasgow College, and a year's study in Edinburgh, 1821-2, he spent the intervening time before he settled at Row in reading and further study, chiefly of a philosophic kind. His father's sympathies were in the main with the 'Moderate' party. He delighted in the study of Tillotson and Samuel Clarke. Young Campbell therefore did not imbibe any hyper-Evangelical doctrine in his youth, and yet there was in him from the first such a tendency. It was always the fear of his old tutor that he would become 'too high.' His early ministry was one of simple faith and conviction. He kept aloof from parties in the Church, and gave himself to his duties with untiring devotion. Never was Christian minister more divinely called. He was born to preach the Gospel, and to counsel and guide others in the Divine life. He had the true Apostolical succession, if ever man had, and, what he had, he retained. The same Divine unction lay upon all his words, and the same blessing followed him wherever he went. It is impossible to conceive a ministry more divinely consecrated and sustained, and yet more in the face of all Church theory. He was as plainly 'called to be a minister of Jesus Christ through the will of God' as any Apostle ever was, and his divine calling remained independent of any ecclesiastical sanction, and even grew richer in his isolation. The fact is beyond question, whatever our theories may make of it.

Difficulties soon arose in the course of a ministry

so earnest and personal as Mr. Campbell's. As he studied the Scriptures diligently, and visited his people constantly, he became impressed with the lack of vital piety. He found many interested in religion, but few living holy lives. The higher the standard he set before his people the less did they seem to reach, in his opinion, a true standard at all. He pondered the cause of this, and came to the conclusion that it was because they did not feel sure of God's goodwill to them as individuals. They required to be taught the very first step in religion, the being 'assured of the Divine love in Christ.' Hence his 'doctrine of the assurance of faith,' by which he seemed at first at least to mean the assurance of an objective fact—the Divine Father's love—rather than of a subjective state, —as if a man could never fall from grace. But here in the nature of his language the first opening was given for heretical charge against him. Then came the further thought, How can any man in particular know that God loves him unless Christ has *died for all*,—unless the Gospel be a 'Gospel' or divine gift to every human being? Otherwise he thought 'there was no foundation in the Record of God for the assurance which he demanded, and which he saw to be essential to true holiness.' Hence his further doctrine of Universal Atonement.

He described, not without a touch of unconscious humour, how those who had been most satisfied with his teaching on the subject of Assurance were particularly displeased with his teaching as to the Universality of the Atonement. It seemed to them that if Christ died for all, then the individual Christian was deprived of assurance in his own case. Others, again, who had been offended by his preaching Assurance, were still more offended by his combining with this doctrine that of universal pardon.

There can be no doubt that there was much confusion both of thought and language lying at the foundation of what is known as the Row heresy. In a certain respect Mr. Campbell's teaching was beyond challenge. That God loves every creature that He has made, that Christ died for all men, are commonplaces of Christian theology—but not so the doctrine that 'assurance is of the essence of faith' or that all men are pardoned in the sense of being saved. Preacher and accusers misunderstood one another, and the longer they argued they misunderstood the more. It would be wrong to lay all the blame of this upon the accusers. Mr. Campbell was not only fond of his own phrases, but he had that tendency common to the dogmatic mind to take his phrases for an essential part of Divine truth. In 1829, when the agitation against his teaching was reaching its height, he makes the remarkable confession, 'I know that I might preach the truth without challenge if I avoided two things; innovations of language such as saying that all are pardoned; and personal interrogations, such as, 'Are you born again?' 'Do you know yourself to be a child of God?' But these modes of speech were necessary, he imagined, to the expression of his own thought. What he meant was that all are pardoned in the amplitude of the Divine love, and *if they would only realise* it all are already by the act of God Himself His own children ; but he was supposed to mean that all are already saved and the children of God, whether they realised it or not,

whether they lived as the children of God or not.
He was speaking of the ideal in Christ—the Church
redeemed and sanctified in Him. Others were
thinking of men and women as they generally are,
unconscious of their Divine privileges. The assertion that all were pardoned was translated into the
notion of salvation without regard to morality, or even
any consciousness of true religion ; and did not Anti-
nomianism therefore hang on the skirts of such
preaching? Nothing could have been further from
Mr. Campbell's thoughts. It was the very intensity
of his desire for holy living among his people that
made him dwell upon the assured love of God to
them as the true and only root of such holy living.
It was his craving after the very life of God in himself
and others which made him so emphasise the love of
God to sinners. But there was none the less a certain
danger in his modes of speech, especially when taken
up and translated by minds with none of his spiritual
insight. Like his friend Erskine, he saw not only to
the heart of the Gospel, but he saw it always as an
ideal whole—faith, hope, charity, love, light, holiness,
all blended in one. His conception of the Divine
was essentially concrete. His assurance of the Divine
Love in the forgiveness of sins already contained in
it the whole idea of salvation. But the common
theological intelligence has abstracted and divided
the several parts of the Divine life. It does not
hold pardon and holiness, love and law, assurance
and conduct, together in their necessary nexus as
he did. And to this state of mind 'universal pardon'
is indiscriminate salvation.

The case was one for forbearance and conference.

Unhappily it developed rapidly into prosecution. There had been growing offence at Mr. Campbell's preaching. He had become marked along with Mr. Erskine as the centre of a new school of thought within the Church. The latter had heard him preach in Edinburgh apparently in the spring of 1828. Returning from church he said with emphasis, ' I have heard to-day from that pulpit what I believe to be the true Gospel.' The same summer found Mr. Erskine at Row united in a close and warm friendship with the pastor. Others joined the brotherhood sooner or later. Mr. Story, minister of Roseneath, across the Gareloch; Mr. Scott, afterwards well known as Principal of Owens College, Manchester; Edward Irving, and others less prominent. They became credited with an attempt to upset the old Calvinistic doctrine. The idea of some such combination undoubtedly possessed the minds of many, and may be held so far to explain the sad series of events which followed.

It is needless to pass any harsh judgment now on what took place, nor is this the place to describe the sequel at length. But it must ever remain a matter of regret that the Church did not weigh more deliberately her line of action, and realise more solemnly all its meaning. No Church was ever more blessed than the Church of Scotland then was in these men of Christian genius whom she rashly cast from her bosom. They were all men of truly prophetic spirit, and who knows what healing might have come to Irving's great but perturbed mind if he had been tenderly cared for and sheltered within the Church of his Fathers instead of being rudely pushed

outside of it! It was a favourite topic with Mr.
Erskine in after years—the great wrong which the
Church had done to herself in this matter. Principal
Shairp has recorded that 'he never ceased to regard
Mr. Campbell's deposition as the stoning by the
Church of her best Prophet, the deliberate rejection
of the highest light vouchsafed to her in his time;'
and that in his eyes all the calamities that soon
befell the Church were as judgments for her wrong-
doing.

The proceedings in Mr. Campbell's case assumed
before they closed a specially interesting phase. He
passed in his defence from the discussion of the
special heretical doctrines with which he was charged
to the higher question, as to whether the doctrines—
admitting them to be beyond the *Confession of Faith*
—were not yet obligatory upon the Church as being
the truth of God? Is the Church not bound to
acknowledge any higher light of truth than she has
hitherto received if made manifest from the Divine
Word? Is it not of the very function of the Church
to declare anew the truth when new light comes to
her? A famous passage in the Scottish Confession
of 1560, which both Campbell and Edward Irving
preferred greatly to the later Puritan or Westminster
Confession, was quoted on the subject, to the effect
that Scripture was acknowledgedly the Supreme Rule
of Faith, and that no sentence or article is to be
received that can be shown to be inconsistent with its
plain teaching. Mr. Campbell did not then allow that
his doctrines were inconsistent with a fair interpretation
of the Westminster Confession of Faith, but granting
there was any doubt of this, he appealed with con-

fidence to Holy Scripture for their authority, and he maintained that the true principle of the Church was, not to put her Confession on a level with Holy Scripture, or to cast any from her bosom except on the ground that they taught what was not according to the Word of God. 'If you show me,' he said, 'that anything I have taught is inconsistent with the Word of God, I shall give it up, and allow you to regard it as heresy. . . . If a Confession of Faith were something to stint or stop the Church's growth in light and knowledge, and to say, "Thus far shalt thou go and no further," then a Confession of Faith would be the greatest curse that ever befell a church. Therefore I distinctly hold that no minister treats the Confession of Faith right if he does not come with it, as a party, to the Word of God, and consent to stand or fall by the Word of God, and to acknowledge no other tribunal in matters of heresy than the Word of God. In matters of doctrine no lower authority can be recognised than that of God.'[1]

The question thus opened was a highly significant one. Half a century ago, however, it was too searching and bold a departure to be likely to help Mr. Campbell at the bar of any Synod or Assembly of the Church, the more so that it was combined in his case with a certain element of dogma offensive to the 'moderate' clergy, and by no means fitted in itself to strengthen Mr. Campbell's position. He did not argue, for example, in favour of a general latitude of interpretation. On the contrary, he expressly

[1] From speech of Mr. Campbell before the bar of Synod of Glasgow and Ayr, which he regarded as the best exposition of his side of the case.

repudiated such a latitude. He did not say, I claim for myself a wider application of the Gospel in the light of the Divine word, as I am willing to allow a similar width of interpretation to others who have departed as far from the letter of the Confession as I may have done. It is of the very nature of a document, like the Confession, to be subject, as time advances, to meanings of a more flexible character than those which may have been in the view of its original framers. This broad and common-sense principle was not only not in Mr. Campbell's mind, but was rejected by him at this stage of his career.[1] He was not content that his views should be tolerated. He claimed recognition for them as 'the truth of God.' Both he and Mr. Erskine, with all their personal humility and insight into the perplexities of the religious mind were essentially dogmatic in their turn of thought. They failed, as all connected with the movement more or less failed, in historical knowledge—in appreciation of the growth of Christian doctrine—and the manner in which higher and lower moments fit into one another in the great progress of the Church. They would have all to stand on the same level as themselves, and they did not hesitate to judge the Christianity of others from their own point of view. They not only had the true light, but all those who opposed them, or who were unable to see the truth as they saw it, were in darkness. There is something painful, I confess, in their readiness of

---

[1] He speaks disparagingly for example in his defence of the 'charity' that is indulgent to all manner of opinions, and which regards 'speaking dogmatically as necessarily an evil.'—*Memorials*, vol. i. p. 80.

judgment, and their incapacity to recognise how much Christian good there may be in opinions differing from their own—in other words, in their failure to perceive the impossibility of any form of words —of one school or another—containing what they called 'the truth of God' to the exclusion of all others. They did not, in short, rise above the dogmatic temper of the time, while they sought to enrich its dogmatic thought. Afterwards they attained higher views. The searching discussions of a later time in England helped them to realise, more than was possible in those earlier in Scotland, the historical conditions underlying all dogmatic statements of Divine truth, the value of free opinion, and of tolerating within the Church the expression of such opinion.[1] Mr. Campbell, indeed, never lost his profound feeling for dogma, or 'the truth of God,' as he called it. His first and main thought as to any new views was always, 'are they true?' Historical criticism, of which he confessed he knew little, never touched the inner sphere of his own conviction; but he came to appreciate its importance, and how much it must affect and to a certain extent limit all conclusions drawn from Scripture.[2]

The same General Assembly which deposed Mr. Campbell deprived his friend, Mr. Scott, of his licence as a preacher of the gospel. They held the same views, with this difference, that Scott acknowledged from the first their inconsistency with the ' Confession

[1] In 1856 he wrote, 'I am sure free discussion *within* the Church is better than the constant necessity to form a new sect, if one has any new thought to utter.'—*Memorials*, vol. i. p. 276.

[2] *Memorials*, vol. ii. pp. 8-43.

of Faith.' It is said that Campbell came to acknowledge this also, as he walked home with his friend
from the General Assembly, 'the dawn breaking upon
them' as they sought their lodgings.[1] It must be
allowed that the current thinking of the Church
fifty years ago was opposed to the doctrine preached
by both,—a conclusive illustration of which is found
in the combination of the two parties, 'Moderate'
and 'Evangelical,' in the sentence passed upon
Mr. Campbell. His aged father interposed at the
end with one of the most touching speeches ever
heard in any Assembly, in which, divesting his son's
doctrine of all novelty of language, he claimed it to
be the same doctrine they all taught. The emotion
of Dr. Macknight, then chief clerk of Assembly, is
said to have been such that he gave utterance to
strange words ominous as to the future of the Church.
But the fiat had gone forth ; and, by a large and
nearly unanimous vote,[2] Mr. Campbell's connection
with the Church of Scotland was severed.

Mr. Campbell's after life, and the quiet course of
earnest thought which led to his great work on *The
Nature of the Atonement*, by which he came to have
an honoured name in all the Churches, and to take
rank as one of the most profound theologians of the
nineteenth century, belong to a later epoch. There
have been few more striking instances of the reward
of the righteous than his life presents. His sweetness
of nature, and the constant indwelling of his 'fundamental faith' in the great love of God to all human

---

[1] Dr. Hanna, *Erskine's Letters*, vol. i. p. 140.
[2] 119 to 6. The words attributed to Dr. Macknight will be found
in Mr. Erskine's *Letters*, Ed. by Dr. Hanna, vol. i. p. 137.

souls, kept him free from all sectarian association in the midst of his isolation. He never ceased to have a warm heart towards the Church which cast him forth. He grew in ever deeper knowledge of Divine Truth ; and his work on the *Atonement*, and a smaller volume a few years later on *Revelation*, remain treasures to the Christian Church in all time to come.

The General Assembly of 1831 not only discarded Campbell and Scott, but also initiated proceedings against Edward Irving. Irving's is too great a name to be omitted in our review of the religious movement of this time—and yet there is a sense in which he hardly belongs to it. With all our admiration of his genius,—and in point of genius he stands in some respects unrivalled among his contemporaries,—he was never at any time of his life a thinker. He was a great power; but the elements of his power lay in the region of spiritual life,—of oratorical impulse,—and not of spiritual thought. His *Orations*, published in 1823 in the second year of his London ministry, taken as a whole, are the highest expression of his mind, and their characteristics are grandeur of imagination, richness of poetic and spiritual conception, and fulness of vivid feeling rather than any glow of higher insight, penetrating to the deeper problems of religion. They fail in clear-sighted intelligence and definite or even suggestive development of ideas. We cannot better mark this than by saying that no one would think now of having recourse to Irving's *Orations* or any of his works—as they would have recourse either to Mr. Erskine's volume, or to Mr. Campbell's—in order to understand the higher aspects of religious inquiry towards which his age was moving. He was the superior of both in much ; the question is not one of personal comparison at all ; but they reached their idea along lines of pure spiritual insight, whereas Irving was caught in the whirl of his own strong emotions, and carried forward by their overpowering rush. The most loveable of men—'the brotherliest human soul,' as Carlyle said of him—he was open to impressions from all sides. Carlyle himself, Chalmers, Coleridge, Campbell, all contributed to give him impulse, till he sunk at last under an order of impressions equally disastrous and unworthy of him. Coleridge he confessed to be his greatest teacher, but he failed to catch the higher spirit of Coleridge's thought. ' You have been more profitable to my faith in orthodox doctrine, to my spiritual understanding of the Word of God, and to my right conception of the Church,' he said to the Highgate philosopher in dedicating to him his famous missionary sermon, 'than any or all the men with whom I have entertained friendship and conversation.'

Yet with all Irving's susceptibility of impression, there was in him from the first not merely the element of dogma belonging to his time, but a supreme dogmatism amounting to priestliness. Docile as a pupil, he was inflexible when once he received any principle into his mind. Constantly craving after what was positive and authoritative in religion, he was ready to welcome new truth, especially if coming from some transcendental region or enforced with high personal pretensions—yet he seemed incapable of revising his accumulated convictions. He was, in short, wholly destitute of the critical intellect. He never knew what it was to hold his mind in doubt or suspense. Of Biblical interpretation he knew nothing in any true sense, or of the historical conditions underlying the whole history of revelation and Christian thought. The modern spirit—liberalism in all its forms—was as hateful to him as to Dr. Newman. The age seemed to him moving towards perdition, and the critics and intellectualists of all sorts only helping it onwards. The talent of Byron and Southey was alike diabolic. Milton was the 'archangel' and Brougham the 'archfiend' of radicalism; the London University 'the synagogue of Satan,' and Catholic emancipation 'the unchristianising of the legislature.'

This was not the temper of a thinker, nor even of a large-minded prophet. It indicated unhealthiness from the first. Grand as was his genius there was a lurid play in it—the working, not of thought, but of spiritual passion. He moved on a scale of lofty but uncurbed emotion. His great ambition for the Gospel was to make it 'more heroical and magnanimous,' but he lacked the balance of philosophy and of common sense for so great a task.

It is hardly to be wondered at that a spirit so high, yet so imperfectly balanced, should ere long have plunged into difficulties. As his fame grew as a preacher, many eyes watched him with admiration; some, like his friend Carlyle, with fear; others with envy. A cry arose that he was preaching heresy as to our Lord's human nature. The truth was, as is now unversally admitted, that in this matter Irving had really reverted to an older and more catholic type of doctrine. It had not been customary in Scotland to dwell on the Incarnation in connection with the sufferings and atonement of Christ. Irving saw, as Dr. Campbell afterwards[1] so powerfully developed, their organic connection. The reality of Christ's human nature, 'as bone of our bone, and flesh of our flesh,' became a cardinal point of his theology. Christ took upon Him our nature, not in any abstract or unreal form, but with all its sinful tendencies. In Him it was sinless, but not through any quality making it to differ from humanity in general, but through 'the indwelling of the Holy Ghost.' That he ever meant to inculcate the actual sinfulness of Christ's human nature, no candid mind can maintain. But he was at fault here, as often, from the rhetorical extravagance of his language. He used unguardedly such expressions as that 'Christ's human nature was in all respects as ours!' 'fallen and sinful'—he meant in the *potency*, not in the fact of sin. But the subject was not one easily understood, while it was easily misrepresented. Notwithstanding all his disclaimers, it was ultimately made the ground of libel against him before the Presbytery of Annan, and, after something of a mock trial, he was deposed in the spring of 1833.

There were other influences, however, at work leading to Edward Irving's deposition. He had not only associated himself with Mr. Campbell from the year 1828, when he came to the Gareloch to visit him ; but he had become identified, in a manner Mr. Campbell never was, with the religious extravagances which arose in this quarter in 1830. First the 'gift of Tongues,' and then the 'gift of Healing' were supposed to have revisited the Church in the person of certain invalids in the parish of Roseneath and the

---

[1] *Nature of the Atonement,* 1856.

town of Greenock.   The phenomena were unquestion-
ably of a singular character[1]—apparently so united
with divine faith and holy lives, that they carried
away Mr. Erskine as well as Edward Irving.   The
healthier nature of the former, however, threw off the
infection.   Irving, with his mind enfeebled by the
morbid study of prophecy, and the exhausting excite-
ments of his London career, was not only taken
captive himself, but under his encouragement, the
delusion extended to his congregation.   'Bedlam and
Chaos,' as Carlyle says, was the result.   The congregation became violently divided.   His friends remon-
strated ; but all was in vain.   The spiritual fever had
gone to his brain.   It was 'impossible to make an
impression on him.'   He was left in hopeless loneliness amidst the fanatics that surrounded him ; and
so passed away from living connection with his age
before he received the sentence of expulsion from the
Church so dear to him.

With all our love and admiration of Edward Irving,
we cannot regard him in any true sense as a leader of
Christian opinion.   But if he did not move its thought,
he greatly helped to deepen its religious consciousness.
All men recognised in him a spiritual power ; a representative, at least in his earlier London years, of religion, as entitled not only to acknowledgment and
sovereignty over all other interests, but as the most
magnificent reality which can claim human attention.
He was, in short, as Coleridge said of him, 'a mighty
wrestler in the cause of spiritual religion and Gospel
morality.'

Our task is wellnigh done in this lecture.   Its

[1] See Mrs. Oliphant's *Life*, vol. ii. p. 102 *et seq.*

chronological limits are to be carefully noted. **Mr.**
Erskine's first book was published in 1820, and Edward
Irving died in 1834. What is known as the Row movement with which the three names we have reviewed
were more or less closely connected, had run its course
by the last of these dates. This was the special
theological interest of the time in Scotland, and in its
higher aspects it was distinctively a movement of
religious thought, the effects of which survive in
many forms. Had we been able to extend our review we might have considered the fresh accession of
Evangelical life which began in the Church of Scotland
at the same time, and rose into continuous and increasing strength for ten years later. Two names above all
represent this movement—Dr. Andrew Thomson and
Dr. Chalmers—to both of whom we have more than
once alluded. The name of Chalmers is in all the
churches honoured as one of Christian genius consecrated to the highest services which any man can
render to his church and his country. His characteristic work, however, was not in the field of Christian
thought. He broke out no new lines in this field.
He initiated no new movement. Both he and Andrew Thomson were powerful leaders on the old
lines—the latter with inferior, although staunch intellectual weapons. Both were great orators beyond
question, the former excelling in massive, sustained,
and overpowering vehemence—the latter in logical
fervour and freedom of utterance. In both the
Evangelical section of the church, which for a time
had succumbed in intellectual repute to the moderate
party represented by men like Principal Robertson
and Principal Hill, received an accession of strength

which carried it ere long to predominance, and told significantly on the subsequent course of events. Chalmers had much the broader sympathies of the two. He was, we have seen, the friend and correspondent of Erskine, and is said to have shared many of his views. It is alleged also that he looked on the proceedings against Irving and Campbell with disapproving eyes. Possibly, if he had been a man of more independent, courageous, and clear-sighted vision than he was, he might have done something to stay these proceedings, or guide them to a more lenient result. But the panic which moved the church at the time was too real to have been easily stayed ; and Chalmers did nothing. Andrew Thomson suddenly died in the midst of his labours in the same year that Campbell was deposed, and left the guidance of the church to younger men, of whom the world has heard, but not in connection with the progress of Christian thought. The great politico-ecclesiastical movement which they led is beyond our province.

There is still one name, however, that deserves to be recalled before we close. There was published during the course of the Row excitement a series of anonymous volumes, chiefly of a devotional character, which excited a good deal of attention from the graceful and interesting style in which they were written. They were felt to be unlike the ordinary devotional literature of Scotland,—even more so in some respects than Mr. Erskine's volumes had been. For Mr. Erskine, layman as he was, used much of the old theological phraseology. It is strange indeed to a modern reader to observe how very technical many of his expressions are,—expressions not much heard now even in the pulpit. The anonymous books in question were singularly free from all this conventional phraseology. Their style was as clear and pure as Dr. Arnold's sermons,—with less substance, but even a more winning and flexible grace. The best known of them was a manual of Prayers under the title of *The Morning and Evening Sacrifice*, which soon established itself as a familiar devotional companion in many households. I remember the leader of the moderate party,—who unhappily moved the sentence against Mr. Campbell,—saying that he had long used this volume at morning and evening prayer without the faintest suspicion that it contained any heresy. Other volumes from the same source were *The Last Supper*, also a devotional manual, *Farewell to Time*, *A Manual of Conduct*; but especially a work in three volumes under the title of *The True Plan of a Living Temple*, published in 1830. This work contained the author's system of thought, and unlike the others, whose quiet and beautiful devotional feeling attracted interest and nothing more, it soon began to excite inquiry and criticism. The *Christian Instructor*, ever on the watch for the orthodoxy of the Church, reviewed it at length in its March number, 1831, expressing admiration of its literary merits, but emphasising its theology as 'not only defective, but positively pernicious.'

It must be admitted that *The True Plan of a Living Temple* presents many features open to criticism. It not only opposes itself confessedly to the prevalent course of religious ideas,—'the current doctrines of divines and moralists,'—but it sets forth at large a philosophy of life little consistent with Calvinistic teaching. The Gospel is viewed mainly as a means, among many others, of generating the principles of order and goodness which are everywhere seen in conflict with the principles of disorder and vice. The world-process is a process of good triumphing over evil,—a Divine kingdom everywhere displacing the rule of evil;—and the great function of Christianity is to reinforce the good against the evil, to extend 'the prevalence of knowledge and virtue and concord and freedom and happiness among men.'

It is enough to quote such a sentence to show how very different a note this book strikes from the usual note of religious orthodoxy. Nor were many of its special ideas less at variance with the latter. Our Lord is represented as speaking only of a 'Father in Heaven' who views all His creatures with love and pity. This is 'the fine idea on which His doctrine is founded—by which it is pervaded;—and by means of it he sought for mankind the three following objects : —First, the improvement of their religious worship ; secondly, the perfection of their moral ideas ; and lastly, the regulation of their social situations.' Suffering and punishment, while entering into the Divine constitution of things—'the true plan of the living temple'—are not 'retributive,' or, to use the author's own expression, 'vindictive,'—only 'corrective.' The book, in short, embodies a contemplative philosophy of human progress rather than any exposition of the Gospel conceived after a Calvinistic model. It is humanitarian rather than theological, the work of a thoughtful student living in a world of his own rather than of a Christian preacher. It contains many fine trains of reflection—thin in texture, and here and there feeble in grasp of moral realities—but beautiful in imaginative feeling and almost always graceful in literary expression. Anything less like the current theology cannot be conceived—and this effect of contrast was greatly heightened by scattered allusions and criticisms in the book. Howe, for example, revered by all Puritan thinkers, was spoken of as having 'a strong tinge of fanaticism ;' Calvin was 'the prince of dogmatists ;' and Bunyan and Wesley are 'notorious specimens of enthusiasm.'

It is needless to say that the book, so far as it excited public interest, was very distasteful to the orthodox clergy. But there were difficulties in the way of meddling with it. While its spirit and many of its reflections were so obviously alien to the Creed of the Church, it did not announce any definite heretical teaching. More than all, its author was invisible. I do not know how far he may have been known at this time to those who were at the pains to inquire ; but his anonymity secured him from public comment ; while he plainly did not claim to be a heresiarch, or to attach, as Mr. Campbell and others had done, vital importance to his views. No steps therefore were taken against the book during all the orthodox ferment of the early time, when not only Campbell and Irving, but others, more or less in sympathy with them, were cast out of the Church. It was not till nearly ten years later that the author became the subject of prosecution, and finally of expulsion from the Church. It gradually came to be known that the writer of the volumes was a quiet country clergyman, Mr. Wright of Borthwick, in the neighbourhood of Dalkeith, a friend of Sir Walter Scott, and spoken of

with commendation in his journal,—a scholarly contemplative man, whose preaching had much of the
same quiet thoughtfulness and pensive beauty as
his books. It would have been well to have spared
him in his advanced years, or at the most to have
admonished him to write no more. But the evangelical fervour, which culminated in the 'Disruption,'
was then running to its height. His Presbytery
was instructed to libel him by the General Assembly
of 1839, and in 1841, the same year in which the
Strathbogie ministers were deposed for contumacy
to the orders of the Assembly, Mr. Wright of Borthwick's ministerial career was brought to an end.
There were circumstances of peculiar harshness in his
case—very unpleasant to recall. He himself declared
that he 'disowned and abjured every one of the errors'
laid to his charge, and that the extracts from his
books on which they were founded, rightly understood,
did not at all sustain them. By a large vote he was
refused any liberty of explanation, and unlike some
who had stood in the same position, surrounded by
their friends—ready to receive them when cast out—
Mr. Wright went forth from the Church a homeless
old man. It was the heyday of evangelical zeal ; but
the blessing of that 'charity that suffereth long and is
kind' certainly did not rest on this General Assembly
or its high-handed leaders.

Nothing seems more remarkable in closing this
review than the brief period within which all these
phenomena of religious thought were crowded. They
are all virtually the product of the third decade of
the century, marked in England by the religious
philosophy of Coleridge and the liberalism of the

early Oriel School. There has seldom been in our national history a more fruitful epoch of religious thought. And the same general character is more or less stamped on all its manifestations, various as these otherwise are. This character may be said to be expansiveness. The theological mind is seen opening in all directions. There is a general breaking up of the old close traditional systems transmitted from the earlier time. The idea of God as the loving Father of all men—of the religious life as having its root in immediate contact with the Divine, rather than in adherence to any definite forms whether of Church belief or Church order ; the recognition of the religious consciousness as a pervading element of human nature with its own rights in the face of Revelation, and especially in the face of the scholastic dogmas which had been based on Revelation ; the desire after a more concrete and living faith merging into one the abstractions of theological nomenclature ; and more than all perhaps an optimist Catholic ideal displacing the sectarian ideals of the older schools of thought ; all these larger features meet us with more or less prominence. Teaching like Mr. Erskine's, Archbishop Whately's, or that of the author of the *True Plan of the Living Temple*,—however unlike otherwise,—unite in taking a more expansive and optimist view of the range of Christianity, and its relation to human nature and life. The change of tone in this respect from the poetry of Cowper, for example, or the theology of Mr. Erskine's uncle, the old minister of Greyfriars, whose portrait survives in *Guy Mannering;* or again, from the piety of such a home as that of Keble's

father, or even of Maurice's father, is immense. One
feels in passing from the one to the other as emerging into wider air and larger room. The intellect
plays with a higher freedom. Religion has grown
grander and 'more majestical.' It emphasises less
the distinction between the church and the world—the
'clean' and the unclean. It claims a wider sovereignty
—a more powerful and extended hold of humanity ;
in short, a more real Catholicism than any church
had yet assigned it. The reaction set in again during
the following decade with the Oxford School in
England and a 'high flying' Evangelicalism in
Scotland. But modern Christianity has never lost
the richer mental tone and broader spirit of love
that infused themselves into it in the earlier decade.
It has shown a larger spirit ever since.

V

THOMAS CARLYLE AS A RELIGIOUS TEACHER.

IN our lectures hitherto we have surveyed the phenomena of religious thought as in the main developed within the Churches. Even Coleridge stands in close connection with the Church of England, of which he was a devoted member, and within whose borders his teaching chiefly spread. Nonconformity, rich as it was in works of philanthropy and evangelical earnestness, did not originate any new lines of Christian thought. Robert Hall was perhaps its greatest name in the first quarter of the century;[1] in massive and brilliant intellectuality he was unequalled; and the fame of his preaching still survives ; but he propagated no new ideas, nor can he be said to have been a new force in religious literature. Nothing can be more barren now-a-days than the doctrinal controversies which divided certain sections of the Presbyterians and Independents, represented by men like Belsham on the one hand, and Pye Smith on the other. The latter was an accomplished scholar and divine, and handled his argumentative weapons with success ; but, with much knowledge as a Biblical critic, he belonged to the purely dogmatic school, and his labours have left no fruitful results.

[1] His ministry at Leicester extended from 1809 to 1826.

During the earlier part of the century higher thought of any kind, save in the poetry of Wordsworth, was dormant. The voice of Philosophy was wellnigh dead. In Edinburgh the old Scottish School had found its last voice in Dugald Stewart ; and Carlyle tells us how little spiritual food of any kind he found at the University.[1] 'There was much talk about progress of the species, dark ages, and the like, but the hungry young looked up to their spiritual nurses, and for food were bidden eat the east wind.'[2] Dr. Thomas Brown, 'eloquent and full of enthusiasm about simple suggestion, relative, etc., was found utterly unprofitable.'[3] Otherwise there was no breath of living movement anywhere. The most hardy imagination could hardly connect Bentham, or any of his speculations, with religious thought. Great as he may have been in his own line as a legislative and legal reformer, Bentham cannot be called anything more than a sciolist in religion. He had but a feeble grasp of the subject either speculatively or historically.

The time was preparing, however, for a revival of higher thinking in more quarters than one, not only within the Churches, but outside their borders. Coleridge planted his thought firmly within the circle of Christian ideas. His religious philosophy, revolutionary as it was for his age, was a philosophy not only congenial to Christianity, but having a footing within it since the days of the Alexandrian School. But there were seeds of thought also growing in other directions. In times of great movement religious questions become pervading ; they spread into the

---

[1] *Sartor Resartus*, B. II. c. iii.   [2] *Ibid.*
[3] *Early Life*, vol. i. p. 25.

general intellectual atmosphere. They lay hold of a class of minds who, while repelling the old solutions and the ecclesiastical connections identified with them, are yet restlessly impelled to new solutions. They are unable to leave religion aside, and frequently exert a powerful influence on its course of development. Such minds, if not religious in the ordinary sense, are full of 'religiosity'; and no picture of the movement of religious thought would be at all complete which did not bring them under review.

Thomas Carlyle and John Stuart Mill were both pre-eminently men of this stamp. Bred in the most diverse circumstances, they have exercised upon their generation a distinctive influence in great part of a religious character. It is not too much to say that the religious thinking of our time has taken a certain direction and colour from both of a highly significant kind, well deserving attention—from the former, as in himself a rich and fruitful if indefinite power—from the latter, as the chief member of a school with a very definite bearing on the course of higher opinion. There is a sense in which both represent the negative attitude to historical religion, which has grown so strong in our day, but there is also a sense in which both, and especially Carlyle, have contributed to enlighten and enlarge the sphere of religious thought. So very different were they that it may seem absurd to class them together; yet they were closely related both by personal, and in some degree by intellectual ties. Their ideals as to religion and everything else became in the end essentially contradictory; but at first they were drawn together by common sympathies and aspirations. My aim in this lecture and the next will be to give some account of both, and of their religious opinions. I make no pretension to judge at length their general intellectual and literary influence. It is only as they seem to stand in close connection with our subject that I venture to sketch their character and teaching.

There are few men of our generation, or indeed of any generation, of whom we have a more detailed and vivid picture than we have of Thomas Carlyle. The only complaint is that we already know too much of him. Carlyle biographic literature has poured so copiously from the press that readers have been satiated with it. The great writer himself is such a master of graphic portraiture, that all the scenes and surroundings of his childhood live before us as if we ourselves had lived in them. His early home at Ecclefechan ; his father and mother, with their frugal and pious ways ; the farm of Mainhill, where he first studied *Faust* in a dry ditch, are all clear as in a photograph. Both father and mother were ' burghers ' of the strictest type, worshipping in a humble meeting-house, having for minister a certain John Johnstone, from whom Carlyle learned his first Latin, and who was the ' priestliest man ' that he ever ' beheld in any ecclesiastical guise.' Even if we allow for a touch of exaggeration in the picture of the ' peasant union ' that gathered in the heath-thatched house, and the simple evangelist that ministered to them, the picture is a beautiful one, and it left abiding traces in Carlyle's memory. ' On me, too,' he long afterwards said, ' their pious heaven-sent influences rest and live.'

Carlyle inherited the qualities of both his parents —the sturdy indomitable promptness of his father, whose feat in taking up an adversary ' by the two flanks and hurling him through the air,' was notable and long remembered, and the passionate intensity and devotion of his mother. The race was a strong race in whom the fighting propensities of the Border were modified, but by no means extinct. The rough, vigorous fibre of the family was transmitted to the grandson, intellectually and morally. It is only too easy to see now in the extended picture of his life and manners that Carlyle remained in much a peasant to the last. Beautiful in some aspects of character, he lacks everywhere gentlehood. His sturdiness becomes too often rudeness, and his independence pure wanton self-assertion. In a fit of petulant fury he could bang the door upon Miss Welsh, who had tormented him in one of her whimsical moods when he offered her the homage of his affection. In the midst of all his love for Irving he writes both of him and his wife at times with a painful touch of vulgarity. It is needless to mention other instances of the same kind,—how he professes his liking and indebtedness to many, ladies among others, and then abuses them roundly on very little provocation. Nowhere does his strange, brusque intolerance burst out more harshly than in his letters when he first went to London in 1824. There may have been a good deal of truth in his graphic picture of the literary men he there met. There is certainly an infinite art in his epithets. But amusing as some of them are in their broad expressiveness, they are painful in their harshness ; while their presumption can hardly be called less than enormous when we remember that Carlyle at this time was himself without any literary reputation. Surely never did a young Scotsman carry such a pair of eyes into the world of London or set such a peremptory mark upon its notabilities. Behind all that he says of Coleridge and Campbell and Hazlitt and De Quincey one instinctively feels that there must have been something higher and more deserving of respect which he failed to see. He makes no allowances; he does not set a single figure in any radiance of past achievement or explanatory necessity. It is the mere ugliness of the passing impression that he transfers to his pages. There is more than recklessness in this; there is a certain rudeness of feeling. And this rudeness at times was more than a lack of manner. It entered into his intellectual judgment and vitiated it. It made him emphasise characteristics opposed to his own, and convert mere traits of strength more or less congenial to his own character into virtues. When there was no play for his visual observation and for the knowledge of the meaner qualities that unhappily mingle in all men when brought within the range of personal knowledge, Carlyle could not only be reverent, but unduly reverent. Cromwell was to him a saint as well as a hero; Danton a patriot; Goethe a great character as well as teacher. They remained glorified in distance and imagination. He holds his breath over a somewhat emptily complimentary letter of Goethe's at the very time that he is abusing his literary contemporaries in London. Had he visited the old intellectual sensualist at Weimar, and seen all his ways there, we should perhaps have had a very different portrait. For admiration with Carlyle was seldom able to withstand personal contact, and all imagery save that of his early home became blackened as soon as the veil of distance was removed.

Carlyle carried from his home a deep sense of religion. His parents were both devout, his father less expressively so ; his mother showing in all her letters a deep, simple, and strong piety very beautiful to Carlyle and in itself. Her faith stands sure in 'the Word of God,' which she never fails to pray her son to read constantly. She entreats him 'to mind his chapters.' 'Have you got through the Bible yet?' she asks in 1817, when he was twenty-two years of age and schoolmastering at Kirkcaldy. 'If you have, read it again. I hope you will not weary, and may the Lord open your understanding.' Again, 'Oh, my dear, dear son, I would pray for a blessing on your learning. I beg you with all the feeling of an affectionate mother that you would study the Word of God.'[1] Carlyle felt forced to excuse himself in the same year that he 'had not been quite regular in reading that best of Books which you recommended to me.' However, he adds, 'Last night I was reading upon my favourite Job, and I hope to do better in time to come. I entreat you to believe that I am sincerely desirous of being a good man ; and though we may differ in some few unimportant particulars, yet I firmly trust that the same Power which created us with imperfect faculties will pardon the errors of any one (and none are without them) who seek truth and righteousness with a simple heart.' His mother did not like the phrase 'imperfect faculties,' nor perhaps the apologetic tone of the

[1] Vol. i. p. 62.

letter, and she says in reply, 'God made man after his own image, therefore he behoved to be without any imperfect faculties. Beware, my dear son, of such thoughts ; let them not dwell on your mind. God forbid. Do make religion your great study, Tom ; if you repent it, I will bear the blame for ever.'

This affectionate exhortation belongs to the year 1819, when Carlyle had already abandoned his intention of entering the Church. This, as is well known, was his original destination, and the earnest desire of both his father and mother. It is remarkable too that, strong seceders as they were themselves from the National Church, the idea does not seem to have occurred to them, any more than to himself, of his entering the Secession ministry. After completing his Arts course at the Edinburgh University, he entered the Divinity Hall there, although he never seems to have attended the classes. It was common at this time for divinity students to pursue their studies by simply enrolling themselves and appearing each session to deliver a discourse. It sounds strange now to hear that in this way Carlyle delivered an English sermon from the text, ' Before I was afflicted I went astray, but now I keep thy word '—a ' weak flowing sentimental piece,' he said, for which however he had been complimented 'by comrades and Professor.' Afterwards he gave a Latin discourse on the question whether there was or was not such a thing as Natural Religion—possibly, we may say almost certainly, from the same theme as James Mill delivered his Latin discourse, ' *Num sit Dei cognitio naturalis.*'[1] It was on this last occasion, when in Edinburgh in

[1] *James Mill:* a Biography by Dr. Alexander Bain, p. 21.

1814, that he first met Edward Irving, and had a 'skirmish of tongue with him' at a friend's rooms. He had indeed seen Irving before when he visited the Annan Grammar School, where, as half-mythically detailed in *Sartor Resartus*, Carlyle suffered much from the tyrannous savagery of his schoolfellows. Irving, as is well known, was a native of Annan, distant only a few miles from Ecclefechan.

The project of entering the Church, dear as it was to the hearts of his parents, seems never to have been cordially entertained by Carlyle himself, and so it gradually drifted out of his mind. His more than friendly association with Irving at Kirkcaldy in the years 1816, 1817, and 1818, had no effect in inclining him in this direction, or in obviating the 'grave prohibitive doubts' which had already arisen in his mind. On the contrary, it seems to have been in Kirkcaldy that these doubts strengthened into a resolve to give up all idea of the Christian ministry: He had found Gibbon's History in Irving's library,[1] and eagerly devoured it with negative results. Yet schoolmastering was also intolerable to him, and so he found his way back to Edinburgh in 1819, to try the Law classes, but really to subsist by private teaching and occasional employment on the *Edinburgh Encyclopædia*, given him by the Editor, afterwards Sir David Brewster.

The character of Carlyle's doubts will appear more fully in the sequel. We may only remark now that there is no evidence that he had at this or any future time fully studied the evidences of the divine origin of Christianity. The very idea of such evidences was

[1] *Early Life*, vol. i. p. 52.

always repulsive to him. But there had gradually grown upon him the conviction that the Christianity of the Church was 'intellectually incredible,' and that he could have nothing to do with it. He has told us himself how he disclosed to Edward Irving the great change which had taken place in his mind on the subject.

He had been to Glasgow, where Irving was then assisting Dr. Chalmers in the spring of 1820, and had some friendly conference with Chalmers, who was full, he says, of a new scheme for proving the truth of Christianity. 'All written in us already in sympathetic ink ; Bible awakens it, and you can read.' The fact dwelt in his memory, but it had not touched his heart, or brought him any light. The 'sympathetic ink' in his case would not take effect. And when the time came for his return to Annandale, he describes how Irving accompanied him fifteen miles of the road, and how they sat among the 'peat hags' of Drumclog moss, 'under the silent bright skies,' with 'a world all silent around them.' As they sat and talked, their own voices were 'the one sound.' Ailsa Craig towered 'white and visible,' away in the distance. Their talk had grown ever friendlier, and more interesting. At length the declining sun said plainly, You must part. 'We sauntered,' he says, 'slowly into the highway. Masons were building at a wayside cottage near by, or were packing up on ceasing for the day. We leant our backs on a dry stone fence, and looking into the western radiance, continued to talk yet a while, loth both of us to go. It was just here as the sun was sinking, Irving actually drew from me by degrees in the softest manner the confession that I

did not think as he of the Christian religion, and
that it was vain for me to expect I ever could or
should. This, if this was so, he had pre-engaged
to take well from me ; like an elder brother if I
would be frank with him, and right royally he
did so, and to the end of his life we needed no
concealments on that head, which was really a step
gained.'

For a time—apparently not more than two years—
Carlyle's state of mind was one of great unhappiness,
in which the foundations not only of Christianity, but
of all natural religion, seemed shaken within him.
'Doubt darkened into unbelief,' 'shade over shade,'
until there was nothing but 'the fixed starless
Tartarean dark.' He was very miserable, and he cried
out in his misery, 'Is there no God then ? Has the
word Duty no meaning ? Is what we call duty no
Divine messenger and guide, but a false earthly phan-
tasm, made up of desire and fear ?' But even in his
worst darkness the ideas of God and of Duty survived,
in a fluctuating way, in his mind. The language
which he used in his letters during the same period
both to his father and mother, leaves this beyond
doubt. It was his constant assurance to his mother,
that his opinions, although clothed in a different
garb, were at bottom analogous with her own. There
were times no doubt when he felt differently and
seemed to lose hold of all truth. There was a
deeper despair—and then some lightening of the
clouds before true light and peace came. It was
not, we shall see, till 1826, after his first return from
London, that he was able, in his own language,
'authentically to take the devil by the nose.'

He has himself described in mystical guise in *Sartor Resartus* the beginning of his spiritual deliverance. The incident is told in the close of the seventh chapter of Book II., and he says it literally occurred to himself—only we have to substitute Leith Walk for the Rue Saint-Thomas de l'Enfer.   It was during the summer of 1821, after three weeks of total sleeplessness, in which his one solace was that of a daily bathe on the sands between Leith and Portobello.   Long afterwards he said he could go straight to the place. The incident happened as he went down to bathe.   As he went on his way in gloomy meditation, 'all things in the Heavens above and the Earth beneath' seemed 'to hurt' him.   The day was intolerably sultry, and the pavement 'hot as Nebuchadnezzar's Furnace.'   Suddenly the thought came to him, "'What *art* thou afraid of ?   Wherefore, like a coward, dost thou for ever pip and whimper, and go cowering and trembling?   Despicable biped !   what is the sum-total of the worst that lies before thee ?   Death ?   Well, death ; and say the pangs of Tophet too, and all that the Devil and Man may, will or can do against thee !   Hast thou not a heart ; canst thou not suffer whatsoever it be ; and, as a Child of Freedom, though outcast, trample Tophet itself under thy feet, while it consumes thee ?   Let it come, then ; I will meet it and defy it."   And as I so thought, there rushed like a stream of fire over my whole soul ; and I shook base Fear away from me for ever.   I was strong, of unknown strength ; a spirit, almost a god.   Ever from that time, the temper of my misery was changed : not Fear or whining Sorrow was it but Indignation and grim fire-eyed Defiance. . . . Then it was that my whole ME stood up, in native

God-created majesty. . . . The Everlasting No had said, " Behold, thou art fatherless, outcast, and the Universe is mine (the Devil's) ; " to which my whole ME now made answer : " I am not thine, but Free, and for ever hate thee." From this hour I incline to date my Spiritual New-birth.'

There is no more significant passage in all Carlyle's writings. It was written long after the event—nearly ten years—but it expresses beyond doubt a great change in his mode of thought. His fears and doubts were henceforth cast behind him, and a clear light of spiritual conviction began to dawn within him. His full deliverance was not yet, but the incident in Leith Walk was its beginning. Five years afterwards the consummation came during a happy summer that he spent in a cottage of his own, not far from his father's farm. There he succeeded in chaining up, finally, the spiritual 'dragons' that had tormented him, and attaining to what he called his conversion. It was nothing less in his view. ' I found it,' he says, 'to be essentially what Methodist people call their conversion—the deliverance of their souls from the devil and the pit. Precisely that in a new form. And there burnt, accordingly, a sacred flame of joy in me, silent in my inmost being, as of one henceforth superior to fate.. This "holy joy" lasted sensibly in me for several years, in blessed counterpoise to sufferings and discouragements enough ; nor has it proved what I can call fallacious at any time since.'

It is difficult to know how far Carlyle's language here, and in many places, is to be taken literally, especially when speaking of himself. No Methodist

—not even John Bunyan—clothes his spiritual experiences in more highly metaphorical phrase. His imagination bodies forth his sufferings, more rarely his joys, in figures of intensity and magnitude altogether disproportionate to the experience of ordinary men. The transformation of Leith Walk in all its prosaic ugliness, into the Rue de l'Enfer, is merely one among many instances of this power of imaginative exaggeration. 'Dragons' and 'Tophet,' 'Eternities,' 'Silences,' 'Immensities,' are the familiar imagery of his mind. He sees everything transfigured in a halo of gloom or of sunshine. The truth seems to be that on this occasion peace of mind came to him largely from a temporary access of health. The summer of 1826, spent in his own cottage on Hoddam Hill, with his mother at command to attend to his wants, and set free from the distractions of the paternal farm, seems almost to have been the happiest portion of his life. He had room ; he had work ; the translation of German Romance, which cost him little trouble, and brought in some money. The view from his cottage over the Solway Firth was unrivalled in extent and grandeur. No other residence seems to have suited him so well, and it was one of the misfortunes of his life that he was unable to retain it. There was freedom, occupation, a wild Irish pony on which to gallop, and roads, 'smooth and hard,' to his taste ; 'ample space to dig and prune under the pure canopy of a wholesome sky.' It was here Miss Welsh visited his mother, and may be said to have definitely sealed her fate. The story of her visit, and all that followed, is beautifully told. He grew for a time strong in health in the midst of such inspirations,—with simple food, and quiet restful nights. This was the true explanation of his spiritual triumph, of his taking the devil so effectually by the nose at this time. These years, he tells us, lay in his memory as a 'russet-coated idyll; one of the quietest on the whole, and perhaps the most triumphantly important of my life. I lived very silent, diligent, had long solitary rides on my wild Irish horse, Larry, good for the dietetic part. My meditatings, musings, and reflections were continual; my thoughts went wandering or travelling through eternity, and were now, to my infinite solacement, coming back with tidings to me. This year I found I had conquered all my scepticisms, agonising doubts, fearful wrestlings with the foul, vile, and soul-maddening Mud-Gods of my Epoch,—had escaped as from a worse than Tartarus, with all its Phlegethons and Stygian quagmires, and was emerging free in spirit into the eternal blue of Ether.'[1]

Had Carlyle only been able to dwell on the top of Hoddam Hill with some fair portion of this world's goods, and his strong peasant mother, who knew all his ways, to minister to his wants, instead of the delicate lady whom he made his wife, we might have heard less of 'dragons' and 'Stygian quagmires.' As it was, the spiritual happiness of this year so far remained with him. Ever since, he says, he had dwelt comparatively in the clear heaven, looking down upon the 'welterings' of his poor fellow-creatures below, and having no concern in 'their Puseyisms, ritualisms, metaphysical controversies, and cobwebberies—no feeling of my own, except honest silent

[1] *Reminiscences*, vol. i. p. 286.

pity for the serious or religious part of them, and occasional indignation for the world's sake at the frivolous, secular, and impious part, with their universal suffrages, their nigger Emancipations, sluggard and scoundrel protection societies, and unexampled prosperities for the time being. What my pious joy and gratitude then was let the pious soul figure. . . . I had in effect gained an immense victory, and for a number of years, in spite of nerves and chagrins, had a constant inward happiness that was quite royal and supreme. . . . Once more, thank Heaven for its highest gift. I then felt, and still feel, endlessly indebted to Goethe in the business. . . . Nowhere can I recollect of myself such pious musings, communings, silent and spontaneous with fact and nature, as in these poor Annandale localities. The sound of the kirk bell once or twice on Sunday mornings (from Hoddam Kirk, about a mile on the plains below me) was strangely touching, like the departing voice of eighteen centuries.'[1]

This is a charming picture ; and it is interesting to note the date of this new birth-time of spiritual life in Carlyle. It is a date, as we have seen already, fertile in religious thought. At centres wide apart, and tending to very different issues, the Divine impulse was moving many minds in those years—Coleridge, Arnold, Milman, Thirlwall, Newman, Erskine, Macleod Campbell. The higher visions of Truth that then came to Carlyle were to himself certainly of the nature of Divine inspiration ; and the creative moments were ever afterwards among the brightest of his existence. His better health

[1] *Reminiscences*, vol. i. p. 286.

concurred with the inspirations of the year, and was a more important factor in the result than he himself realised; but the time was also big with spiritual excitement; and the Divine afflatus came to him as to others amidst his silent wanderings and communings with nature.

This year—1826—with its 'rustic dignity and beauty,' passed for Carlyle too rapidly away. He was back at his father's house at Mainhill before it was out. Nay, before the last month of autumn was yet finished, he was married—after no end of negotiation—and settled at Comely Bank; and then, two years later, he was at Craigenputtock, 'the dreariest spot in all the British dominions.' His life there—his disappointments, and weary work at article-writing, his encouraging letters from Goethe, and his composition of *Sartor Resartus*—are all written in Mr. Froude's volumes. With *Sartor Resartus* Carlyle's message to the world may be said to have begun. It was composed at Craigenputtock in 1831, given to the world in *Fraser's Magazine* in 1833, but not published separately till 1838. The story of his attempts to find a publisher, his interviews with Mr. Murray and Messrs. Longman, make a series of pitiful adventures, all very pathetic. We cannot wonder at the difficulties he encountered, for the world has ever been slow to recognise new prophets, and Carlyle assumed in *Sartor* the *rôle* of a prophet. It was written with his heart's blood,—a wild and solemn sorrow 'running through its sentences like the sound over the strings of an Æolian harp.' In this book, too, for the first time, he assumed his characteristic style. The new message seemed to demand a new language; and Teufelsdröckh poured forth his wailings and his aspirations in words that caused the ears to tingle, if not exactly in the sense Carlyle meant.

Carlyle's style, it is needless to say, has been much criticised. To writers like Macaulay and Jeffrey it was intolerable ; and Jeffrey did not hesitate to bid him ' fling away his affectations, and write like his famous countrymen of all ages.' A strange, and we think erroneous, suggestion has been made recently that he adopted 'a studied and ambiguous phraseology' with a view to conceal opinions which would have been fatal to his success as a writer. The public, it is said, 'put their own interpretation on his mystical utterances, and gave him the benefit of any doubts.' Not only is there no evidence of such an intention in Carlyle, but in point of fact his peculiar style, instead of in any degree helping the circulation of his opinions, undoubtedly retarded it. Carlyle, moreover, was so far from having any such object in view that his style is nowhere so obscure and mystical as in fragments written for his own eyes alone. The truth plainly is, that Carlyle's style was partly modelled on that of *Jean Paul Richter* among his favourite studies at this time,[1] and partly a natural growth of his mind as he wrestled with the problems of the universe, and fought himself free from the dragons and the dismal abysses of Tartarus. It is only when he takes up his prophetic message that he fully dons, so to speak, the prophet's mantle. His

---

[1] His famous study of Jean Paul in the *Foreign Review* belongs to 1830. He had previously written on the same subject in the *Edinburgh Review* in 1827.

translations of the *Wilhelm Meister*, and his *Life of Schiller*, were written mainly in the current style of his time, and even his article on Burns, in 1828, is comparatively simple in style, although Jeffrey objected to its diffuseness and length for the *Edinburgh Review*. Carlyle was not the man, either privately or as a writer, to mask his opinions in a feigned style, or to deliberately design to mystify his readers. The mystification, if any, lies in the character of the message, as well as in the language in which it is conveyed.

The twenty years or so that followed the publication of *Sartor Resartus* mark the era of Carlyle's chief influence. He was of course a great name long after this. But his prophetic phase culminated with the *Life of Sterling* in 1851. From this time people ceased to look to him as a religious teacher. He passed into the literary patriarch—the great Father of contemporary letters, under which aspect an increasing veneration gathered around his name, receiving perhaps its most memorable expression in the Edinburgh Rectorship of 1866, and the enthusiastic welcome which was then given him by the students and public. He was at this time seventy-one years of age, a truly venerable figure, bearing in his worn and sad, yet heroic, face the impress of all the struggles he had gone through. And as he appeared surrounded with many new and some old faces—among the latter that of his friend Mr. Erskine from Linlathen, like himself a striking figure in his old age—the sight was both a grand and touching one. Many warmed to the ' heart-worn ' old man as they listened with beating hearts to his words but faintly caught at times, and heard from his own lips the lessons of his life.[1] ' There was not a word in his speech,' Mr. Froude says, ' which he had not already said, and said far more forcibly, a hundred times.   But suddenly and thenceforward, till his death set them off again, hostile tongues ceased to speak against him as hostile pens to write. The speech was printed in full in half of the newspapers in the island.   It was received with universal acclamation.   A low-priced edition of his works became in demand, and they flew into a strange temporary popularity with the reading multitude. *Sartor*, " poor beast," had struggled into life with difficulty, and its readers since had been few, if select.   Twenty thousand copies of the shilling edition were now sold instantly on its publication.   It was now admitted universally that Carlyle was a " great man."   Yet he saw no inclination, not the slightest, to attend to his

---

[1] I may be pardoned for mentioning here that I happened to be the first to convey to Mrs. Carlyle the personal assurance of the splendid reception which her husband received on this occasion. I left Edinburgh on the evening of Mr. Carlyle's address on a visit to Mrs. Oliphant, at Windsor, where I found Mrs. Carlyle among Mrs. Oliphant's visitors.   I had some acquaintance before both with her and her illustrious husband.   She was of course greatly interested in what I was able to tell her about the enthusiasm with which the students had received Mr. Carlyle; and made us all (Mrs. Oliphant, Mrs. Tulloch, and myself) promise to visit her a few days later at Cheyne Row to meet Mr. Froude, as mentioned by him in his concluding volume, p. 34.   In fulfilment of our engagement we were on our way to Cheyne Row when we observed Mr. Froude run hastily along the street in the direction of Mr. Carlyle's house ; and we then learned for the first time the sad news of Mrs. Carlyle's sudden death.   It was a terrible shock to all, and the incident remains engraven on one's memory.   She had been bright beyond measure at Windsor, elated by her husband's triumph—dealing wittily but kindly with many things, and glancing with playful sallies at Carlyle himself and his ways.

teaching. He himself could not make it out, but the explanation is not far to seek. The Edinburgh Address contained his doctrines, with the fire which had provoked the animosity taken out of them. They were reduced to the level of Church sermons ; thrown into general propositions which it is pretty and right and becoming to confess with our lips, while no one is supposed to act on them. We admire and praise the beautiful language, and we reward 'the performance with a bishopric if the speaker be a clergyman. Carlyle, people felt with a sense of relief, meant only what the preachers meant, and was a fine fellow after all.'[1]

So far Mr. Froude. The cynical allusions are after his manner, and need not concern us. The truth is that there now happened to Carlyle what more or less falls to all writers of distinction. His name, as the favourite of the Edinburgh students, was for the time 'up.' It drew a widespread general attention, and his writings inevitably grew in temporary popularity with his name. But Carlyle, we fancy, was too wise a man to concern himself much with such a result. He could not well have imagined that a popularity of this kind was likely to extend the real influence of his teaching, which had reached its height some time before. The freshness of his doctrines was past. The generation which had been deeply moved by *Sartor Resartus*, and the lectures on *Heroes and Hero Worship*, was growing to maturity. The *Life of Sterling*, with all its beauty and interest as a composition, had repelled many—and rightly so. It was felt to be offensive to the Churches and to

[1] Froude, vol. ii. (*Carlyle's Later Life*), pp. 306-7.

doctrines independent of all Churches, and to reveal
a bitterness which is never near to wisdom. The
Edinburgh enthusiasm was a tribute to the man
of letters rather than to the prophet of any doctrine
whatever. And it was all the truer and higher tribute
on this account. Carlyle will be remembered in
literature when his 'philosophy of clothes,' and all his
philosophy, is forgotten.

But let us now try to estimate his position as a
thinker. What were those 'doctrines' of which Mr.
Froude speaks, or in other words the 'message' which
the prophet himself thought he bore to his generation? There are two ways in which we may consider
this question. First of all we may ask what was the
general influence of Carlyle as a writer, and then
what, so far as we can make out, were the contents of
his 'message,' or the principles of conviction underlying all his teaching? The two questions are closely
connected, and indeed hardly separable. But it will
be convenient to look at them in succession.

I. Carlyle spoke with two different voices about
literature. As a profession he held it in contempt.
He has no words too hard for the poor literary man,
in London or elsewhere. 'Good Heavens,' he says, 'and
is this the literary world—this rascal rout, the dirty
rabble, destitute not only of large feeling and knowledge or intellect, but even of common honesty. They
are not red-blooded men at all. They are only
things for writing articles.' But at other times he
spoke of literature with divine enthusiasm. The
writer of a true book was the real 'Primate of England and of all England.' 'Literature, so far as it is
literature, is an Apocalypse of Nature. The dark

scornful indignation of a Byron, so wayward and perverse, may bear touches of the god-like ; nay the withered mockery of a French Sceptic—his mockery of the false alone, and worship of the true ; how much more the sphere harmony of a Shakespeare and a Goethe ; the cathedral music of a Milton ; the humble genuine larknotes of a Burns—skylark starting from the humble furrow far overhead into the blue depths, and singing to us so genuinely there.' Even writers of newspapers, more frequently objects of his scorn, are sometimes spoken of as ' the real working effective Church of a modern country.'

The world's final judgment upon Carlyle, we feel certain, will be that he was himself above all a man of letters. He had the graphic faculty more than any other. He could not help putting pen to paper. The 'pictured page' came forth from him naturally, and grew under his hand irresistibly—yet always under the impulse of a high ideal. This is the explanation of the different ways in which he speaks —or at least it is the chief explanation—for no doubt also mere mood sometimes swayed him. Literature was to him ' the wine of life.' It should not be converted ' into daily food.' Above all, it must not be confounded with the ' froth ocean of printed speech, which we loosely call literature.' This must be said for Carlyle—no less than for Milton,— that he never ceased to claim a high ideal for litera-ture, and to vindicate for its theme ' whatsoever in religion is holy and sublime, and in virtue amiable and grave.'

In this respect Carlyle's influence has been good without exception. It brought an element of thoroughness, of depth and reality, into the literary thought of his time which was of great value. It did so in more ways than one. His own writings were all more or less penetrating and earnest. He took up subjects from the inside with a view to their vital comprehension in their essential and not merely their ordinary meaning. His papers on Burns, on Jean Paul, on Voltaire, on Novalis, on Samuel Johnson, as well as on Goethe and others, were all of this kind. His famous article on 'Characteristics,' 'more profound and far-reaching even than *Sartor* itself,' and his previous article on the 'Signs of the Times'—both in the *Edinburgh Review*,[1] were also of the same stamp. His style of work is better illustrated by such examples, because they do not raise, so directly, the question of the principles underlying his general works. These principles may be disputed; but no one can well dispute that the themes handled by Carlyle in these miscellanies were handled with a *soul* which was new in the literature of our century. Thoughtful readers were arrested and made to feel that they were brought face to face with spiritual facts, with the realities of life and thought, as in no other writings of the day. This was of the nature of religious influence,—more truly so than much that professed to be religion. It tended to deepen thought, to cleanse the spiritual eye, to go down to the roots of questions, and bring their complexities into some organic shape. Imperfectly as the writer was still understood in his earlier years, he exercised so far a vast influence, and of the best kind. The 'mysticism' of which he speaks in his letters of this time

---

[1] *Signs of the Times*, 1829.   *Characteristics*, 1831.

was a quickening power to all opening minds. One can see how it attracted John Stuart Mill when Carlyle visited London in 1831 with a view to the publication of *Sartor*. Different as was their point of view, and widely as they afterwards separated, Mill was then strongly drawn to Carlyle, as Carlyle was drawn to him. He tells us how 'the enthusiastic yet lucid calm youth' walked home with him the first time they met,[1] and seemed as if he had been 'converted by the head of the mystic school.' Carlyle indeed soon discovered that he had not found 'another mystic' in Mill, but his startling intuition, his intellectual downrightness, and clear, strong grasp of realities made an obviously great impression upon the young 'Spirit of the age,'[2] as Carlyle called him. The same power was felt by others even thus early, although it was ten years afterwards till his full influence began to tell. And the influence thus exercised was largely independent of his special doctrines. Whether these doctrines were true or not, it was plain that here was a mind of rare force—of stern truthfulness—to which it would do well for the world to take heed. And the result was undoubtedly to lift many questions not only of literature and history, but of social, moral, political, and religious importance, into a higher atmosphere, and invest them with a higher meaning than heretofore.

But it was not only by the tone and spirit of his own writings that Carlyle accomplished this result. He was the first who brought home to the British mind the great storehouse of higher thought that

[1] September 1831.

[2] The title of a series of Articles by Mill in 1831.

existed in the literature of Germany. Attempts had been made in the same direction by Taylor of Norwich in his *Translations* and his *Survey of German Poetry*, which is now however chiefly remembered from Carlyle's review, by Sir Walter Scott, and by Coleridge ; but it cannot be said that the treasures of German poetry or reflective fiction were really known in this country before Carlyle's *Life of Schiller* and his translation of *Wilhelm Meister*, and his articles on Richter and Goethe. To what extent Carlyle borrowed his own so-called 'mysticism' from Germany need not be considered. He professed himself, as all know, endlessly indebted to Goethe. But there can be no question of the extent to which his own mind was stimulated and enriched by Germanism. Coleridge had drawn wealth from the same source, chiefly from the German philosophical writers, which had no particular attraction for Carlyle, notwithstanding the paper on Novalis; but it cannot be said that anything that Coleridge had done in this way had spread the knowledge of German thought and literature. Carlyle for the first time made us alive to the power, beauty, and genuine depth of meaning there were in the great German poets and writers, their freer and richer views of life, their higher and more comprehensive canons of criticism. In this knowledge too there was an element of religion. Religious aspiration was seen to rest on a wider basis than our insular narrowness had been accustomed to place it. It was acknowledged as a powerful element in all life—in art, in speculation, in every intellectual growth. 'In all human hearts there is the religious fibre'[1]—was the lesson which Carlyle had learned himself and preached to others. No human product, and least of all literature, can be divorced from religion. This was a higher and better view of literature than had prevailed during the eighteenth and the early part of the nineteenth century. It is liable no doubt to abuse. It may be turned by literary libertinism into an assertion that any kind of religion is good enough—that mere sentimentalism may stand for religion. But the thought in itself is true and valuable, and not to be measured by its abuse. It both elevates humanity and enlarges religion. It claims all intellectual activity as rightfully belonging to God and not to the devil, and casts over it a sacred lustre. It brings man as man within the light of the Divine, and shows him in his truly supernatural life—'An infinite happiness and an infinite woe not only waiting him hereafter, but looking out upon him through every pitifullest present good or evil.'[2] This deeper way of looking at human nature with all its products, liable to loose and feeble exaggeration as it may be, was a real gain to the higher thought of the time. It was a true advancement of literature. It vindicated a wider sphere for religion. It failed to arrest the progress of the mechanical philosophy against which it was chiefly directed; but it still operates as a pregnant force in British thinking.

But we must consider Carlyle's religious attitude

---

[1] Always and everywhere this remains a true saying—'Il y a dans le cœur humain un fibre religieux.' Man always worships something. Always he sees the Infinite shadowed forth in something finite.—*Review of Goethe's Works—Miscellanies,* vol. iii.

[2] *Ibid.*

more particularly. What were his own special doctrines?

Mr. Froude speaks repeatedly of Carlyle's 'Creed,' and of the effect it exercised upon himself and his contemporaries in the agitating years in which Puseyism had outrun itself, and evangelicalism as a power was wellnigh extinct. These were the years in which Mr. Froude himself began life as an author, and along with other young souls was 'determined to have done with insincerity, to find ground under their feet, to let the uncertain remain uncertain, but to learn how much and what we could honestly regard as true.' Tennyson 'became the voice of this feeling in poetry.' Carlyle stood beside the poet as a prophet and teacher, and his words were 'like the morning reveillé' to the new searchers after truth. 'They had been taught to believe in a living God. They heard of what he had done in the past. Carlyle was the first to make us see his actual and active presence now in this working world. To know God's existence was not an arguable probability, a fact dependent for its certainty on church authority or on apostolic succession, or on so-called histories, which might possibly prove to be no more than legends; but an awful reality to which the fate—the fate of each individual man bore perpetual witness. Here, and only here, lay the sanction and the meaning of the word *duty*. We were to do our work because we were bound to do it by our Master's orders. We were to be just and true because God abhorred wrong and hated lies. Religious teachers, indeed, had said the same thing, but they had so stifled the practical bearing of their creed under their doctrines and traditions that honest men had found a difficulty in listening to them. In Carlyle's writings dogma and tradition had melted like a mist, and the awful, actual fact burnt clear once more in the midst of heaven.' As for himself, Froude adds that he was saved by Carlyle's writings ' from Positivism or Romanism or Atheism. The alternatives were being thrust upon us of believing nothing or believing everything, or worse still, of acquiescing for worldly convenience in the established order of things which had been made intellectually incredible. Carlyle taught me a creed which I could then accept as really true ; which I have held ever since with increasing confidence as the interpretation of my existence, and the guide of my conduct so far as I have been able to act up to it. Then and always I looked and have looked to him as my master.' [1]

We need say nothing of the assumption underlying this passage that sincerity was a supreme if not exclusive note of the band of young truth-seekers who in those years (1842-4) had broken loose from traditionary and historical religion, and could find no rest in any existing form of Christianity. The talk of *sincerity* is too much in the mouth both of the prophet and his disciple. It is an evil weapon, and may be turned with too great facility many ways. We know after all but little in any case—sometimes even in our own case—of the real motives and state of mind underlying religious belief or unbelief. And it is the wiser as well as the humbler course to credit each other with sincerity, save when conduct and belief are in too glaring contrast. There may be a cant

[1] *Later Life*, vol. i. p. 291 *et seq*.

about sincerity, as about other things, and it comes near to being this when used thus recklessly.

Of Carlyle's deep sincerity there can be no question. When he told Irving, under the 'western radiance' on Drumclog Moor, that he had ceased to think of the Christian religion as his friend did, he was evidently moved by the irresistible honesty of his nature. Then, and ever afterwards, he found himself unable to believe in Revelation, 'technically so called'—a revelation, that is to say, supposed to be established by historical miracles. The fullest expression of his disbelief in Christianity is to be found in his *Life of Sterling ;* but Mr. Froude has published an interesting fragment in the opening of the second of his earlier volumes on Carlyle's Life, bearing on the same subject.[1] In this fragment he explains, in characteristic fashion, his views of all historical religions as being in their day loyal efforts, according to the light of their time, to explain the problem of the Universe, and the reality of human duty—efforts however, in their very nature, neither exhaustive nor permanent. For a time they seem to fill the whole orbit of spiritual vision, and all things to move in harmony with their contents. But the Universe itself is greater than any theory that can be formed about it. It was natural for the Jewish people to fancy that 'the set of convictions' which they had worked out for themselves were of universal import, and that the world was revolving round them, while they were motionless, as a centre. But in their case, as in others, the story of Galileo and the Heavens applies—they were really in motion, while the world

[1] *Spiritual Optics,* vol. ii. p. 8, *et seq.*

in its divine beauty was still and peaceful around
them. They, no more than others, have read all its
meaning, or fixed it for ever. The universe itself, and
man as its prime figure, form the true Revelation.
Religion cannot be incarnated and settled once for
all in forms of Creed and worship. It is a continual
growth in every living heart—a new light to every
seeing eye. Past theologies did their best to interpret the laws under which man was living, and to
help him to regulate his life thereby. But the laws
of God are before us always, whether promulgated in
Sinai Thunder, or otherwise. ' The Universe is made
by law—the great Soul of the world is just, and not
unjust. . . . Rituals, Liturgies, Credos, Sinai Thunder,
I know more or less the history of those—the rise, progress, decline, and fall of these. Can thunder from
the thirty-two Azimuths repeated daily for centuries of
years make God's laws more godlike to me? Brother,
No ! . . . Revelation, Inspiration, yes, and thy own
God-created soul: dost thou not call that a Revelation ?
Who made thee ? Where didst thou come from ?—
the voice of Eternity, if thou be not a blasphemer, and
poor asphyxied mute, speaks with that tongue of
thine. Thou art the latest book of Nature ; it is the
Inspiration of the Almighty giveth thee understanding, my brother, my brother.'[1] Again, ' God not only
made us, and beholds us, but is in us and around us.
The age of miracles, as it ever was, now is. . . . This
is the high Gospel begun to be preached : Man is
still man !'[2]

It is evident that Carlyle's repulsion to Christianity

---

[1] *Past and Present*, pp. 307-9.
[2] ' Characteristics'—*Miscellanies*, iii. p. 32.

arose out of the general tendency of his mind to throw
aside all dead forms of thought, as he conceived them
to be. With a creative imagination, unexampled almost
in the history of literature, his highest gift was yet
strangely limited.   He could make the dead live again
in feature and character—every aspect of life, society
and manner, glow upon the canvas in a way no writer of
our time, or perhaps of any time, ever rivalled.   Lock-
hart said that he excelled every one in this respect,
except Scott.   Mr. Froude, and many will agree with
him, will not allow the exception.   But with all this
intense imaginative realism in the description of facts
—in the portraiture of character and events—he had
little or no power of realising systems of thought, and
recognising what is great and still living in them.
Philosophies and theologies, merely because they are
past, are all dead metaphysics—putrescent stuff—to be
cast out and trodden under foot.   Any manifestation
of forceful life—of energetic personality—in the past
as in the present, interested him—Luther, Knox,
Mohammed, Samuel Johnson, Burns, Edward Irving,
so far ; but movements of thought, apart from the
personalities concerned in them—movements which,
after their first life, had clothed themselves in systems
and institutions, he nowhere shows a capacity of understanding, still less of estimating in their surviving
life and power, as embodied in Institutions, Churches,
articles, Liturgies, or other symbols.   The mere fact
that they were no longer in their first freshness, but
had become traditional, implied to him that they
were dead, and that there was no more good in them.
With all his historic vision, so intense of its kind,
there is no evidence that he ever saw what a marvel-

lous and exceptional movement Christianity had been—what life still stirred in it—what an historical as well as spiritual grandeur there was in the Church —and the witness it still was for a living God in the world. He could not accept its miraculous framework ; but neither could he accept its inner spirit. He was too obviously repelled by the essential character of its teaching as a Gospel for the poor, weak, and sinful. He was blind, with all his heroic instincts, to the most heroic history that has ever been enacted in the world. Calvinism was to him respectable, not because it was a great intellectual or theological phenomenon, with a continuous historical life of its own, but because it was the faith of his father and mother, and he saw how it had moved them with the strong hand of its purity, and given their lives a certain grandeur and stern kind of beauty. When he talks of 'unbelievability,' and the impossibility of any man of veracity taking up with traditional Christianity, it is necessary not merely to say that he never gave the subject of its credibility any adequate attention ; but that he failed to understand its simple greatness as a fact, or rather a great procession of facts—the power of its thought in moulding human life all through the Christian centuries—the stamp of tender heroism which it alone still gives to this life. He failed, in short, on this side, as a student of that very human nature which in its essential elements was to him professedly Revelation, to the exclusion of the dead theologies which hung around it.

But opposed as Carlyle was thus to Christianity, he was still more opposed to Materialism in all its forms. This is evident enough in his writings, vague as they often are, but Mr. Froude's statements place the matter beyond all doubt. They have a special value as professing to be founded on much personal converse with him during his last years, when his thought was fully matured in the light of the successive efforts made in our time to account for man's nature by materialistic evolution. All such efforts were to him mere ' mud philosophies.' ' God was to him the fact of facts.' Again, his biographer says Carlyle ' was a Calvinist without the theology. The materialistic theory of things—that intellect is a phenomenon of matter, that conscience is the growth of social convenience, and other kindred speculations, he utterly repudiated. Scepticism on the nature of right and wrong, or on man's responsibility to his Maker, never touched or tempted him.' [1] He discredited Christianity as a professed revelation ; but he not only never doubted the Divine Government of the world,—it may be said that all his writings, historical, political, and biographical, appealed incessantly to this Government as the surest reality in the Universe. Opposition to it and to the plain facts everywhere witnessing to it, was the explanation of all personal, social, and political corruption. It was even because in his view religion, as represented by the Churches, had so much lost sight of the inexorable Moral law lying upon all human life, that it had lost so much of its power, and had become dead and useless as he supposed. There was never a sterner Apostle of Divine Law than Carlyle, or any one more opposed to the idea of a Godless world in which man was his own chief end.

[1] *Life*, vol. ii. p. 2 (years 1795-1835).

But strongly as Carlyle seized the divine side of things, clearly as he recognised that there is a spirit in man, and that the Almighty alone giveth him understanding, he refused to look steadily at spiritual as distinct from natural life. There is a lack both of reality and discrimination in his conception. His dualism of spirit and matter, much insisted upon in general terms, and in opposition to all 'mud philosophies,' had a constant tendency to vanish on application. Nature and man were divine to him now and here. Nothing is more touching and beautiful than the way in which he vindicates the divine meaning of all nature, the simple streamlet or *Kuhbach* that ran by the home of his childhood, 'flowing, gurgling from beyond the earliest date of History,' no less than the Jordan or Siloa of Scripture; the lives that were dear to his heart no less than the lives of Patriarchs or Apostles. All in idea were sacred,—a Revelation to him. But the Divine in Nature and in Man—all-significant in Carlyle's imagination—was but imperfectly apprehended by him in particular fact. Here as everywhere to him the ideal and the actual failed to harmonise. Nature was before his eyes at Craigenputtock no less than Hoddam Hill; yet the former was a God-forgotten wilderness—'a devil's den' when he was out of humour. 'Man was still man,'—Godlike,—but man the individual, save in rare instances, was intolerable to him. No one has ever written more eloquently of man in the universal, and abused more dreadfully the individuals with whom he was brought in contact.

There is not only this gap between the ideal and the practical; but with all Carlyle's talk of God,—

of the Divine,—he everywhere shrinks from any definition of God as distinctively moral. There is everywhere to him a Divine meaning. But what does this come to? 'Matter, were it never so despicable, is the manifestation of spirit.' But what is spirit? What is the Divine that moves in all things,—'all thinking things, all objects of all thought'? He used the common name of God. At other times he refused to use any definite name, and fell back upon his well-known 'Eternities,' 'Immensities.' He veiled his meaning in metaphors. But whether he did this or used the name of God he did not mean what the Christian or the Theist means by God. He did not mean a Personal Being, judging the world in righteousness; and still less a 'Father in heaven.' He spoke in abundance of a law of judgment,—of a righteous rule that will not let the wicked go unpunished. The 'Veracities' and their unfailing sentences were ever in his mouth. The liar, the time-server—the impostor in every form—social, political, or religious—cannot hope to escape. There is laid up for all such a fearful looking for of judgment, which will yet crush them and all their works. Here there is in full force the Biblical, or Calvinist element of Carlyle's early education. But he was only too good a Calvinist, or rather he took up merely with one side of Calvinism—the side which emphasises the bare will, the naked power of God. He could not conceive himself made save by a being who had a moral sense like his own. But he refused to acknowledge a Personal Life above his own life, a Life pitiful as well as just, Love as well as Law. And so his idea of the Divine readily sank into the idea of

Supreme Force. He scouted the materialist who denied spirit, but no less he scouted the Christian who sought to realise the relation of the Supreme Spirit to himself as an individual,—who recognised the idea of Personal Love as the only adequate conception of Spirit. He delighted in the vagueness which lies necessarily in this higher region, and clung to it with scorn of all who would give to the Supreme a more concrete meaning. And so Spirit with him constantly passes into Force, Law into Might—Righteousness into mere order. The world is divinely governed, no doubt; but a Danton, a Cromwell, and a Frederick the Great are the special representatives and executive of this government. It is plain that the Carlylean and the Christian ideas of the Divine are not the same. When it is right to have done with the negro at whatever hazard, and to clear the earth of wretches by whatever process, you feel that the Divine righteousness to which he appeals is not the righteousness of the Gospels. It is Calvinism not only without the theology, but without the morality which clung to it in the religion of his youth. It is a *Divine* kingdom—let us be thankful for Carlyle's inflexible insistence that there is a righteous order in the world which will vindicate itself against all deceptions and evasions of man—but a Divine kingdom without mercy for the penitent or pardon for the guilty—an Order of judgment girdling the earth rather than a Father's Love seeking the sinner while condemning his sin.

Upon the whole we may venture to sum up the relation of Carlyle's teaching to Christianity as follows. It was negative in the following points:—

(1.) In denial of miracle;[1] (2.) in denial of the
Divine Personality; and (3.) in his disposition to
exalt strength,—to set forth the mighty in intellect
and character rather than the 'poor in spirit,'—as the
Divine ideal. On the other hand, his teaching had
an affinity with Christianity—(1.) In his continual
assertion of a Divine Power behind all matter; (2.)
his representation of man as the offspring of such a
Divine Power or Being; (3.) his earnestness on
behalf of a Moral Law or eternal distinction between
right and wrong; and (4.) his belief, vague though it
may have been, in immortality. When his wife died
so suddenly in his absence, his heart seemed breaking at the thought that he could never see her again.
'Yet then and afterwards, when he grew calm, and
was in full possession of himself, he spoke always of
a life to come, and the meeting of friends in it, as a
thing not impossible.'

Carlyle was great as a Moral Teacher in so far as
he preserved certain elements of his early creed. In
his earnestness he honestly believed that he had discovered the truths he proclaimed. They seemed to
him to have vanished from Christendom, sunk into
dotage and formality. But, truly speaking, every
genuine element of his moral teaching, overlaid as it
may have been by churchly traditions, was still living
in Christianity. The eternal 'Veracities,' every one
of them, were Christian ideals, however obscured
by convention or reduced in practice; and no teacher,
certainly not Carlyle, has been able to convert the
ideal everywhere into fact. Convention, cant, re-

---

[1] Mr. Froude represents him as saying quite definitely, 'It is as
sure as Mathematics such a thing never happened.'

asserts itself in the soil of human nature—springs like a noxious weed amidst the growths of human passion and self-deception. The ideals of conduct require to be constantly reasserted and applied with renewed earnestness to the individual, social, political, and religious life of mankind. Carlyle did a noble service in this way as a Preacher of the Kingdom of Divine Righteousness in a world ever lapsing both from the idea and the realisation of such a kingdom. But he not only did not advance the moral ideal ; he rather retrogressed, by abstracting from it the spiritual conditions most fitted to nurture it and make it living and aggressive. By lowering the thought of God from that of a Sublime Personality whose highest name is Love, to a mere impersonal conception—whether in the singular or plural form, such as—' The Divine,' ' Silence,' the ' Eternities,' ' Immensities,' [1] he relapsed into a species of Stoicism which has long ago proved itself ineffectual both as a guide of human conduct and a response to the human heart. Like many noble minds he shrank from the fussiness and what he considered the degradation of religion as embodied in churches and their multiplied and mixed activities. The Divine seemed to him formalised

---

[1] This old phase of religious thought is known to every student of its history not only in Stoicism but in Gnosticism. In the very Judaism which Carlyle so much repudiated the same disinclination which he himself had to fix the idea of the Divine and *name* it was powerfully present, and had a significant influence in the development of the Christian conception of God. We fear it must be said that to Carlyle in some respect is due the modern habit, conspicuously exemplified in *Natural Religion* and Mr. Matthew Arnold's writings, of using the name of God without any note of its Christian meaning,—a habit in every respect pernicious, as both leading to moral confusion and ignoring the living growth of moral and religious ideas.

and belittled in their narrow restrictions; but the remedy for this can never be found in turning the Divine into a mere vague generality which may mean anything or nothing. This is really to fall back in the progress of moral ideas, and to end, as it has done in all our modern endeavours after a Natural, —or, as he would have called it, 'Natural-Supernatural' Religion,—in an idealisation of Force as the last word both of morality and religion. The idea of Personality embracing alike righteousness and love, order and pity, can alone make the Divine a living power to the human conscience—a Life above, redeeming and sanctifying as well as controlling human life.

VI.

JOHN STUART MILL AND HIS SCHOOL.

NOTHING can be greater than the contrast between the upbringing of Thomas Carlyle and John Stuart Mill. Yet both were of Scottish blood, and the father of the one and grandfather of the other were very much in the same social position. James Carlyle was originally a mason, and then a farmer. James Mill—the father of the author of the *History of British India*—was a Kincardineshire shoemaker, more or less prosperous in his earlier years. Both lived in a cottage, and partook of the same simple rough diet which nurtured the Scottish peasant in the end of last century. Not only so; but the same ambition, so common to the Scottish peasant of the time, inspired both families. Carlyle's father and mother wished him to become a minister of the Scottish Church. James Mill the shoemaker, and especially his wife, who seems to have been originally of a higher position, as she was of a somewhat higher character than her husband, brought up their son— or he was brought up by others under their special sanction—to the same ministry. Unlike Thomas Carlyle, James Mill not only studied for the Christian ministry, but became a preacher in the Scottish Church, and officiated as such for three years.

With these similarities in their origin there was the most marked difference in the early life of the two men. James Mill, as is well known, not only abandoned the profession to which he had been trained, but he definitely and entirely abandoned Christianity; and in the wonderful education which he gave his famous son religion had no part. Among all the books which the latter read—so appalling in number and variety—the Bible had no place. Carlyle's early thought and imagination were fed upon the Bible. It was originally, and remained more than Goethe and all else, the basis of his varied culture. Not only in the Scriptures—but in the person of his mother particularly—religion was steadily before the mind of Carlyle as a youth. On the contrary, the very idea of religion was carefully excluded from John Stuart Mill's mind. 'I was brought up from the first,' are his own words, 'without any religious belief.'[1] 'I am one of the very few examples in this country of one who has not thrown off religious belief, but never had it. I grew up in a negative state with regard to it.' This of course implies that his mother, whatever may have been her own sentiments, did nothing to make up his lack of religious education. James Mill, indeed, was not the man to permit any interference, even from such a source, with the remarkable plan of education which he had sketched for his son, and which, amidst all his own hard work, he persistently carried out. We hear little or nothing of the wife and mother in this strange household. She was good-looking, it is said, with 'a small

[1] *Autobiography*, p. 38.

fine figure, and an aquiline type of face, seen in her eldest son.' The marriage was one of affection, and the household became a large one, and was admirably managed by her. But the singular hardness of James Mill's character, and the failure on the part of his wife to prove a companion to him in his intellectual enthusiasm, led to early disappointment, and 'the union was never happy.'[1] The surprising thing is that the son, in his *Autobiography*, should never mention his mother when dwelling with such minute detail on his father's character and opinions—here, as in other respects, differing so much from Carlyle. The greatest beauty of Carlyle's biography would undoubtedly be gone if the figure of his mother, and his passionate devotion to her, were absent from its pages. His love for his mother, as her love to him, are more than any other the golden threads that run through his struggling life. In Mill we find nothing of this. There is no tenderness even in the feeling which he expresses towards his father, loyally as he was devoted to him,—and of his mother not a word. This speaks volumes as to the different character of the families, and of the great men who came from them. This typical difference will be seen on many occasions in their respective careers.

There is a strange onesidedness in John Mill's account of his father's views on religion, or—to put it otherwise—in James Mill's religious opinions as represented by his son. It is evident from this account alone that Christian preacher as James Mill had been, he had not studied Christianity either in its substance or evidences, in any large spirit. He

[1] Bain's *Biography of James Mill*, p. 60.

had looked at it closely as a definite creed or set of opinions, but without any recognition of its development as either a speculative or ethical system. God was conceived by him after the Deistic fashion of last century as holding a purely external relation to the world, and, as its Creator, directly responsible for all its evil and good alike. Religion was to him a mere device, or at best a growth of imaginative passion, for the most part evil rather than good. He is represented as affirming 'a hundred times' 'that all ages and nations have represented their Gods as wicked in a constantly increasing progression—that mankind have gone on adding trait after trait till they reached the most perfect conception of wickedness which the human mind can devise, and have called this God, and prostrated themselves before it.' Such an opinion could only have been entertained by a man who, whatever other things he knew, did not know religion in any intelligent manner, who had not even conceived intelligently what religion means. It would be hardly possible to condense into a single sentence a series of grosser misconceptions. Whatever be the origin of religion it certainly does not come out of the mere wickedness of man's heart, nor grow worse as history advances. It is infinitely more true to say that it springs out of the higher imagination and spiritual side of human nature, whatever grosser elements may also mingle in it, and it is certain that its progression has been, as surely as the progression of morality, from lower and more imperfect to more elevated and perfect forms. James Mill's dogmatism was at all times narrow and one-sided; but dogmatism so ignorant and superficial as that now quoted touches the very sanity of his intellectual conceptions on the side of religion.

James Mill's infidelity evidently sprang from ignorant misconception of the Christian idea of God. He fell into the very snare which Philosophy such as his is fond of attributing to popular religion. The God of his imagination was anthropomorphic and nothing else—a Being supposed to sit in the heavens and to apportion, directly after the manner of a man, all the issues of good and evil in the world. There was no wonder that he came to reject such an idea —or with such a mechanical conception of Divine agency he should have plunged into Manichæism as the only possible solution of the problem of the universe. He found it impossible to believe that a world so full of evil could be the work of an Author at once almighty and beneficent. It appeared to him a far more feasible theory that the world was the production of an Evil as well as Good Power struggling for mastery. Christian theism, according to him, instead of being an advance was really a retrogression from the old Sabæan or Manichæan theory. St. Augustine was profoundly mistaken when he abandoned the latter theory for the former. We have been so accustomed to crudities of speculation in our day that we write these sentiments without a shock. But coming as they did from the mouth of a philosopher they are not the less nonsense. Of all conceptions of the government of the world the Dualistic is one of the coarsest and most untenable. It ignores alike the laws of reason and the comprehensive meaning of facts—both of which irresistibly point to a unity. All the lessons of Science and the hopes of life point in the same direction.

But what are we to say of the Evil in the world? It is there. And is not the idea of an allotted place of Evil to which the wicked are doomed a Christian conception? 'Think of a Being,' Mill was accustomed to say, 'who would make a Hell—who would create the human race with the infallible foreknowledge, and therefore with the intention that the great majority of them were to be assigned to terrible and everlasting punishment.' Even if there be a hell in Mr. Mill's sense, it does not follow that God made it. Still less does it follow that the human race were 'created' with the intention that 'the great majority of them' should be consigned to it. A cruder explanation, ignoring a whole world of Christian argument, can hardly be imagined. Mr. Mill had no right to substitute his own mechanical conception of Deity, and no less of good and evil, and then from his own point of view to condemn Christianity, which rests on quite other conceptions. There is no resemblance between the Divine Ideal of the New Testament, whose will is that 'all men be saved' and 'an Omnipotent Author of Hell.' Nor is there any resemblance between the evil which condemns men in the Gospel, and the evil to which Mr. Mill supposes them to be condemned. Evil is a great fact in the world, beyond all question, but it is not more a fact than the consciousness that the worst evil is always the fruit of our own will. To make God the author of it because man is the doer of it is a generalisation not only crude but self-condemned on the very testimony of the doer himself. To speak of God as making

Hell, when the worst hell is that which a man makes for himself, is a poor fallacy as well as a gross caricature. It does not come out of the region of Christian thought at all, which it is evident James Mill never entered. There was no room in his philosophy for the mystery of Will—Divine or human—and the very conditions of the Christian problem were therefore not before him. His caricature may find its justification in pulpit rhetoric—for what extravagances may not the popular imagination reach? But one does not expect to find the philosopher rivalling and even outdoing the street preacher on his favourite ground, and the Christian apologist is not bound to bandy arguments of such a nature.

In order to judge any religion fairly it must be judged from its highest point of view. James Mill seems never to have understood this, and his son, with a much fairer and broader mind, which constantly owns the difference between certain popular notions of Christianity and Christianity itself, is yet apt, with all his school, to argue from the lower rather than from the higher level. Nothing is easier than to give a thing a bad name, and then show how worthless it is ; in other words, to debase the Christian ideal, and then point out how unworthy of credence it is. In no other subject save religion would such a mode of argument be allowed. On any other subject men feel bound to accept its highest interpretation as the only true interpretation. The students of a special subject are allowed to be the judges, and the only judges of its right meaning. But every one thinks himself capable of sitting in judgment upon religion although he may have given no study whatever to the subject. And the whole class of philosophical writers to whom the Mills belonged were in the habit of fighting with unfair weapons of this kind. We do not suppose and do not affirm that they were conscious of any unfairness ; but the effect of their arguments is not the less unfair. In treating past systems of morality they would carefully endeavour to find their essential principles in their best modes of expression; and it was therefore a singular perversity which led them, whenever they approached the subject of religion, to take up with its flimsiest and most unworthy expressions. But a man so non-religious as James Mill could hardly be expected to understand Christianity any more than a man without any soul or faculty for music could understand harmony. There are men, and James Mill was one of them, so utterly lacking in spiritual instinct that their judgments as to religion really merit no more attention than other men's judgments about music. We by no means say the same thing of John Stuart Mill. We shall have occasion to show that he possessed far higher instincts. But he was trained in a school which not only knew nothing of religion, but may be said deliberately to have despised it. It was outside the whole range of his experience and culture. Men are not supposed to be and cannot be experts in anything the very rudiments of which they have never learned; and we have no right therefore beforehand to look to John Stuart Mill's writings as possessing any special authority on this subject.

Of John Stuart Mill's general education under his father we need not speak. He has himself given us the most ample and detailed account of it. It is a marvellous story, the interesting effect of which, however, is impaired by its great singularity. Not only was John Mill beyond all other boys ever heard of in his aptitude for learning, and in the amount and variety of his acquisitions, while still a bare youth. He lived to wear all his knowledge and learning as the flower of a rare and noble intellect. Any other boy we fancy must have broken down and become effete before manhood under such a pressure of education. He could read Greek fluently when about six years old, at the time young people in general are beginning the first standard. Before he was eight he had read the whole of Herodotus and a considerable part of Xenophon. He had read six of Plato's Dialogues, including the Theætetus in 1813, while still only seven. It takes away one's breath to speak of such achievements, and they represent a mere fraction of the story which he tells us.[1] Father and son together, the former as teacher, the latter as pupil, present in the first chapter of the autobiography a picture which is incomparable—the tenacious firmness of the father in urging the son along the pathway of knowledge, severely testing every step in his progress as if a matter of course needing no acknowledgment, and the eager responsiveness of the son, honouring rather than loving the hand which led him onwards with such rigid resolve. Besides the Classics, Greek and Latin (Latin after Greek) and Mathematics, he studied diligently and copiously History, English Poetry, although with a less universal interest, Chemistry, Logic, Political

[1] *Autobiography*, pp. 5-25.

Economy. He read Aristotle's Analytics, in the original of course, when about twelve. In all he was more or less a proficient before he was fourteen, when he went abroad (1820) for a six months' sojourn in the south of France. Withal, he tells us, and we believe him, he was not self-conceited. His father, he says, completely succeeded in keeping him out of the way of hearing himself praised, and so he was not at all aware that his attainments ' were anything unusual at his age.' In personal manner, in mature years, he was certainly free from all self-assumption. It may be more doubtful whether his intellectual manner, as shown in his writings, does not all along bear trace of a certain conscious mental superiority, especially when controverted on any of his favourite topics. It could hardly be otherwise.

In all the variety of his studies, as already indicated, Biblical or religious literature had no place. His mind had no religious aspirations. It found all its satisfaction in secular acquisition, and in speculation and logical analysis. From the first he was a ' master of sentences,' writing out under his father's eyes elaborate abstracts of the books he read, especially in history and philosophy. No youth, I should think, ever wrote so many digests, or prepared himself so carefully, by mastery of the thoughts of others for the work of thought himself. He describes the great influence exercised upon him by his first direct contact with Bentham's speculations. His whole previous education had been in a sense ' a course of Benthamism ;' but, after his return from abroad, he began the study of Bentham on his own account, as interpreted in Dumont's *Traité de Législa-*

tion. The reading of this book was 'an epoch' in his life. The classifications, 'more clear and compact than in Bentham's original work, were illuminating in the highest degree.' He felt taken up to an eminence,' from which he could survey 'a vast mental domain, and see stretching out into the distance intellectual results beyond all computation.' And to this intellectual clearness there seemed to be added 'the most inspiring prospects of practical improvement in human affairs.' 'When I laid down the last volume of the *Traité*,' he goes on, 'I had become a different being. The "principle of utility," understood as Bentham understood it, and applied in the manner in which he applied it, fell exactly into its place as the key-stone which held together the detached and fragmentary component parts of my knowledge and belief. It gave unity to my conception of things. I now had opinions ; a creed, a doctrine, a philosophy, in one among the best senses of the word,' he adds, 'a religion.'

In the following year he began to write independently. In 1823 he was appointed a clerk under his father in the office of Examiner of Correspondence in the East India Company, in whose service he gradually rose to be chief conductor of the Correspondence with India in one of the leading departments—that of Native States. Finally he became Examiner, but only two years before the abolition of the Company (1858). His first essays in authorship were, as in so many other cases, in the newspapers, in the end of 1822 and beginning of 1823 ; and when the *Westminster Review* was launched in April 1824, he became a regular contributor from the second number

till the year 1828, when through some misunder-
standing with the editor, Mr. Bowring, afterwards
Sir John Bowring, he ceased to write for it. He
describes his own early performances in literature
as 'dry,' and 'entirely argumentative.' He could
manage argument as the natural fruit of his education.   But no other mode of composition came to
him naturally at this time.   He admits, indeed, that
the phrase applied to the Benthamites in general of
being merely reasoning machines—'inapplicable' in
some cases—was by no means untrue of himself in
those years.   His great object in association with
others was to draw them into argument.   In the
winter of 1822-3, he formed a society of young men
'agreeing in fundamental principles,' to meet together
once a fortnight to read essays and discuss questions.
He gave it the name of the 'Utilitarian' Society,
which was the first usage of the word he believes in
its current philosophical sense.   He disclaims invent-
ing it, however, and says he found it in one of Galt's
novels, where a Scotch clergyman warns his hearers
'not to leave the Gospel and become Utilitarians.'
He was evidently also the inspiring spirit of meetings
which were held for several years at Mr. Grote's
house, for reading and conversation chiefly in Political
Economy and Logic.   The meetings were from half-
past eight till ten in the morning, and appear to have
been highly fruitful, so far as his own speculations
on both these subjects were concerned.   'I have
always dated from these conversations,' he says, 'my
own real inauguration as an original and independent
thinker.'   He was an active member of still another
association, the object of which was to cultivate the

gifts of speech, rather than of reasoning. Roebuck, he, and some others, met in 1825 at the 'Co-operative Society,' composed of Owenites which met for weekly public discussions in Chancery Lane. They went to this Society, not as approving of Owenism, but with a view of discussing the principles which it involved, some of the chief Owenists acting in concert with them, nothing loth to have a controversy with opponents, rather than a tame debate among themselves. Charles Austin, Charles Villiers, and a once well-known educational writer, Mr. Ellis, were among the number of the speakers ; but the speaker that struck Mill most, although he dissented from nearly every word he said, was Thirlwall, the historian, afterwards Bishop of St. David's, 'then a Chancery Barrister unknown, except for a high reputation for eloquence acquired at the Cambridge Union before the era of Austin and Macaulay.' 'His speech was in answer to one of mine,' the autobiography continues. 'Before he had uttered two sentences, I set him down as the best speaker I had ever heard, and I have never since heard any one that I placed above him.'

These debates led to a new combination, in imitation of the Edinburgh Speculative Society, where Brougham and Horner were known to have contended. This Society lasted for many years, and occupied much of Mill's time. The chief difficulty at first was to secure a sufficient number of Tory speakers. Almost all the members were Liberals of different orders and degrees, such as Macaulay, Thirlwall, Praed, Lord Howick, Samuel Wilberforce (afterwards Bishop of Oxford), the two Bulwers (Edward and Henry), and Fonblanque, the well-known editor of

the *Examiner*. It was difficult in such circumstances
to maintain the life of the Society ; but in 1826-7, two
young Tory speakers of great ability were found—the
late Mr. Hayward and Sergeant Shee—while Cockburn,
the late Chief-Justice, and Charles Buller, Carlyle's
pupil, joined the Society on the Liberal side.   The
result was the most lively discussions between the Tory
lawyers and the 'philosophic Radicals,' attracting a
wide attention.   A new element was added to the
Society in 1828 and 1829, when the Coleridgians, in
the persons of Maurice and Sterling, made their
appearance as a second Liberal and even Radical
party, on totally different grounds from Benthamism,
and vehemently opposed to it. ' Our debates were very
different from those of common debating societies, for
they habitually consisted of the strongest arguments
and most philosophic principles, which either side
was able to produce, thrown often into close and
terse confutations of one another.'[1]

A life of such incessant and severe intellectual
application—with no out-door exercise except long
walks in the country—led with young Mill to the
inevitable consequence. He fell into a state of ill-
health and depression of spirits. He has himself
described this at length in his autobiography as ' a
crisis' in his mental history. He had set before himself the great object of being ' a reformer of the world.'
He had found all his happiness—he was still only
20 years of age—in this high ambition.   Suddenly,
in the autumn of 1826, he felt as if this great object
no longer interested him. He was 'in a dull state of
nerves,' and became uneasy and dissatisfied.   He

[1] *Autobiography*, pp. 128-129.

compares his condition, just as Carlyle did a few years earlier, to that 'in which converts to Methodism usually are' when smitten by that first 'conviction of sin.' He asked himself, What if all after which he aspired were realised? Would his happiness be secure? The answer of 'an irrepressible self-consciousness within him' was distinctly 'no.' At this his heart sank within him' and the whole future of his life seemed to fall to the ground. Neither sleep nor distraction could chase away the cloud which rested on him. He awoke to an ever-renewed consciousness of his misery. For months the cloud 'seemed to grow thicker and thicker.' Mill treats this unhappy crisis of his as mainly if not entirely mental, and the inference he would have us to draw is that he then underwent—as Carlyle, we also saw, supposed—a new birth or conversion. There is indeed in Mill's case no pretence of any religious change. There was really no basis for such a change in his mental experience and association. All thoughts of sin or moral shortcoming were entirely absent from him. What the Methodist means by 'conviction of sin' was unintelligible to him then and at all times. But a change we believe of a thorough character did come to him, partly moral and partly intellectual. After long suffering a ray of light broke in upon his gloom. He was reading Marmontel's *Mémoires*, and the picture of self-sacrifice there brought before him in the resolution of the young Marmontel after his father's death to be all that his father had been to the family, moved him to tears, and woke within him brighter hopes. From this moment his burden was lighter. The cloud gradually drew off, and he was able once more to enjoy life.

It is remarkable how the language of religion comes to Mill's lips as it did to Carlyle's with still more touching force, at such a period of inward conflict. There was apparently, however, less of a conflict in the one case than the other. Two important results are attributed by him to this crisis. He modified his theory of life so as no longer to pursue happiness as a conscious object, but duty rather, in the conviction that happiness was sure to follow ; and he learned that true culture was to be found in a wider range of experience than he had previously aimed at. Feeling had hitherto little to do with his education. His father's idea had been that the feelings would always take sufficient care of themselves, and did not require to be specially cultivated. But now he saw how inadequate his former purely intellectual or logical standard had been ; and the cultivation of the feelings became henceforth one of the cardinal points in his ethical and philosophical creed.

Such is, very briefly summed up, Mill's own account of this phase of his mental history, to which he evidently attached great significance. More widely viewed, there can be little doubt that, as in Carlyle's case, the state of his physical health had far more to do with the crisis than he was disposed to allow. Dr. Bain indeed, who lived in such close association with him for many years, although not at this early time, is disposed to attribute all his dejection now and on subsequent occasions in his life, which were not unfrequent, to purely physical causes, the 'chief of which was of course overwork of the brain.' If ever a young brain was overtaxed, Mill's certainly was, and there seems every reason to conclude that

Dr. Bain's explanation is the correct one, although we may allow more than he does for accompanying mental perplexities. In his unhappiness there was nothing, strictly speaking, of the higher spiritual order ; but the loss of his youthful ideal was so far akin to a consciousness of spiritual loss and insufficiency ; and it worked as all such losses do—baffled hope, defeated ambition,—like 'madness in the brain.' Overstrain, no doubt, as in so many other cases, was the root of the suffering. But who shall measure in the inner chamber of consciousness how far the spiritual interlaces itself with the physical, and contributes to the intolerable misery that accompanies such nervous depression !

There can be no doubt that John Stuart Mill emerged from his mental crisis a richer and broader-minded man than he was before. Music, poetry,—especially the poetry of Wordsworth;—the association with Maurice and Sterling, both of whom—he owns, while deploring in the former a greater waste of intellectual power (as he thought) than in any of his contemporaries—were of considerable help in his development ; and finally Carlyle ; all assisted to enlarge his thought and rescue him from the narrow intellectual groove in which he had been trained. His father looked askance at all these wider studies and influences. Many of his father's friends did the same. It is amusing, yet in a way melancholy, to read of the anxieties he excited, lest he should forsake 'the true faith' of the experience-philosophy. He was watched with more jealousy than the promising Christian neophyte by old theologians, lest he should stray from the fold. George Grote, Dr. Bain tells us, had always certain misgivings about him. It was he, as we shall see again, who chiefly watched for his backsliding. 'Much as I admire John Mill,' he used to say, 'my admiration is always mixed with fear.' So soon does the old leaven of Sectarianism, erroneously supposed to be a special property of Christendom, assert itself in the most alien creeds, and blend its noxious power with the boldest freethinking.

James Mill died in 1836 of pulmonary consumption, the year after the starting of the *London Review*, which in its fifth number became the *London and Westminster Review*, the old Westminster being merged with it. John became editor of this Review, of which Sir William Molesworth was the proprietor. He continued editor for five years, during which the Review became a powerful organ of public opinion. It was designed to represent the 'philosophic Radicals' of whom great hopes were for a time entertained by Mill, not a few of them, including Mr. Grote, having been returned in the Reformed Parliament. These hopes, however, soon vanished, and the Review continued more memorable during the time of his editorship, for his own articles on Tennyson, De Tocqueville, Armand Carrel, Carlyle, Bentham, and Coleridge, than for anything else. In these papers the author gave full vent to his altered and enlarged range of thought. He drew off from the narrower Benthamism of his earlier writings, with a result very distasteful to many of his early friends. They in their turn drew back from the Review.[1] But Mill was now in the full maturity of his powers, and was able to stand on his own feet without special encourage-

[1] See *J. S. Mill: a Criticism*, by Dr. A. Bain, pp. 56-7.

ment from any quarter. He felt himself a power both in the intellectual and political world ; and although he did not continue beyond the year 1840 to edit the Review, he never flinched from any of the broader convictions of which he had made it the vehicle. He remained especially proud that he had vindicated so successfully Lord Durham's Canadian policy, and contributed to establish Carlyle's long delayed fame.

During all this time Mill was elaborating his great work on Logic. He may be said to have begun this book as far back as 1830, when he first put upon paper certain ideas, afterwards worked into his preliminary chapter. He busied himself with the subject from time to time, till in the summer of 1838 he set about its systematic development ; and in the end of 1841 he had the book ready for the press. It was his habit, he tells us, in connection with the preparation of this work, to write all his books and articles twice over. A draft was first prepared to the very end of the subject—and then the whole begun again *de novo*—an admirable plan for giving proportion and due effect to the several portions of a book. The *System of Logic*, ready by the end of 1841, was not published till the spring of 1843. It immediately attracted wide attention. The author confesses himself astonished at its success. On this book more than any other his fame will rest.

The publication of his *Logic* may be said to open what Mill himself calls the third portion of his career, when he became an established reputation in philosophy, and rose to be head of the school which his father founded. For whatever changes of opinion he underwent, and however far he enlarged his general ideas in literature and education, he remained substantially true to his father's philosophical standpoint. He is at particular pains to point this out in his *Autobiography*, and to show that he lost nothing that was good in his old mode of thought. But it was unnecessary to give any assurance of this. The *System of Logic* is in itself the satisfactory evidence that he stood in philosophy where his father stood. It was, and in some respects continues to be, the most complete manual of the experience-philosophy, even after all that has been done in that line during the last forty years. With Mr. Herbert Spencer and others that philosophy has entered on a new departure, by the help of the principle of Evolution. But the *Logic* is still the most complete text-book of the doctrine which, according to the author's own statement, 'derives all knowledge from experience, and all moral and intellectual qualities from the direction given to the associations.' It is at the same time the best polemic against 'the opposite school of Metaphysics —the ontological and "innate principles" school.' The ideas which it embodies, and which give its chief interest to the work, strike, as we shall see, all spiritual philosophy at the root, and lead to the subversion of revealed religion.

The *System of Logic* was followed in 1848 by the *Principles of Political Economy*, which more than rivalled the success of the former work, and has also taken its place among the great books of the time. With the publication of this volume Mill's creative activity as a writer may be said to cease.

Some of his most interesting writings appeared after this, as his volume on *Liberty* in 1859, and his *Examination of Sir W. Hamilton's Philosophy* in 1865 ; but in none of these writings is the constructive effort so great as in these main works. *On Liberty* was probably the most popular of all his books, as it is the most charming to read. There are few minds of a liberal turn who can have perused it for the first time without a thrill of delight, even if the continued advance of liberal thought has now made some of its eloquence comparatively commonplace.[1] There are none of his writings again more acute, subtle, and in part strong, than his attack on the Hamiltonian philosophy. Yet, as Dr. Bain admits, he had spent his force as an originator on his two larger works. They contain all the pith of his thinking ; and his after labours were in the main expository and polemical, rather than constructive. By the date of his *Political Economy* (1848) he had acquired all the elements of his thinking, accumulated all his stores, among the last of which were the fertile ideas he derived from the study of Comte. His mind remained fixed from this time, while his reputation rapidly grew. He certainly brought nothing further to the support of his special principles. The three posthumous *Essays on Religion*, interesting as they are, form no exception ; for our purpose they are more valuable, perhaps, than any other of his writings. They enable us, along with his autobiography, to see

---

[1] Charles Kingsley, when he first took up the volume in Parker's shop, became so entranced with it that he sat down and read it through without stopping. As he left the shop he said it had 'made him a clearer-headed, braver-minded man on the spot.' I read it first on the railway between Oxford and London with something of the same ennobling effect.

more clearly into the peculiar characteristics of his religious opinions. But not even Mill's greatest admirers—these admirers, indeed, least of all—would claim for them any peculiar intellectual merit among his productions. There are, in fact, prominent traces of weakness in all of them, and if he had never written anything bearing with more penetration and strength of argument upon the foundations of religion than these essays, they would hardly have claimed a place in these lectures. They demand from us, however, some special notice.

But we must first endeavour to fix Mill's main significance in the modern development of religious thought. This significance is almost exclusively derived from the fundamental principles of which he was the expositor, as the chief teacher of the experience-philosophy in his day. John Mill inherited this philosophy quite as much as most Christian thinkers inherit opposite principles. His *Essays on Religion*, his volume on Hamilton, as well as many of his special papers, show that his life of thought was a continued advance from the narrower notions of his school. Yet, as we have already implied, he was, from the first, and continued to the last, true to its main principles, notwithstanding all the advances he made in mere intellectual and poetic feeling. The doctrine of the absolute uniformity of Nature, or to put it in the language which he himself chiefly adopts in his autobiography—the doctrine of the necessity of all human character and conduct, no less than of all material phenomena—was his cardinal doctrine. His love of liberty in all human affairs, and his eloquent defence of Individualism, never touched the root principle on which all his philosophy, no less than his father's philosophy rested, and which came to him as a sort of religion. He never ceased to be the Apostle of Circumstance,[1] as opposed alike to Free will in human conduct and the freedom of Divine Action in Nature, although with a wider knowledge and a more candid perception of the difficulties of the doctrine than most of his school had.

His doctrine is most fully expounded in the famous chapter 'of the Law of Universal Causation' in his *System of Logic.*[2] From his own point of view, and the postulate which lies at the foundation of all his thinking,—the postulate, namely, that all our knowledge is derived from sensation,—this chapter is admirably reasoned and conclusive. But like Hume's famous argument about miracles, it gets all its force from the assumption of the very thing to be proved. If it is true, as Hume maintained, that the Laws of Nature are established by an *unalterable* experience, of course such a thing as a miracle can never have happened. No testimony can be of the slightest value against an *unalterable* experience. But then this was the very point in question. Has experience been *unalterable?* That a philosopher says so does not settle the question. No amount of induction—in other words, no conclusion drawn from any amount

---

[1] He himself well says of his father in his *Autobiography :*—' His fundamental doctrine was the formation of all human character by *Circumstances*, through the universal principle of association, and the consequent unlimited possibility of improving the moral and intellectual condition of mankind by education. Of all his doctrines, none was more important than this, or needs more to be insisted upon.'—P. 108 (2).

[2] Chap. v. B. III.

of observation and experiment can constitute an absolute truth, or convert a generality of science into a universal principle. Even so, Mill's Law of *Universal Causation*, which on his own philosophical basis is irrefragable, ceases to be so when looked at more comprehensively. If all our knowledge is derived from sensation—from the observation and generalised experience of our senses—we cannot of course have any knowledge that does not come under the law of scientific induction. The unbroken continuities of Nature in *co-existence* or *succession* are all that we can ever learn in this way. Nature and human life present themselves to us as an endless surface, linked by apparently indissoluble sequences. It has no life but the life of circumstance. But then this is the very question. Is all our knowledge so derived? Nay, can *knowledge*, strictly speaking, arise in this way at all? Could we even get experience, properly so called, on such a basis? Experience implies unity, cohesion, co-ordination. But is not sense in itself a mere repetition of vanishing particulars, which come and go without any cohesion? What brings order into the accidental chaos? Mere association? as supposed by Mill. Is it not rather a certain creative power of the mind itself, which builds up mere sense-accumulations into experience, and then into knowledge? To speak of knowledge apart from experience is of course absurd. To speak of experience apart from sense is equally absurd. All our knowledge goes back to sense—to our contact with the outer world. It is primarily dependent on sense. But mere sense could never yield it. The synthesis of the inward and outward is 'the essential fact in all cognition.' And this analysis of cognition, which recognises an inward creative as well as an outward accumulative element, cannot be disposed of by mere ridicule of 'innate principles.' 'Innate principles' may be exploded, but an innate power, which is itself not the product of sense, cannot be dispensed with.

Mill might not have denied this analysis so far. He came in the end, in his criticism of the Hamilton philosophy, to a species of Idealism, or 'possibility of sensation' as the root of knowledge. But the inner mental, no less than the outer material factor, was to him a mere evolution of circumstances. It had no originality. It was itself a new circumstance, the outgrowth of physical conditions. This is the fundamental antithesis between the materialistic and spiritualistic schools, and needs always to be broadly stated. To the one school man in his whole nature is the mere growth of physical forces. To the other he is endowed with a mind which may or may not have grown along with Nature—although all attempts to trace a mere natural growth of life or mind have utterly and confessedly failed—but which is in itself, in its essential character, absolutely distinct from other natural products. It is conscious, whereas they are unconscious. It is free, whereas they are bound. It is responsible, whereas they are without any sense of obligation. It stands, therefore, not merely by any religious claim made for it, but by its own intrinsic being—all that makes it what it essentially is—outside the alleged law of 'Universal Causation.'

Not only so. But the idea of Causation itself has its root in the very distinction of mind and matter.

It arises only from our self-consciousness—our personal experience of ability to move our limbs, or to resist our natural impulses. We have no other index of power. Will, in short, is the suggestion of Cause, which we transfer to the world at large. And in making such a transference, we follow strictly, as it has been recently said, 'the scientific instinct and the scientific process. We are putting into the same class the motions that we observe in other things and the motions we observe in ourselves.'[1] The idea of Cause thus originated 'becomes expanded into law, as we recognise its communication from one thing to another,' and so on indefinitely in continuous and regular succession. This is what Mr. Mill calls the 'invariableness' of the order of Nature. But 'invariableness' first of all is not the true note of Causation. This note is origination and not order, invariable or otherwise, as he constantly makes it. The word retains to the last the traces of its origin, and when men speak of a cause they do not mean the mere antecedent of a phenomenon, but the original power which called it into being. Secondly, 'invariableness' can only be predicated, even of the order of Nature, by assuming that there is nothing behind this order, and that our experience of its uniformity has never been broken and never can be broken. But no experience can justify a conclusion of this kind. It may justify a presumption; it cannot generate an absolute and necessary truth; and especially in the face of the suggestion of a Power behind phenomena that lies within the very idea of Cause from the first. We cannot,

[1] Bishop Temple's Bampton Lectures on the *Relation between Religion and Science*, p. 21.

without inverting the order of knowledge, convert the external uniformity of Nature into an iron necessity, which *de facto* excludes the fact through which alone we have been able to rise to the apprehension of Causation or uniformity in Nature at all.

When we look at this great question from the moral side, Mr. Mill's cardinal doctrine becomes still more untenable. As even science may be said to begin with will, so all morality and religion not only begin, but end with the same central fact of human life. The moral law has no meaning, save as applied to that self-consciousness within us which is ever the same amidst all the changes of our external life, and the modifications of our moral growth. The commands which it lays upon us are commands addressed to our wills—in other words, to ourselves—ever the same in virtue of the mysterious gift of personality. It is only thus we become responsible, and in contrast with all other creatures enter within the circle of moral and religious aspiration. If the will be a fiction, a mere cluster of hereditary instincts indissolubly bound together by the law of association, and the growth throughout, therefore, of circumstance, it seems unintelligible how the ideas of right and wrong should cling to us as they do—how in short what we mean by conscience should arise. The sense of right and wrong rests on an absolute feeling that we are free to choose the good and avoid the evil. Moral ideas are no doubt largely developed by association and circumstance, but moral acts come from our own free choice in such a sense at least as that the deepest misery may spring from wrong action. It seems impossible to explain this save by recognising Will

as an original power within us, and conscience as its
Divine guide. If Will be the growth of circumstance,
conscience can only be a calculation of chances. And
how in such a case should it ever accuse and condemn
us? We can never really act otherwise than we do.
And yet that we can so act, and have frequently
failed so to act, is the experience of every higher
nature. The sting of a lost good is that we ourselves
lost it. The misery of a present evil is that we ourselves did it. Once admit the thought that the good
was never in our power, and the evil a necessary
sequence in our life, and the whole fabric, both of
religion and morality, disappears. Responsibility in
any true sense vanishes. Nay, self-consciousness becomes a dream. For the very essence of this consciousness is that it erects itself against the law of
causality, which is supposed to bind all being in order,
and to explain all. It refuses this explanation. It
says, 'I am not bound. I am free to choose the evil or
the good. I am more than nature, or any product
of nature. I may be crushed by its laws, but I am
more than any of its laws. I have that within me
which no mere circumstance has given. I have will
and conscience, and divine reason. I am the child
of God, and the inspiration of the Almighty hath
given me understanding.'

All true morality and religion, therefore, imply in
man a breach of Mill's law of natural causation. In
other words, the experience-philosophy, of which he
was the great teacher, is a philosophy inadequate
to grasp the realities of human nature and life.
There is more in man than is dreamt of in this
philosophy; and the whole course of its expositor's

own intellectual development was so far an evidence of this. He maintained to the last that character, like all natural phenomena, is born of circumstance; but he allowed for what he called the action of the will upon circumstances, and seemed to himself in this way to discriminate between his doctrine of necessity and the common interpretation of that doctrine as fatalism. But his reserves were merely sentimental; they were forced upon him by the urgency of facts to which he could not shut his eyes. They did not spring from any change in his point of departure; and his system was really fatalistic, whatever he thought of it. He held it with less clearness and firmness the longer he lived. He had neither the hardihood nor the coarseness of *the true faith* which animated his father and his father's unhesitating followers. This really argued that he had higher elements of character and more comprehension of thought than they had, although they did not think so. His very hesitations in the full acceptance of his father's creed were tributes to a more expansive philosophy, and although he never reached the clear heaven of such a philosophy, he left behind him enough to confound the partisans of that narrow no-faith which have made such a boast of his name.

This brings us to the consideration of his special view of religion, as explained in his posthumous essays. It is evident from these essays that the subject of religion fascinated him, studiously as he had been trained without any knowledge of it. Not only so, but he came to realise—with all his loyalty to his father's main teaching—that religion was a far more important factor in human life than he had been led

to believe.   All the same the savour of his hereditary
teaching remained, and mixed itself with all his
thought.   His father's pessimism, for example, in-
tensified by a vein of intellectual pride, partly inherited and partly his own, appears prominently in
the first essay on 'Nature.'   James Mill thought very
little of the world.   It was to him upon the whole a
bad world.   Human life was 'a poor thing at the
best.'   The son turned the father's thought—which
was also his own—into a sort of philosophy.   It is difficult to say whether Christianity was more obnoxious
to him than 'the optimistic Deism or worship of
the order of Nature,' to which modern scepticism
has so much inclined, and more than ever since his
time.   A 'natural religion' like that recently expounded under this name, would have seemed to him
essentially unreasonable.   Nature, so far from being
to him an object of admiration, as it was to Wordsworth and the author of *Natural Religion*, was, on
the contrary, a cruel and mischievous power.   'All
the things which men are hanged or imprisoned for
doing to one another, are,' in his opinion, 'Nature's
everyday performances.'   No writer of sane mental
comprehension has ever drawn such an indictment
against nature.   He does not even give it the credit
of that 'order' of which he elsewhere speaks so
much.   Disorder is rather 'a counterpart of Nature's
ways,' he says.   'Anarchy and the Reign of Terror
are overmatched in injustice, even as death, by a
hurricane and a pestilence.'

This tone of superiority to the world,—as if it
might have been better if they had had the making of
it,—is a remarkable feature in the intellectual char-

acter of both the Mills. They seem to have been unconscious of the strange intellectual presumption it implied, and its essential inconsistency with the fundamental principle of their own philosophy. For if Nature be supreme in its facts and laws, and there be nothing but a development of Nature, it seems, to say the least, to be an unreasonable philosophical attitude to indulge in abuse of it or its manifestations. Mill not only does this, but in the most elaborate of his essays—that on Theism—he may be said to construct a Theistic theory on his recognition of the imperfections of the world. It was this essay which, more than the others, proved a stumbling-block to the school which looked to him as its chief apostle. It is a tribute so far to the candour and openness of mind which characterised him beyond all the other members of his school, but it is in some respects the least successful of all his writings. In his treatment of the argument for a First Cause, he recurs to the old thought which pervades the chapter on Causation in the *Logic*, and which we may be excused therefore from still further glancing at. 'All the power that Will possesses over phenomena,' he contends, 'is shared by other and far more powerful agents,' such as heat and electricity, which evolve motion on a far larger scale than human volition. And what right have we therefore, he virtually asks, just as Hume did, to conceive of intelligent will or mind as the original cause of all things? 'what peculiar privilege has this little agitation of the brain which we call thought, that we must make it the model of the universe?' None at all, we admit, on a mere phenomenal basis. But once suppose that there is more in heaven and earth than we can gather from the knowledge of phenomena—that man is more than matter—that mind is more than any combination of matter, and all analogy between mental force and other forms of force disappears. Does it not even disappear when the facts are looked at in themselves ? All forms of material force are obviously in themselves mere transformations. They operate unconsciously ; they are merely *changes*—transferences. *We* recognise force in them because we have experience of force in ourselves ; but they do not themselves yield the idea of force. We could never get the idea from them ; and therefore Comte, the most consistent of all phenomenalists, would have the term disused as misleading—as implying something of which we have no knowledge. The idea of force is only given in the action of mind ; it is the product of self-consciousness—of nothing else. And does not this separate conscious Will from all other facts in Nature ? It is confessedly intranslatable. No process of merely natural change can generate it. Does it not, therefore, by its very character, stand apart from the category of matter, and compel us to recognise its distinction ? Does not, in short, the purely scientific view of mind, as something in experience absolutely apart from all other motor forces in the world, lead us up to the theological view that mind, as self-conscious, is a singular power—an efflux from a higher Source than matter ?

It may be impossible to prove Mind to be what the Christian heart believes it to be, and so to infer that the Primal Force or First Cause of the Universe must be a Supreme Mind—and nothing less. Facts are so far in favour of the theistic hypothesis. So far as experience extends, Mind cannot be generated from any other or inferior force, or any combination of Matter and Force. On this ground the Theist holds it to be *sui generis*—a Divine particle implying a Divine Author. But even if this cannot be proved, it seems evident that a Divine Author or Creative Mind can only be argued on the basis that Mind is something more than any mere function of matter. What otherwise comes of the principle of Design?— with which Mr. Mill, no less than the Theist, largely works. He is greatly in favour of Design in Creation. Repudiating all other evidences of Theism, he thinks that the argument from marks of Design in Nature is ' of a really scientific character.' He does not allow the argument to the extent of the Christian Theist. The ' marks of Design' appear to him to imply an Evil as well as a Good Power, or at least an imperfect Power. There is evidence of benevolent Design, but it is also evident he thinks that benevolent Design has been hemmed in and hindered by lack of adequate power or intractableness of material. But leaving aside the character of his conclusion, of which we have already said enough, is there not a radical weakness at the root of any Design argument in his hands? for if mind be a mere quality or outcome of matter, we may certainly ask, with Hume, why should it be made ' the model of the universe'? What right have we to transfer it to natural phenomena at all as their explanation? Design is only intelligible as the purposeful operation of an intelligent will. It is essentially the expression of such a will. And is this not already to own an intelligence behind the order of Nature? Does not Theism of any kind, in short, even such Theism as Mr. Mill's, imply a metaphysical basis—an intelligent will operating behind the changes of experience; while a philosophy like Mr. Mill's, which *ab initio* denies that there is anything at all behind experience, and makes the will itself merely a phenomenon, really leaves no room for Will in Nature at all. No analogy of mere experience can enable us to find in Nature what we do not recognise in ourselves. The whole fabric of Mr. Mill's Theism therefore tumbles to the ground. It is the old story again of *Nullus spiritus in Microcosmo, nullus Deus in Macrocosmo.* Blot out the Divine in Man, and no Divine can be found in Nature. Soul and God are essentially co-relative, and if soul is denied, God, or a Creative Mind, can nowhere be found.

It is remarkable how far Mr. Mill is disposed to recognise Design in Nature—as in the formation of the eye for example. Sight not being precedent, but subsequent to the organic structure of the eye, this structure can only be explained by an antecedent idea as the efficient cause. 'And this at once marks the organ as proceeding from an intelligent Will.' But is not the idea of an intelligent Will essentially metaphysical? It has no meaning as a mere educt of experience. Intelligence may be predicated on a mere basis of observation, but an intelligent Will—Mind as a creative or original agent—is something deeper than any mere experience, and lies at the background of all experience. We cannot play with words in this manner; we cannot use 'Design' and speak of 'an intelligent will,' and yet maintain a merely phenomenal basis.

The distinction of the two systems of thought is radical, and there is no binding the two together. Atheism is the consistent result of Phenomenalism, and by its very premises shuts out the Divine both in Man and Nature. It holds all life throughout in its everlasting grasp, and there is no getting behind it. Because, *ex hypothesi*, there is nothing behind,— there is no metaphysic.

There can hardly be a doubt therefore that what were supposed to be Mill's earlier views were the true logical outcome of his mode of thought, far more than the pallid Theism propounded by him in his posthumous essay, which recognised a Creator, but denied to Him either full benevolence, or the power to carry his benevolent purposes into effect. A God thus limited—whose hand is shortened that it can not save, is no God at all, and no religion worth speaking of could rest on such a basis.

It may be asked, then, What is the value of Mr. Mill's thinking upon religion? Is it not purely negative? Even if it were so, it would claim our attention. The advocates of a thesis can never overlook the anti-thesis, and those who defend it. The very breadth of Mr. Mill's negations and the negations of his school has been of service to religious thought. The thoroughness of his logical analysis on one side has led to a more thorough analysis on the other side. The ideas of Order, of Miracle, of Free Will, have all come forth from his searching logic more clear and intelligible. They have been set in a higher light, and Christian reason has come to see how unworthy were some of its old conceptions on such subjects.

But Mr. J. S. Mill has not merely done this negative work in religious thought. He has done much more. The effect of his thoroughgoing criticism has been to make clearer than before the roots of the great opposing lines of thought, on which all higher speculation rests. In the end, on either side, a postulate stares us in the face. Man is either divine from the first—a free spiritual being standing apart from all nature,—or he is essentially material. On the latter basis, no religion in the old sense can be based. All attempts to find spirit in matter, if spirit is not already presupposed as prior to matter, is a mere futile imagination. All attempts to reach God through Nature, the Unseen through the seen, must necessarily fail. We can never gain from natural law anything but some product of that law. Once bring man within the chain of causation binding the life of nature, and there is no rational outlet towards the Divine. The Divine may be held by faith as an hypothesis running parallel with the natural ; but it cannot in such a case be established on any grounds of reason. This result was apparent enough long ago, when Hume delighted to emphasise the absolute separation between faith and reason ; but it has been scientifically exhibited by Mill. He shrank from the downright atheism to which his principles inevitably lead ; but the real drift of these principles is nowhere obscure. Determinism in philosophy lands in the negation of all religion. Religion may be tacked on by faith or superstition to a Determinist Philosophy or Doctrine of Necessity; but it cannot be rationally evolved from it. And thinkers like Baden Powell in our own time, or Chalmers and Jonathan Edwards in former times, who attempted to combine Determinism with Christianity, have all failed, with whatever power of argument. They started from a wrong beginning. The marches between the great lines of thought have been thoroughly cleared by help of Mill's logic and other books of the same school. They are not likely to be obscured again; and this of itself is to have done a great service to religious thought.

But yet, again, Mill has done service in vindicating everywhere the moral side of religion. It was in fact his tendency in all his writings to confound morality with religion. Setting aside, as he did, the Divine as an imaginary sphere, and yet recognising so strongly the moral and social bonds that make so large a part of religion, it was inevitable that he should exalt these human aspects of the subject. They were estimated not unduly in themselves, but disproportionately in comparison with others. But the very emphasis with which our philosopher dwelt on moral attributes in relation to the Divine Being, as well as to human society, was of great value. If it tended to bring down religion from heaven to earth, it also tended to purge the Heavenly Ideal of all grosser taint. Nothing could be further from the truth than the picture of the Christian God given by both the Mills; but it is not to be denied that there lies in all religious systems an inclination to conceive of God more or less after an arbitrary manner, as dealing with mankind on other principles than those of pure Morality, notwithstanding that this moral conception of the Divine is everywhere supreme in the

Gospels. This is a perilous inclination, and not undeserving the indignation it excited in their minds. The famous passage in the *Examination* of Hamilton's Philosophy, which sent a thrill through many Christian hearts, had a tinge in it of that intellectual pride of which we have already spoken ; but it also breathed a fine moral intensity.[1] Nothing but degradation can come to religion from lowering the Divine Ideal beneath the Ideal of the highest good that we can ourselves conceive. The true ideal of Christian thought is not only more real, but more perfect and beautiful than any human ideal whatever.

We have spoken in the main of Mr. John Stuart Mill throughout this lecture, and rightly so ; for all the special influences of his school were concentrated in him. He was himself more than all its other members. Two other names, however, claim to be mentioned before we close.

The first of these, Mr. Grote's, is by itself, and in

[1] 'If, instead of the "glad tidings" that there exists a Being in whom all the excellencies which the highest human mind can ever conceive exist in a degree inconceivable to us, I am informed that the world is ruled by a Being whose attributes are infinite, but what they are we cannot learn, nor what are the principles of his government, except that the highest human morality, which we are capable of conceiving, does not sanction them, convince me of it, and I will bear my fate as I may. But when I am told that I must believe this, and, at the same time, call this Being by all the names which express and affirm the highest human morality, I say in plain terms that I will not. Whatever power such a Being may have over me, there is one thing which he shall not do. He shall not compel me to worship him. I will call no Being good who is not what I mean when I apply that epithet to my fellow-creatures ; and if such a Being can sentence me to Hell for not so calling him, to Hell I will go.'—*Exam. of Sir William Hamilton's Philosophy*, pp. 123-4.

connection with his own special province of Greek literature and history, a great name, inferior to none in the nineteenth century. But it has little bearing comparatively upon our subject. Mr. George Grote was in philosophy and general intellectual spirit the pupil of James Mill. He came under his influence about 1819, when Mill was about 46 years of age, in the very height of his intellectual power, and Grote himself was 25 years of age. Previously he had been devoted to his profession (banking) and study, but without showing any marked religious or political tendencies. His mother is said to have been strongly inclined to Calvinistic religion, of which there is no trace in the son. Possibly it may have inclined him, by way of reaction, as in similar cases, to the opposite principles which he soon imbibed. The original bond of union between Mill and Grote was Mr. David Ricardo, the well-known political economist, in connection with whose studies the younger mind chiefly sought instruction at the hands of one whom he felt to be a master. But the ascendency of Mill's influence soon showed itself, not only in such subjects, but still more in the views adopted by Grote regarding Political Philosophy, Theology, and Ethics. According to Mrs. Grote, her husband soon found himself 'enthralled in the circle of Mill's speculations, and after a year or two of intimate commerce, there existed but little difference in point of opinion between master and pupil. The pupil not only imbibed what may be reasonably called the opinions, but no less the prejudices of his master.' Mr. Mill entertained a profound feeling against the Established Church, and a corresponding dislike of its members, and Mr. Grote was carried away in the same 'current of antipathy.' There is an unconscious irony in Mrs. Grote's description. She seems to think it creditable to her husband, rather than otherwise, that he should have shared Mill's narrow dogmatism and prejudices, no less than his reasoned conclusions.

There is no evidence in Grote's life, as related by his widow, that he himself ever examined the religious problems whose negative settlement he accepted with such a curious deference from James Mill. Masterly and critical as his intellect was in his own departments of study, he is a striking example of a common characteristic of the course of modern negative speculation. The basis of this speculation is professedly inquiry. It is supposed by those whom its current has swept away so abundantly in recent times to be the result of the irresistible progress of the human intellect. Yet no body of religious disciples have ever followed the voice of authority with more unhesitating decision than a large proportion of the professed army of Modern Unbelief. They have surrendered themselves with the most melancholy monotony to the voice of some master or other, without any genuine inquiry on their own part, or even any knowledge sometimes of the real character of the conclusions from which they dissent. It is indeed a pitiful comment on the weakness of human nature that the anti-Christendom of modern times has reproduced in flagrant forms two of the worst vices of Mediæval Christendom—its intolerance and vulgar deference to authority.

Apparently the negations as to religion into which George Grote's mind settled thus early, under the teaching of James Mill, never left him. He dismissed altogether and with contempt the subject of Theology from his mind. The 'antipathies of his teacher,' it is admitted by Mrs. Grote, 'coloured his mind through the whole period of his ripe meridian age, and inspired and directed many of the important actions of his life.' This is a somewhat sad confession to make, but it is made without any shame, and is, no doubt, honest. There was a certain element of loyalty in Grote's devotion, and a certain simplicity—it is impossible to say, largeness of mind—in the enthusiasm with which he maintained the negations of his early creed, and even quarrelled with James Mill's illustrious son, as being a comparatively unfaithful advocate of 'the true faith,' according to his father. If there are any of John Stuart Mill's writings more nobly creditable to him than others—more marked by luminous and truly wise comprehension, it is his two articles on Bentham and Coleridge, which appeared respectively in 1838 and in 1840, in the *London and Westminster Review*, and are found in the first volume of his collected *Discussions*. But for the very reason that all open minds must admire these writings, they were particularly offensive to the 'straitest sect' of his father's school, and to none more so than to Grote and his wife. There is an unpleasant revelation on this subject—to which we have already adverted—in Dr. Bain's volume.[1] No orthodox teachers, at variance on some abstruse point of their common divinity, could use more disrespectful language to one another than Mrs. Grote does in conveying her own and her husband's opinion of what

[1] *J. S. Mill: a Criticism*, pp. 56-57.

she is pleased to call ' the stuff and nonsense' of these papers.

Mr. Grote must be pronounced, therefore, more of a Millite than John Stuart Mill himself. His attitude in the well-known controversy as to the Chair of Logic in University College in 1866, when Dr. James Martineau was a candidate, and was defeated almost entirely by his influence, is an unpleasant illustration of the same extreme tendency. The event is not one on which we are called to dwell ; but it is highly significant, as showing how thoroughly so great an intellect can shut out all the influence of higher religious speculation, and intrench itself with undeviating complacency within the narrowest limits on so great a subject. This very intensity of negative dogmatism made Grote, to some extent, a power in his time even in relation to religion ; it is the warrant of our touching his career at all in a manner in which we would rather have refrained from doing, seeing how great a figure he is otherwise. But the limits within which he confined his mind on this subject prove sufficiently that he was not, in any real sense, a teacher, and he can hardly be said to have exercised any definite influence on the development of religious thought.

George Henry Lewes was in all respects a different type of man, versatile, accomplished, in a sense learned—acute and ingenious as a philosophical thinker. We have no means of tracing the growth of his negative convictions, but they were fully matured in 1845, when the first volume of his *Biographical*

History of Philosophy appeared. One of the chief notes of this book—in its earliest and latest form alike,[1] its characteristic note—was its antipathy to philosophical theology, and to all the fundamental conceptions on which it rests. Mr. Lewes's idea of the history of philosophy was very like the popular notion of the play of Hamlet with the part of Hamlet missed out. He did not believe in any higher or spiritual thought. All metaphysic was to him an absurdity. It was merely ' the art of amusing one's-self with method '—' l'art de s'égarer avec méthode.' No definition can be wittier or truer, he thought.

Mr. Lewes had studied John Stuart Mill's *Logic* and Comte's *Cours de Philosophie Positive*, and these he accepted as his philosophical Bible. All his earlier teaching—for he assumed in all his graver writings more or less the *rôle* of a teacher—was drawn from those two sources. He originated no special line of thought. He was the bold usher of the modern scientific spirit, and his influence chiefly consisted in the unalloyed enthusiasm with which he pushed its premisses to their legitimate conclusion. His popular *Exposition of the Positive Philosophy*, which first appeared in a succession of papers in the newspaper known as *The Leader*, probably introduced the name and the principles of Comte for the first time to many readers in this country. He had admirable gifts as a writer, whatever we may think of his powers as a thinker. His exposition was marked by a rare lucidity, and had the charm of interest, even when

---

[1] It was first published in four small volumes in Knight's Shilling Series, and finally in two large library volumes in 1867. The History was greatly enlarged in its latest form.

least satisfactory. Much of a Frenchman in many of his ways, he had the French gift of facile and happy expression.

We do not touch Mr. Lewes's later philosophical writings beginning with his important work on *Problems of Life and Mind* in 1874. They do not come within our present period of review. But he was certainly a recognisable factor in the formation of negative opinion during the fifth and sixth decades of the century;[1] nor is there any reason to doubt—doubtful as the fact long remained in many minds looking at his earlier writings—that he was a really earnest thinker almost religiously interested in the doctrines he expounded. Under the persiflage of his style he seems to have hidden a laborious and earnest purpose. This is placed beyond doubt by the reflected light which the recent life of George Eliot throws upon him as her studious companion for so many years. No candid reader can refuse to admit,—whatever estimate he may otherwise form of these volumes,—that Lewes's character and mental ambition both appear in a better aspect than many before would have been disposed to regard them. We may differ from him and the principles which lay at the root of all his mental work, but he was plainly a man who had convictions, and who devoted his life with an increasing devotion to their propagation. He was by no means an original, nor perhaps, even in his latest efforts, a

[1] 'Mr. Lewes had a letter from a working man at Leicester who said that he and some fellow-students met together on a Sunday to read the book aloud (*Biographical History of Philosophy*) and discuss it.'— *George Eliot's Life*, vol. i. p. 467.

profound worker in the great modern anti-theological school. But at any rate it was not out of mere lightness of heart that he joined the army of Negationists. He believed he had something better than any theology to give his generation, and if his belief was delusive it was at least no unworthy motive that inspired it.

Christian thought may learn a good deal even from works like Lewes's. There was an admirable directness and lucidity in many of his anti-theological arguments. His very exaggerations,—as in his frequent antitheses of law and will, science and moral freedom,—served to bring out confusions apt to underlie forms of Christian opinion, just as George Eliot's trenchant exposure of Cummingism served to bring out the crudities of popular religion. Thought that is really true and well founded never suffers from such exposures. Its weaknesses are cast out in the fierce light that is made to beat upon it. Whatever it may have to throw away as useless encumbrance in the conflict, it comes out tried as by fire, and hence purified and enlarged in its central and essential principles.

VII

FREDERICK DENISON MAURICE AND
CHARLES KINGSLEY.

I T is remarkable within how brief a period all the
forces of thought which we have reviewed in the
preceding lectures were comprised. Our earliest
starting-point was 1820, when Mr. Erskine's first
book was published. But it can hardly be said that
there was any movement of fresh intelligence in
religion till the appearance of Coleridge's *Aids to
Reflection* in 1825. This third decade of the century
also marks the rise of the early Oriel School. The
next decade gives us not only the rise but the
decline of the original Oxford movement. Carlyle's
characteristic principles were all worked out when he
went to London in 1834; and John Stuart Mill, the
latest factor in the series of movements, had elaborated his Logic and his cardinal doctrines by 1843.
Even the *Biographical History of Philosophy*, if it
deserves to be mentioned, does not bring us later
than the year 1845-6. It is true that the modifications of religious opinion which began with Mr.
Erskine and Coleridge had still, as we shall see in
this lecture, a definite course to run; while the
negative mode of thought which had set in with

the Mills, and was diligently propagated by Lewes and others, was far from having spent itself. New and fertile developments were awaiting it in the writings of Mr. Herbert Spencer and others. But these developments belong to what may be called the scientific epoch of Negativism or Agnosticism, with which our present lectures are not concerned. What especially deserves notice at present is the rapidity with which a crowd of new ideas which only commenced with the end of the first quarter of the century developed themselves. It was 1825 before they had begun to move the national mind ; by 1845 they had not spent their strength, but had attained to their full *momentum*. A period of about twenty years had seen them rise in quick succession and grow to their full height. There has been no more vital or germinant epoch in the history of British thought.

The natural result followed. With the significant exception,—which now awaits our attention,—there set in a period of sceptical languor. The failure of the Oxford movement especially produced a strong reaction, which worked powerfully in many minds to the distrust of all religious truth. This was the time of which Mr. Froude speaks in his life of Carlyle, when he and a companion band of truth-seekers were driven into the wilderness in search of something in which they could believe—some certainty on which they could stand. He and others found a refuge in Carlylism, but many found no such refuge. His own early volumes—now rarely met with—*The Shadows of the Clouds* (1847) and the *Nemesis of Faith* (1849) ; the poems of Clough,

who at this time broke away from Oxford and resigned his fellowship ; the *Phases of Faith* of Francis
Newman (1849), who then also parted with his early
Evangelicalism ; the struggles after a higher belief
which meet us in the lives of Kingsley and Frederick
Robertson ; all testify to the sceptical weariness
which in these years overtook many minds of the
younger generation.   No finer spirit than Clough's was
ever wrecked on the ocean of doubt, and Frederick
Robertson, we shall see, bore to the last the impress
of the suffering through which he then passed.   It
was in the same years that John Sterling's faith
disappeared ; and Matthew Arnold's first poems,
with all their divine despair, although not published till a later date (1853), were born of the
same time of spiritual darkness, when the sun of
faith went down on so many hearts.

The recent life of George Eliot has served to
bring into prominence some of the special disinte-
grating influences of this time.   George Eliot herself
belongs upon the whole to the later or 'Scientific'
era, which marks itself off from the period now under
review.   It was not till after 1855, and her conjunction with such fellow-workers as Mr. Herbert Spencer
and Mr. Lewes, that her unbelief assumed a definite
form.   But she and her friends the Hennells and
Brays bear ample testimony to the disintegration of
belief in the preceding decade.   An ardent Evangelical in 1840, she had left off her old faith in the
following year, influenced in the main by a book of
Charles Hennell's entitled *An Inquiry concerning the
Origin of Christianity.*   There is no evidence of her
having been attracted by the Oxford Theology ; but

she had read with interest, and some disturbance of thought, Isaac Taylor's animadversions on that Theology in *Ancient Christianity* (August 1840). Probably the contrast between the faith in which she had been brought up and the opinions of many of the Fathers was a somewhat harsh awakening to her, and while in this state of mind the views presented by the Brays and the line of inquiry started by Mr. Hennell laid hold of her, and led her in the purely sceptical direction which she followed for the next ten years.

Miss Evans herself, whatever we may think of her conclusions, was strong as a sceptic, as in all other respects. There is no weakness in any of her work. Her translation of Strauss, begun in 1843 and published in 1846, is a masterpiece of its kind, and no less her subsequent translation of Feuerbach's *Essence of Christianity.* But the influences that surrounded her in those years were not of a high order. The Brays and Hennells were people of more than usual intellectuality ; but the *Philosophy of Necessity* by Charles Bray and Charles Hennell's *Inquiry* are neither of them very profound or interesting books. Mr. Bray reminds us, as a writer, of George Combe, and is a less original thinker of the same school. He was, as his recent biography shows, full of that singular self-elation characteristic of second-class intellectual men when they hit, as they suppose, upon new veins of thought. Hennell's volume opened a line of inquiry in this country akin to that of Strauss and the Tübingen School in Germany. It was translated into German under Strauss's own direction, and is not without a certain bald

acuteness ; but its historical criticism, notwithstanding the commendation of George Eliot, is shallow and
meagre,—one of its main features being the derivative
connection of Christianity with the Essenes—a supposition now proved quite baseless,[1] as indeed, to any
one who understood either Essenism or Christianity,
it was always a bad guess.

Of all the sceptical group which surrounded George
Eliot in those years there is not one save herself who
will be remembered for anything that they did.   The
world had indeed forgotten them till brought to life
again in her letters.   Even Mackay's *Progress of the
Intellect*, a work which she much admired, and
reviewed for the 'Westminster' in 1859, is not only
a dull book, but to a large extent on false lines.   It
seems strange that lesser *illuminati* of this kind,
known to the world at the time mainly in connection with Mr. Chapman the publisher of the
'Westminster,' and the series of anti-Christian
volumes which issued from his press, should have
influenced so much as they did a mind like George
Eliot's.   Sara Hennell,[2] notwithstanding her chaotic
style, is the only one besides George Eliot herself
with any real genius.   There is a sense of power in
her, inarticulate as it often is, which explains her
long mental association with the translator of Strauss
and the author of *Romola*.   In none of them, however—not even in George Eliot—can we trace any
large knowledge of the Christianity they so readily

[1] See Bishop Lightfoot's elaborate discussion of the subject,—*The
Epistle of St. Paul to the Colossians*, p. 114 *et seq.*

[2] Particularly in Sara Hennell's *Thoughts in Aid of Faith* (1860)
there are some striking and interesting trains of reflection.

abandoned, or any genuine historic insight into the problem of its origin. The originality of Christ's character, in absolute distinction from all else in the Jewish thought or imagination of the time, is unappreciated. The spiritual side of Christianity in its sense of Sin and revelation of Divine Pity and forgiveness is unfelt. The transcendency of the Divine Life depicted in the Gospels finds no echo in their hearts. Religion even to George Eliot is not an inner power of Divine mystery awakening the conscience. It is at best an intellectual exercise, or a scenic picture, or a beautiful memory. Her early Evangelicalism peeled off her like an outer garment, leaving behind only a rich vein of dramatic experience which she afterwards worked into her novels. There is no evidence of her great change having produced in her any spiritual anxiety. There is nothing indeed in autobiography more wonderful than the facility with which this remarkable woman parted first with her faith and then with the moral sanctions which do so much to consecrate life, while yet constantly idealising life in her letters, and taking such a large grasp of many of its moral realities. Her scepticism and then her eclectic Humanitarianism have a certain benignancy and elevation unlike vulgar infidelity of any kind. There are gleams of a higher life everywhere in her thought. There is much self-distrust, but no self-abasement. There is a strange externality,—as if the Divine had never come near to her save by outward form or picture,—never pierced to any dividing asunder of soul and spirit. Amidst all her sadness—and her life upon the whole is a very sad one—there are no depths of spiritual dread (of which dramatically—as in *Romola*—she had yet a vivid conception), or even of spiritual tenderness. We do not look to minds of this stamp —into which the arrows of conscience make only slight wounds—for a true estimate of Christianity either in its Divine character or origin.

But amongst all the scepticism of this time, and in direct connection with it, there arose a new and powerful religious influence. This has received the name of the ' Broad Church' movement, and, for the sake of convenience, we shall use the expression. It is necessary, however, to say that the name is not only apt to mislead, but was entirely disowned by the chief theologian to whom, with others, popular usage has applied it. As late as 1860 Mr. Maurice says that he does not know what ' Broad Church' means, but that if it means anything it must apply to followers of the Whately school,—of which he was certainly not one. He was, beyond all doubt, right in this. Mr. Maurice's great deficiency as a theologian, as we shall have occasion to point out, is just his deficiency in certain critical qualities that belonged to Whately and others, and gave an historic breadth to many of their conclusions. But the name ' Broad Church ' has also come to denote a species of universalism—or breadth of doctrinal sentiment— which was not only not at variance with Mr. Maurice's standpoint, but may be held characteristic of the men to whom it is commonly applied.

The name ' Broad Church' is said to have been first used by Dean Stanley in an article in the *Edinburgh Review* in July 1850 on the Gorham controversy. His words were to the effect that the Church of England was 'by the very condition of its being neither High nor Low, but Broad.' In the original use of the word, therefore, there was no intention of characterising any party. The meaning rather was that the Church of England was of no party, and embraced by its constitution and history all the different sides of spiritual truth. In this sense the name would not have been repudiated, but would have been willingly accepted by Mr. Maurice.[1] His whole teaching was a protest against party spirit or sectarianism of every kind. A few years after Dean Stanley's article, however, there appeared in the same review a striking paper by Mr. Conybeare on 'Church Parties,' and here the name was distinctly applied in a party sense as denoting a succession of Liberal no less than Anglo-Catholic and Evangelical teachers, which have always prevailed within the English Church. This is the historic and best sense of the word, if it is to be used in a party sense at all. It will be apparent, as we proceed, how far Maurice and Kingsley are rightly identified with the great succession of liberal thinkers in the Church of England.

Maurice's early associations identify him with the broadest principles of the Church of England. No less than his friend Sterling he was an admiring student of Coleridge, and deeply indebted to his writings. Mr. John Stuart Mill welcomed them both

---

[1] This is plain from his own language in speaking of the English Church being *broad* enough to comprehend persons so unlike as Whately and Julius Hare, meaning thereby, as he is careful to explain, that 'she can claim their talents and different qualities of mind for her service.'

as Coleridgians to the debates in which he delighted
in 1826. In those debates Maurice himself tells us that
'he defended Coleridge's metaphysics' against the utilitarians. He elsewhere says that Coleridge [1] had done
much to preserve him from infidelity. In dedicating
the second edition of his first work, *The Kingdom of
Christ*, to Mr. Derwent Coleridge, he speaks at length
of his indebtedness to his father, while at the same
time saying that he had never enjoyed the privilege
of personal intercourse with him, and offering certain
criticisms on his writings. To the *Aids to Reflection*
especially he expresses ' deep and solemn obligations.'
Whatever other influences, therefore, affected Maurice,
he struck his mental roots deeply in Coleridge. Not
only so ; but in contrast to his friend John Sterling,
he never abandoned the impulse thus communicated
to him. He remained Coleridgian in the basis of
his thought. It was the Coleridgian movement,
under whatever modifications, that he and Kingsley
really carried forward. The life of Coleridge's
thought survived the ecclesiastical turmoil of the
fourth decade of the century, and the scepticism
that followed, till it emerged strong again in their
hands. It became a new birth of religion in many
of the stronger minds of the age when Anglicanism was discredited and for a time in arrest, and
Evangelical Christianity had sunk into such teaching
as that of Dr. Cumming and the slanderous orthodoxy of the *Record*. It was the virtue of what has
been called ' Broad Churchism' that it attracted
such minds. It came as a religious power to
them, when the power of religion was at ebb-tide

[1] *Life*, vol. i. p. 177.

in other directions. Maurice and Kingsley and Frederick Robertson became the religious teachers of a generation in danger of forgetting religion altogether. They were strong while others were comparatively weak. Tennyson himself, in the whole spirit of his poetry, is the sufficient evidence of this powerful wave of religious tendency, and its ascendency over the higher minds of the time. 'Strong Son of God, Immortal Love,' might be taken as the keynote of the movement, and the closing verse of 'In Memoriam' as a summary of its thought—

> 'That God which ever lives and loves,
> One God, one law, one element,
> And one far-off Divine event
> To which the whole creation moves.'[1]

While Coleridge formed the basis of Maurice's thought, there were other and powerful influences of a peculiar kind, that mingled in his religious culture. Few men have had a stranger religious up-bringing. His father was a Unitarian minister of the tolerant unaggressive type, which preceded Priestley and Belsham, a man of varied culture, and self-sacrificing if not zealous life. Calmly restful in his own convictions, he was content to preach the great moralities and duties of religion, as was customary in his time. His enthusiasm went out, like that of so many others of his class, into politics rather than religion. He would have been glad to lead a peace-

---

[1] See other verses still more significant of the 'Broad Church' point of view, LIV., LV., LVI., and the well-known lines—

> 'Our little systems have their day ;
> They have their day and cease to be :
> They are but broken lights of Thee,
> And Thou, O Lord, art more than they.'

ful, busy, religious life after his own fashion, farming, preaching, and keeping a school for boys. He was devoted to the good of his children, and worked hard for them, but all the while a singular trial was preparing for him in the bosom of his own family. His elder daughters (there were three older than Frederick), and then his wife, abandoned his Unitarian creed, and withdrew from his ministry. They wrote to him that they could no longer 'attend a Unitarian place of worship,' or even 'take the Communion with him.' The picture, as presented by Colonel Maurice, is a very painful one, on which we would rather not comment. If there was any type of religious thought more obnoxious than another to the Unitarian father and minister, it was Calvinism, yet to Calvinism they all betook themselves, though by different roads. Each daughter 'took up a position peculiar to herself.' The eldest joined the Church of England; the second (Anne) became a Baptist under Mr. Foster, the famous Essayist; and Mary, the third, was not 'exactly in sympathy with either of the others.' After various experiences, however, she also joined the Church of England, as all the younger members of the family seem to have done. This strongly marked religious individualism—an inheritance from the mother—explains a good deal in Mr. Maurice. No man could be in a sense less self-asserting than he was. His shy humility was from early years a marked feature of his character. But along with an almost morbid self-depreciation there was also from the first—certainly from the time that he turned his thoughts to the Church—an intense spirit of religious confidence.

Generalising from his own family experiences, he was led to certain conclusions which he held as absolute truths. These conclusions were entirely unlike those to which his sisters and mother had come. But they were held with the same tenacity and disregard of consequences. If more enlightened, they were not the less downright. When his mother assured her astonished husband that 'Calvinism *was true*,' she said what her son would never have said—but the spirit of the saying may be traced in many of his utterances.

More than this, the singular bigotry of his sisters —we cannot give it any lesser name—reappears in at least one act of his life—his rebaptism at the age of twenty-six, when he at length finally joined the Church of England, and began to prepare for her ministry. This is a truly painful incident in Mr. Maurice's career—of itself enough to show how far he was from theologians of the Whately and historical Latitudinarian school. What would any of them, Bishop Butler, or Tenison, or even Tait in our own time, have thought of such an act? If the baptismal rite of his father—always, as we are told, performed ' in the name of the Father, and of the Son, and of the Holy Ghost '—was not enough, what made it not enough? His father's imperfect faith. But is the efficacy of a rite to be judged by the precise faith of the celebrant? Or was the rite only efficacious in the Church of England? But what was this but to fall into the worst error he attributed to Dr. Pusey and the Tractarians? 'I think I was directed to do it by the Holy Spirit,' is all he says in defence of the act in a letter to one of his sisters. But what

is this but an assertion of his own private judgment
in a form which admits of no answer?

In addition to the influence of Coleridge and
of his own peculiar family experiences, there was a
third and very important factor in the formation of
Maurice's theology. If Coleridge laid the foundation,
and the strong religious individualism which he
inherited gave direction to his thought, it ultimately
took much of its form from Mr. Erskine's writings
and the theology in Scotland with which Mr.
Erskine was identified. It is difficult to fix the precise period when Mr. Erskine's mode of thinking
began to touch Mr. Maurice; but very early in his
career, before he had turned his attention to theology
as a study, it was brought under his notice in connection with his mother's religious difficulties and his own
painful feelings arising therefrom. For a time, and
while still a youth, these difficulties so clouded his
own mind, that he wrote to a lady in an extremely
gloomy tone as to his own spiritual condition and
prospects.[1] The lady was a friend of Mr. Erskine,
whose first book had then appeared, and she replied
questioning his authority for the dark suggestion
he had made of his being *destined* to misery, here
and hereafter. Her argument was exactly in the
spirit of Mr. Erskine, and obviously impressed him.
Later, when at Oxford in 1830, he formed the
acquaintance of Mr. Bruce, afterwards Lord Elgin,
Governor-General of India, and through him became
directly acquainted with Mr. Erskine's books, notably
at the time with the volume entitled *The Brazen
Serpent*, which produced a very important effect upon

[1] Vol. i. p. 43.

his mind. Long afterwards, in an autobiographical letter written for his son,[1] he says of the impressions he then received, ' I was led to ask myself what a Gospel to mankind must be; whether it must not have some other ground than the fall of Adam, and the sinful nature of man. I was helped much in finding an answer to the question by Mr. Erskine's books—I did not then know him personally—and by the sermons of Mr. Campbell. The English Church I thought was the witness for that universal redemption which the Scotch Presbyterians had declared to be incompatible with their Confessions.'[2]

From this time onwards he was deeply pondering the prospect before him of becoming a minister in the Church of England, which he became three years later.[3] All the influences which had mingled in his life continued to work powerfully, and none more so than the larger view of the Gospel, which was opened to him as he believed in Mr. Erskine's writings. In letters to his father and mother, he explains at length ' the firmly fixing basis ' of his thoughts ; and it may truly be said, as is virtually said by his son, that he never swerved from this basis. There are few, even of his after controversies, the germs of which cannot be found in these letters. He was already nearly thirty years of age, and multiplied as were his subsequent activities, the position in which he now stood when he began his ministry, was the position in which he always stood. Let us endeavour then, if we can, to state this position clearly. Of all writers there is none to whose fundamental principle it is more necessary to get an initial clue than to Mr.

[1] In 1878.   [2] Vol. i. p. 183.   [3] In January 1834.

Maurice's.   Even with such a clue his marvellous subtlety is often evasive ; without it, it is hopeless to read a coherent meaning into his several writings and controversies.

There are at least two fundamental principles that lie at the basis of all his thought. The first and most important of these, as well as the most pervading, is nowhere more clearly expressed than in a letter to his mother at this time (December 1833). His mother, as we have already seen, had embraced with his elder sisters an extreme type of Calvinism.   She had done so, however, like Cowper, without deriving any comfort from her supralapsarian doctrine.   Believing in Election as absolutely fixed, she could not yet realise that she was one of the Elect.   A more painful state of mind can hardly be imagined. His mother's spiritual distress was a constant pain to the son, while it increased his love and reverence for her.   It was especially painful in the light of the larger views that he believed had come to himself.   Nay, how far may those larger views not have been welcome to him as a reaction from the narrow and dreadful doctrine which had fascinated the minds of both his mother and sisters, and even for a time thrown a shadow over himself ?   In any case it is against the background of such a doctrine that he draws out the great antithetic principle on which all his own theology lay—the principle it may be called of 'universal redemption.' We use this expression because it is used by himself.   But like many general expressions it is misleading and indefinite.   It is necessary to clear it up therefore in his own language, if not exactly his own order of expression. 'Now, my dearest mother,' he says, 'you wish or long to believe yourself in Christ, but you are afraid to do so, because you think there is some experience that you are in him necessary to warrant that belief. Now if any man, or an angel from heaven, preach this doctrine to you, let him be accursed. You have this warrant for believing yourself in Christ, that you cannot do one loving act, you cannot obey one of God's commandments, you cannot pray, you cannot hope, you cannot love if you are not in him. . . . What then do I assert? Is there no difference between the believer and the unbeliever? Yes, the greatest difference. But the difference is not about the *fact*, but precisely in the belief of the *fact*. God tells us " In Him, that is in Christ, I have created all things, whether they be in heaven or on earth. Christ is the head of every man." Some men believe this, some men disbelieve it. Those men who disbelieve it walk after the flesh. They do not believe that they are joined to an Almighty Lord of Life— One who is mightier than the world, the flesh, and the devil—One who is nearer to them than their own flesh. . . . But though tens of hundreds of thousands of men so live, we are forbidden by Christian truth and the Catholic Church to call this the *real* state of any man. The truth is *that every man is in Christ;* the condemnation of every man is that he will not *own the truth*—he will not act as if it were *true* that except he were joined to Christ he could not think, breathe, live a single hour.'[1]

Here, in these emphatic words to his mother, we

[1] Vol. i. pp. 155-6.

get to the heart of Mr. Maurice's theology.   It is the
very antithesis of that of his mother.   Men generally,
she believed, were not related to Christ.   Man, as
man merely, was 'under the wrath and curse of God.'
With him, on the contrary, man is divinely created
in Christ from the first.   Man, as man, is the child
of God.[1]   He does not need 'to become a child of
God;' he needs only to recognise the fact that he
already is such.

Maurice's quarrel with the popular theology
through all his life was mainly on this fundamental
ground.   It taught, he supposed, whether in the form
of High Church Anglicanism or Calvinism, that man
had 'to become a child of God.'   Instead of beginning with the divine constitution of man in Christ,
it began with the fallen evil condition of man out of
which Christ came to redeem his people, and so went
wrong radically from the first.   In one case man was
represented as becoming a child of God by baptism,
in the other by conscious conversion.   The theology
of the Bible and of the Catholic creeds was in his
view against these extremes alike.   Both were
untrue ; but popular Protestantism still more so than
Anglicanism.   He himself was 'never a Calvinist,' as
his son truly says, although its shadow passed over
him.   He had certain affinities with it, especially with
the manner in which—in contrast, as he supposed,
with Arminianism—it sets forth God and not man[2]
in the forefront of salvation.   He also appreciated
its strong grasp of moral realities.   But all that
was cardinal in his own theology was opposed
to it.   On the other hand, it seemed for a time

[1] See *Erskine's Letters*, vol. ii. p. 322.   [2] *Ibid*. p. 93.

as if he might have been caught in the High Church enthusiasm which prevailed just after he began his ministry. The High Church party had certain hopes of him at first, so much so that they did what they could in the beginning of 1837 to promote his election to the Chair of Political Economy at Oxford. They recognised his spiritual genius, and they were grateful for the help he had given them by his pamphlet *Subscription no Bondage*. But Dr. Pusey's tract on *Baptism* drove him from their side. He recurs over and over again to the pain this tract gave him. Baptism was, as may be imagined, a sensitive point with Maurice. Much of his argument in his first book, *The Kingdom of Christ*, turns upon its true meaning. He attached infinite importance to it as 'the sign of admission into a spiritual and universal kingdom grounded upon our Lord's incarnation' (of which he considered the Church of England the true representative). But the doctrine of an *opus operatum* was peculiarly repulsive to him. It implied the subversion of his fundamental principle still more than the necessity of conscious conversion. For it presupposed the communication of a new nature instead of the recognition of an original and real relation. In his own words it converted a sacrament into an event.[1] To him this was the destruction of the spiritual life and of the idea of the Church as a communion of self-renunciation and holy discipline.

The second great principle which may be said to lie at the foundation of Maurice's thought was his desire for unity.[2] He was 'haunted all his life,' he

---

[1] *Kingdom of Christ*, vol. i. p. 428.
[2] *Life*, vol. i. p. 41 ; vol. ii. p. 632.

says, 'by this desire.' He had seen the evils of dis-
union in his father's family. He thought he could
also trace there the true secret of unity. In a letter
as early as 1834 :[1] 'I would wish to live and die
for the assertion of this truth; that the universal
Church is just as much a reality as any particular
nation is; that the Church is the witness for the
true constitution of man as man, a child of God,
an heir of heaven, and taking up his pardon by
baptism; that the world is a miserable accursed
rebellious order which denies this foundation, which
will create a foundation of self-will, choice, taste,
opinion; that in the world there can be no communion; that in the Church there can be universal
communion—communion in one body by one spirit.
For this our Church of England is now, as I think,
the only firm consistent witness.' So thought also the
Newmanites. With them too—with Newman himself in particular—the note of unity was ultimately
the governing note in the idea of the Church. But
the ideas of unity were entirely different in the
two cases. Newman and his followers sought unity
in a great external organism, uniform in doctrine,
government, and worship. All outside of this
organism was heretical and schismatic, and so, as
Maurice thought, in the very effort to reach unity,
they restricted and endangered it. They imperilled
the very thing they so much prized. The true idea,
according to him, was to be found not in any negations or hard lines of demarcation indicating the
true Church, but in the conciliation of what was
positive in all Christians, and the rejection of their

[1] *Life*, vol. i. p. 166.

negations. This was how his peculiar family experience worked. Divided as his sisters were, they were in the substance of their faith united. It was their negations alone that divided them. In their affirmations they were at one. And so, out of the training of his home, as he himself admits,[1] there came the very depth of his belief in that which he declared to be 'the centre of all his belief.' He sought everywhere in the positive side of thought a source of unity very much on the old principle attributed to Leibnitz, and laid down by J. S. Mill in his paper on Coleridge, 'that thinking people were for the most part right in what they affirmed, wrong in what they denied.' In similar language Maurice says of the Anglo-Catholics, 'I sometimes feel a longing desire to set them right when I think they are misapprehending or frightening away sincere dissenters ; to say "you need not weaken one of your assertions, you may make them stronger, and yet by just this or that little alteration give them a (really) Catholic instead of an exclusive form."' Again his pupil, Mr. Strachey, makes the principle very clear, writing of Maurice's views on Baptism.[2] 'His object,' he says, '(and this is his method on all subjects), is to show that in each of the party views there is a great truth asserted, that he agrees with each party in the assertion, and maintains that it cannot defend them too strongly ; but he says each is wrong when it becomes the denier of the truth of the others, and when it assumes its portion of the truth to be the whole.'

This principle, that true Catholicity lay in leaving

[1] *Life*, vol. i. p. 41. [2] *Ib.* p. 203.

aside negations and bringing together the positive
aspects of truth, entered deeply into Maurice's whole
turn of thinking.   Applied to religion in general,
and not merely to different parties within the
Christian Church, it is the germ of the higher thought
of one of his best books, *The Religions of the World*,
to which many young thinkers were indebted nearly
forty years ago (1847), before so much was known as
now upon the subject.   It runs through all his most
elaborate work, *Moral and Metaphysical Philosophy*.
It was always springing up as a genial and fertile
seed in his varied life of thought and controversy.   It
has a latitudinarian side, and to many minds will seem
inseparable from the ordinary idea which would
make room within the Church for a variety of opinions.
But this was not Maurice's interpretation of his own
principle.   He had no patience with the inclusion of
' all kind of opinions.'   This is of the nature of profane liberalism.   Unity must come from the centre—
Christ.   On this positive ground all may unite, but
there can be no union otherwise.   Christ, as being the
head of every man, is the centre of universal fellowship, and there is no other centre.   And so the two
main principles with which he worked run into one
another.   They are not independent but inter-
dependent principles.   He expresses this plainly in
the following very characteristic passage :—' If the
person whom I then meet fraternises elsewhere on
another principle, that is nothing to me.   But if the
same person said to me, " Let us meet to-morrow at
some meeting of the Bible Society : I am an Independent, or a Baptist, or a Quaker ; you, I know, are
an Episcopalian ; but let us forget our differences and

meet on the ground of our common Christianity,"—I should say instantly, I will do no such thing. I consider that your whole scheme is a flat contradiction and a lie. You come forward with the avowal that you fraternise on some other ground than that of our union in Christ, and then you ask me to fraternise with you on that ground. I consider your sects—one and all of them—as an outrage on the Christian principle, as a denial of it. And what is the common Christianity which you speak of? The mere caput mortuum of all systems. You do not really mean us to unite in Christ as being members of his body ; you mean us to unite in holding certain notions about Christ.' [1]

Here again we get to the very core of Mr. Maurice's thought—his strange mixture of universalism and yet dogmatism—of generousness and yet severity. He could embrace all men in his Christian charity, but they must not bring their opinions to him to be tolerated. His own faith does not rest on any opinion or ' notions,' as he maintains, but on certain divine facts. That Christ *was the essential ground* of all human life, that man is created in him from the first, and has only to recognise his creative birthright ; that all men being thus equally in Christ are members of his body, united in his fellowship, if they will only own the ground of their common life—these were not opinions with him, they were of the nature of facts admitting of no question. They run through all his theology. They reappear in sermons, essays, and treatises. They furnish the key to most of his work as a Christian philanthropist as well as a Christian

[1] *Life*, vol. i. p. 258-259.

preacher.   His profound faith in them moulds all his
thought, philosophical as well as religious, explains
his views about creeds, about the Church, about sects ;
his indignation alike at the *Record* and at Mansel's
Bampton Lectures.

There never was a more mistaken idea of any man
than that which associated Maurice with a negative
or half-believing theology.   He was the most positive if not the most definite of thinkers.   He was
essentially affirmative, starting from Christ as the
great affirmation both of thought and life.   Man only
finds himself in Christ, only finds his brother there; the
true life of the individual, of the family, of the nation,
of the Church, all come from the same centre and
rest on it.   The Catholic creeds witness to this Divine
reality in all its comprehensive meaning ; he can
see nothing in them but this glorious witness.   Their
very negations become glorified in the light of this
faith.   The Scriptures everywhere speak with the
same voice.   Scholar and thinker as he was, no man
was ever less of a purely historical critic.   He saw
everywhere a reflection of his favourite ideas.   No
Alexandrian divine of the second or third century
—no Evangelical or Anglican traditionalist of later
times, ever dealt more arbitrarily with the development of Divine Revelation, or imposed his own meanings more confidently on Patriarchs and Prophets.   His
vivid faith in the Divine—the strength of his root-
convictions, amounting to a species of infallibility—
made him see from Genesis to Revelation only the
same substance of Divine dogma.

Maurice's theology was therefore profoundly dogmatic.   It was wide, generous, in a sense universal,

but it took its rise in positive principles of the most absolute kind. He is often accused of haziness and uncertainty. His idea of God was supposed by Dr. Candlish to vanish in a mere mist of ' Charity' which left no room for a Moral Governor of the universe. There is a certain ground for this assertion when we examine the details of his theological system ; but no theological system could rest more on certain great propositions, which were, as we have said, of the nature of *facts* rather than propositions to Maurice himself. They were realistic in the highest degree, like the general ideas of Platonism. He supposed himself to have a far greater regard for facts than Coleridge ;[1] but his very facts were realised abstractions rather than objective certainties.

There was beyond doubt a certain analogy between the school which gathered around Mr. Maurice and that of the Cambridge Platonists in the seventeenth century. It is not only that many common ideas lay at the root of their thinking, but they had many of the same personal excellencies and defects. They had the same elevation, the same wide tolerance and charity, the same ideal enthusiasm, but also something of the same esoteric character, the same consciousness that they were a group by themselves, pursuing a common object. With all his hatred of sects Maurice had something in him not indeed of the spirit of the sectary (no man could be freer from all the baser qualities which that name denotes), but of the spirit of an inner brotherhood. He and those who worked with him were all more or less a 'peculiar people' with special sympathies and

[1] *Life*, vol. i. p. 203.

special aims in common.   This same spirit is rife in
the Cambridge Platonists, and one of the 'notes' of
of the group.   But in a far higher respect they had
also much in common.   The truly great work of the
Cambridge Platonists in the seventeenth century was
apologetic and not dogmatic.   This was also the
special mission of Maurice and his school.   They
advanced theological inquiry by their rational spirit—
their openness to intellectual movement on all sides—
their fearless assertion of the rights of Theology in
the face of Modern Science, more than in any other
way.   Just as Cudworth and More were the living
witnesses to the Divine reasonableness of Christianity
against the fashionable Empiricism of their day, so
Maurice and Kingsley, in the midst of an atmosphere of low-breathed Scepticism on one side and
of mere formal theology on the other, were witnesses
for a Christianity which had nothing to fear from
the progress of Knowledge.   To the unbelief and
traditionalism of their time they presented a lofty
front of Christian ideality—a reassertion of Divine
fact—of man's essential Divinity in Christ, as lying
at the basis of all true thought.

This, as it appears to us, is the true point of view
from which to regard the early Broad Church movement.   It was essentially a reconstructive movement
of Christian ideas which were losing their hold on
contemporary minds.   Evangelicalism for the time
had lost its power.   Anglicanism was passing through
a crisis.   The moment of creative influence was gone
for both.   As Kingsley says in one of his letters,[1]—
' Decent Anglicanism and decent Evangelicalism

[1] *Life,* vol. i. p. 143.

were each playing the part of Canute to the tide rising around them. Men were despairing both of the religion and the social life of the country.' The real struggle was no longer, as in the preceding decade, 'between Popery and Protestantism, but between Atheism and Christ.' This may or may not be an exaggerated picture, but it was the picture that presented itself to many living and strong men like Kingsley just entering upon his career in 1846. It was the aspect in which he and many others saw the world around them.

In such circumstances the Maurice - Kingsley school elaborated their thought and took up their work. Under similar pressure as to whether Christianity remained any longer living, we shall see that Frederick Robertson spent his noble energies as a Christian preacher. It is as Christian Apologists, therefore, that they ought to be viewed and estimated in the history of modern religious thought. Unhappily they were taken by the old orthodox school for the most part differently. The prophetic side of their character and work, their truly divine insight, their living hold of the Divine Constitution of man and the world, were overlooked, and all the details of their theology polemically examined—examined and condemned from a point of view which they themselves deliberately rejected. It was Mr. Maurice's aim, in view of the half Christian or wholly materialised forms of thought around him, to reconstruct the Christian ideal that it might take its place once more in the human heart as the only power by which men can live and die. This was what he sought after more

than anything else. It was the aim in which he succeeded so far as he succeeded at all. His teaching
came as a new life-blood to many who could accept
neither Anglicanism nor Evangelicalism. It gave
them a Divine Philosophy by which they could work.
It helped them not only to believe in God, but to
realise God as the fact of facts, and Christ as ' Strong
Son of God, immortal Love,' the 'Divine Archetype
of Humanity,' in whom all human wellbeing lies.
But the religious world, so far from being grateful for
this service, for the most part assailed him and
those who agreed with him as dangerous teachers.
They looked upon them as imperilling the Ark of
God rather than rallying to its defence.

The case cannot be more clearly put than in relation to Maurice's Essays, and the painful discussions
which they raised. In these Essays Mr. Maurice was
thinking, as he tells us, of the Unitarians. It was
his aim to convince the Unitarians that if they held
to Christ and Christianity at all they must hold to
them in a deeper sense than they did. Christ is
more than they professed to own if he is the Christ
at all—the manifestation of the Father—the revealer
of His will and character to man. The author may
or may not have been successful in his aim and argument. But at any rate the issues which were raised
against him by Dr. Candlish and others were irrelevant
issues. They virtually came to this : But you are
utterly wrong in so far as you disagree with the old
Theology, and fail to recognise that God is the Moral
Governor of the universe as well as the Creator
and Father of men, and that in order to uphold
the great principles of his government sin must

be dealt with quite differently from what you suppose, and the offices and the work of Christ quite
differently conceived. The hostile critics were right
in many respects. They were able to make
many points against Mr. Maurice in the light
of the Puritan theology. But then it was not the
Puritan theology that Mr. Maurice was thinking of.
He had deliberately set aside Calvinism at the outset
of his ministry. He could find no life for his own
soul either in the Evangelical or the Anglican tradition. It was not the theology of either, but theology itself that he was contending for. He was
thinking of those who had not got the length of
St. Paul, still less of Calvin—who did not see God
as he did in the light of a Father at all, and who,
however they might reverence Christ, did not recognise in him any kind of a Saviour.

Even if it were true that Mr. Maurice's theology
fell short of the Puritan, or even of the Pauline theology, it would by no means follow that it was to be
reprobated as these critics reprobated it. If it did
rest, as some of them contended, on Platonic or Neo-
Platonic forms of thought, it may be asked, Did it do
so more than the theology of Clement of Alexandria
and Origen ; and must we deem these teachers less
Christian because they adopted certain ideas of
Platonism in the expression of Christian doctrine ?
What ancient theologian did not do so ? Is Tertullian
more orthodox than Clement, or St. Augustine than
Gregory of Nazianzus ? Is St. John not a quite
different type of theologian from St. Paul ? and St.
James from either ? And even so, is Mr. Maurice
less Christian as a theologian because he does not

speak in the same language or expound the same ideas as those which belong to a wholly different school ?

If I am asked to pronounce an opinion I must often agree with his orthodox critics against Mr. Maurice. Sin is certainly more than selfishness, and the atonement more than the perfect surrender of self-will to God. It is a satisfaction of Divine justice as well as a surrender to Divine love. God is not merely Love but Law, and Divine righteousness is strong not merely to make men righteous but to punish all unrighteousness. If it be a question between the Maurician theology and the Pauline theology, there can be no doubt that there are elements in the latter, the full significance of which Mr. Maurice failed to see. But then there are no less elements in the popular theology which St. Paul would have disowned, and St. John certainly not have understood. The idea that theology is a fixed science, with hard and fast propositions partaking of the nature of infallibility, is a superstition which cannot face the light of modern criticism.

The true attitude of the Christian thinker to Maurice and his teaching is that of gratitude and not of controversial cavil. He became a power in the spiritual world when other powers were comparatively inoperative. Whatever may have been the errors of his theology, they were errors of Divine excess. Instead of minimising man's relation to the Divine, he emphasised it. It required this note of emphasis to draw men's thoughts to theology at all, and to make it once more a factor in human thought and life. In adopting such a line of argument I am aware that

I am doing what Maurice himself would not have
done. He was too intensely dogmatic in his own convictions to accept any explanation of the peculiarities
of his creed. His creed was, as he always maintained,
the Church's creed. He was not content to be tolerated. He was right. Other theologians were wrong.
His intense spiritual activity, his theological courage,
came out of his unwavering dogmatism. He would
have repudiated, therefore, any apology for the peculiarities of his dogmatic system arising out of the circumstances of his time, and the character of his own
education. But while I feel bound so far to vindicate
his position as a Christian thinker, I am not bound to
do so on his own terms. I can see how his dogmatic
position arose, and what force there was in it in a
time of materialistic scepticism, but I also see wherein
it was undue and onesided. My business is to judge
him, and the other thinkers who have passed under
our review, historically and not dogmatically. I can
acknowledge, therefore, what was good in his theology without accepting it ; I feel bound to set forth
his value as a Christian thinker without agreeing with
him. If there is one lesson more than another that
the study of Christian opinion enforces, it is how
far men, equally Christian, may differ in theological
opinion, nay—how inevitably in the progress of
thought, theology, like philosophy, changes its point
of view without losing its essential Christian character. It is but a poor weapon to fight with when
you disagree with a theologian, to tell him he is no
longer a Christian. It is a weapon, moreover, which
can be too easily exchanged in conflict. Both
Maurice and Kingsley were really, as Bunsen said of

them, exponents of 'the deepest elements' of contemporary religious thought, and it was this, and nothing less than this, that gave them their significance and influence.

But it is now more than time to sum up certain facts of Maurice's life, and to glance at his relations with Kingsley, in so far as they illustrate the movement associated with their names. Maurice's theology was virtually complete from the outset of his career as a clergyman. A student first at Cambridge (1823-6), and then at Oxford (1829-32), he spent the interval in London as editor first of the *London Literary Chronicle*, and then of the *Athenæum*, with which the *Literary Chronicle* was united (1828). His great abilities had been recognised at Cambridge. He was the inspiring spirit there of a society called the 'Apostles' Club;' and there is an interesting letter from Arthur Hallam to Mr. Gladstone in June 1830, speaking of his influence over many of his companions. Mr. Gladstone himself witnesses to the fascination which he exercised later at Oxford over those who came in contact with him.

After his ordination (1834) he was much disturbed, with others, by the proposal to abolish the subscription at the Universities of the Thirty-nine Articles. It was at this crisis that he was brought for a time into close relation with the leaders of the Oxford movement. Considering that it was the necessity for subscribing these Articles which had precluded him from taking his degree at Cambridge, he might have been supposed favourable to the intended legislation. But, on the contrary, he now showed at the outset that strange turn for paradox which never left him in connection with public movements. The Articles had acquired to him a sudden importance as 'a declaration of the terms on which the University proposed to teach its pupils, and upon which terms they must agree to learn.' It was 'fairer to express these terms than to conceal them.' They had appeared to him at Cambridge prohibitory, as binding down the student to certain conclusions beyond which he was not to advance, but now they seemed 'helps to him in pursuing his studies.' This extraordinary refinement in argument, the tendency to see things in a different light from other people, and even from his own first plain impression, was an unhappy characteristic of Maurice all through his life. It led him, at a later time, to glorify the Athanasian Creed as peculiarly inclusive of his own faith and deepest conviction. There was nothing disingenuous in this ; but there was an absence of plain sense and of that historical point of view, of the excess of which he complained in his friend Dean Stanley. Hailed by the Oxford School for the time as an ally, he soon found how much at variance he was with them. They were thinking in the main of how Subscription kept all but themselves out of the Church. He was thinking as usual of the good that might be got out of the Articles as guides to higher study. They availed themselves of whatever help was to be got out of his early pamphlet, *Subscription no Bondage ;* but he and Dr. Pusey soon came to blows ; and the latter is said to have denounced him and his assumed zeal for Church privilege in no measured terms.

Maurice's first charge was the chaplaincy of Guy's

Hospital, which he held for eleven years,[1] during a portion of which time he was also Professor of English Literature at King's College. In the latter year he became Chaplain of Lincoln's Inn, and one of the Professors of Theology in King's College. He is particularly careful to point out in one of his letters that he was chosen to the latter post without his own seeking. It deserves also to be said that before his appointment he had already made known[2] his peculiar interpretation of the phrase 'Eternal life,' which was afterwards concerned in his dismissal from the College. Before that time he had been both Warburton and Boyle Lecturer; and it was as Boyle Lecturer that he produced the most popular of all his books already referred to, *The Religions of the World.*

In 1844 he made the acquaintance of Charles Kingsley in circumstances related in the lives of both of them. Kingsley had been working at Eversley as curate for about two years in the midst of lovely scenery, but in an utterly neglected parish. Not a grown-up man or woman in it could read when he began his ministry. The church was nearly empty; the communicants few; the water for Holy Baptism held in a cracked kitchen basin; and the alms collected in an old wooden saucer. No wonder that the parish was overrun with dissent of an extremely ignorant type. When Kingsley was settled in it as rector in the summer of 1844, he set himself with characteristic vigour to redeem the parish and the church. He was then twenty-five years of age, four-

---

[1] June 1835 to 1846.
[2] In a pamphlet on Mr. Ward's case at Oxford.

teen years younger than Maurice. He had passed
through a wholly different order of experience.
Brought up within the Church, and at Maurice's
earlier university, he had felt the spirit of the time.
The scepticism that was in the air, as the first life of
the Oxford movement died down, strongly assailed
him. The doctrine of the Trinity especially, and
what then seemed to him the 'bigotry, cruelty,
and quibbling' of the Athanasian Creed—to which
strangely, like Maurice, he too afterwards became
vehemently attached—formed his special difficulty.
His doubts, as told by himself, do not interest us
greatly. They were hard and painful, as they were
truly earnest ; but there is also a superficial air—an
absence of deeper questioning—about them. His
mind as yet evidently had not got beyond the outside of theological questions. He balances the alternatives between Tractarianism and Deism—but, in
point of fact, the former never attracted him. He was
repelled by its ' ascetic view of sacred ties,' an aspect
in which it continued to be always repulsive to him.
The books that chiefly helped him in his difficulties
were, in addition to Carlyle's writings, which were a
significant factor in his intellectual development,
Coleridge's *Aids to Reflection*, and Maurice's *Kingdom
of Christ*,[1] just then published. He had thought of a
colonial life in his temporary despair ; but already, in
1841, he could say that he was 'saved from the wild
pride and darkling tempests of Scepticism.' His
ordination and settlement at Eversley took place in
the following year.

[1] He always said that he owed more to Maurice's *Kingdom of
Christ* than to any book he had ever read.—*Life*, vol. i. p. 84.

In the midst of his parish difficulties he naturally turned to the author of the *Kingdom of Christ* for advice. Strangely, Mr. Maurice was living, in the summer of 1844, in the elder Kingsley's rectory at Chelsea, where he had gone from Guy's Hospital for change of air for his wife and children. In writing to Maurice he apologised for addressing one so much his superior ; 'but where,' he added, ' shall the young priest go for advice but to the elder prophet ? To your works I am indebted for the foundation of any coherent view of the word of God, the meaning of the Church of England, and the spiritual phenomena of the present and past ages.' There was no exaggeration in this statement. The more the lives of the two men are studied together, the more completely does it appear that Maurice was really, as styled by himself, Kingsley's ' Master ' in Theology. There was much in the Eversley Rector with which Maurice had nothing to do,—his eye for nature and colour, his love of sport, his revels by the side of a country stream or by the sea-side,—all those poetic elements which were un- doubtedly the highest in Kingsley, and made him the man of genius that he was. He had also an objective turn, both scientific and historical, which Maurice barely understood. Kingsley, in short, was a poet —which no imagination can conceive Maurice being, with the deep reflective involvements of his mind, always returning upon themselves with a torment- ing ingenuity. But there was little in Kingsley's theology which did not come more or less directly from Maurice, as he himself confesses. When he first began to feel the need of a theology, he applied to Maurice. In 1853, when the Theological Essays appeared, he wrote: 'Maurice's Essays will constitute an epoch. If the Church of England rejects them her doom is fixed. She will rot and die as the Alexandrian did before her. If she accept them not as a code complete, but as hints towards a new method of thought, she may save herself still.' And twelve years later, in 1865, when both had done the best they were ever to do, in theology and other things, it is still to Maurice he looks as his theological master. 'Your letter comforted me,' he writes, 'for (strange as it may seem to me to say so) the only thing I really care for—the only thing which gives me comfort—is theology in the strict sense; though God knows I know little enough of it. I wish one thing, that you would define for me what you mean by being "baptized into a name." The preposition in its transcendental sense puzzles me. I sometimes seem to grasp it and sometimes again lose it from the very unrealistic turn of mind which I have. As to the Trinity I do understand you. You first taught me that the doctrine was a live thing, and not a mere formula to be swallowed by the undigesting reason; and from the time that I learnt from you that a Father meant a real father, a Son a real son, and a Holy Spirit a real spirit who was really good and holy, I have been able to draw all sorts of practical lessons from it in the pulpit, and ground all my morality and a great deal of my natural philosophy upon it, and shall do so more. The procession of the Spirit from the Father and the Son, for instance, is most practically important to me. If the Spirit proceeds only from the Father, the whole theorem of the Trinity as well as its practical results fall to pieces in my mind. I don't mean that good men in the Greek Church are not better than I. On the contrary, I believe that every good man therein believes in the procession from both Father and Son, whether he thinks he does so or not.'

This letter is very interesting both on its own account and as showing how Kingsley retained the attitude of a theological pupil to Maurice. And the attitude remained to the end. In the Christian Socialist movement which brought them into such intimate fellowship in 1850, Kingsley is the inspiring as well as the inspired. He almost takes the place of leader for a time in his young and eager enthusiasm. But in theology he is throughout dependent on Maurice, and many letters pass between them on the subject. There is especially an interesting series in 1855, following Maurice's expulsion from King's College. Kingsley was then again under grave doubts concerning, among other things, Maurice's views of Sacrifice, published in reply to the attacks made upon him by Dr. Candlish. Addressing his ' dear, dear Kingsley,' Maurice takes comfort in his friend's struggles after clearer views, assured that being true to himself and to God, He will guide him into all truth. ' Do not be in the least disturbed,' he says, ' because books of mine about Sacrifice, or anything else, do not satisfy you, or show you the way out of your confusions. Why should they ? Is not the death of Christ, *and your death and mine*, a depth immeasurably below my soundings ? And what have I done, if I have done anything truly and honestly, but beseech people not to try and measure it, but simply cast themselves upon the love of God which is manifested in it, and trust it when there is nothing else in heaven above or earth beneath to rest upon?' Again he says, 'I am a Puritan almost incapable of enjoyment, though in principle justifying enjoyment as God's gift to his creatures. God has given you infinite faculties of enjoyment. But he has given you with these the higher part of being manly, and of caring for your fellow-men, and their miseries and sins. What I fear (perhaps most unreasonably) for you is that the first gift may devour the second, and that your sympathy with what is beautiful in nature and human society should make you less able to stand out against these, more tolerant of that which is eating into the hearts of individuals and nations. Godliness I am certain is the true support of manliness.'

Kingsley's name had become associated with what was called 'muscular Christianity.' The elder teacher evidently desires to caution him, as well as to emphasise his own peculiar point of view. The two men now, and at all times, stand before us in clear contrast, if the light around Maurice be wavering, as it often is. The precise contents of his thought, even in this familiar letter, are not easy to give. How singular and even more than usually vague the manner in which he speaks of the death of Christ! But then what an intense spiritual glow there is in his words! Whatever may be his intellectual hesitations, however difficult it may be to fix him down to definite propositions which any one could venture to repeat, there is never any hesitation as to his own intense faith, his realisation of the Divine love as a solid reality—a ' rock,' as he says in the same letter, ' to hold fast by, although the whole world and himself should be lost out of sight and go to the bottom.' All his subtleties and inconsistencies, as they appear to us, about the forms of Divine truth, never for a moment darken his spiritual vision. And this is Maurice throughout. The Divine Foundation · is never doubtful to him, however strange, wavering, or paradoxical the expression of his formal opinions may sometimes be. Of all men of our time he seems to me to have realised God most vividly. I do not say in his personal life—I do not venture to judge him or any man in this respect—but as the centre of all knowledge and all life, as the core of all human good, personal, domestic, social, ·national, ecclesiastical. Everything was from God with him, and all its strength came straight out of God. Religion above all he never allowed to shut out God from him as many do, as he constantly complained all religious parties did. The Bible had all its meaning to him as a direct revelation from God. It was God he everywhere saw moving through its pages and instructing him—a living God, with whom he could converse, and to whom he could go as having the words of eternal life. It was this that made him so jealous of certain modes of historical criticism, which it must be confessed he did not fully appreciate. It was this that made him prefer the word ' theology' to religion, which always seemed to him to have something of a Pagan meaning. It was this also that made him so often say that all his knowledge and thought began in theology. It was said of Novalis that he was a ' God-intoxicated man,' but of all modern men Maurice seems to me to have most deserved this name. He lived as few men have ever lived in the Divine. He was, as Mr. Gladstone has said of him, applying words from Dante, 'a spiritual splendour.' The Divine embraced him. He did not need to strive after it like most men. It was the Alpha and Omega of all his being—the only reality in comparison with which all other things were shadowy. It was this more than anything that made him the spiritual power that he was. In the presence of Maurice it was hardly possible to doubt of a Divine sphere,—of a spiritual life. While the commercial world by its selfishness was denying God, and the religious world by its slanders degrading Him, and the scientific world by its theories hiding Him from view, or proclaiming Him unknown, there was a reality in Maurice's faith that left no room for doubt. I know of no life, with all the intellectual puzzles which it presents, so intensely and powerfully Divine.

Kingsley was far less intense and *theological.* He had a broader nature, which took in more of the variety and beauty of life. He had, as Maurice acknowledged, a far higher capacity of natural enjoyment. But he too in everything—in his novel-writing, in his social efforts, in his history and science, as well as in his sermons—was a witness to the Divine. He did not glow, as Maurice did, with a Divine radiance in all he did ; he had neither his 'Master's' subtlety nor his profundity ; but he was more intelligible, healthy, and broad-minded, and he carried the spirit of Christianity as

heartily, if not as profoundly, into all his work.
Maurice was more of the Prophet both in his tenderness and occasional fierceness—Kingsley more of
the Poet. Yet with all his more concrete poetic
sympathies, the pupil was earnest as the theological
master he delighted to honour. One who knew him
well has said of him—' The two most distinctive
features of his religious teaching were that the world
is God's world and not the Devil's, and that manliness
is entirely compatible with godliness.' The former
was the manner in which he applied the great principle of his teacher that humanity and the world are
originally constituted in Christ and belong to God,
whatever footing the Devil may have got in them ;
the second was, in a sense, his own peculiar gospel,
springing out of his own high courage and love of
natural life. There was a true message in both
truths for his generation. They taught that Nature
and life were from God at a time when science on
the one hand, and asceticism on the other, tended
to sever them from His presence. If Maurice discerned more deeply the Divine constitution of things,
Kingsley, by his poetic and living sympathies, made
the Divine more visible everywhere around us.

VIII

FREDERICK W. ROBERTSON AND BISHOP EWING.

THERE is no life that mirrors more completely the spiritual conflicts of the fifth decade of our century than that of Frederick W. Robertson. And yet at first his opinions seemed set in a fixed groove. Trained in an evangelical family, he remained more or less an Evangelical till he was 27 years of age. He passed through Oxford at the time when the Anglo-Catholic movement was rising to its height. He was fascinated by it, but remained firm to the principles of his youth. He carried the same principles into the exercise of his early ministry, and it was not till after he had been a clergyman for some years that he was caught and carried away by the spirit of his time. He was of Scottish parentage, and partly educated at the Edinburgh Academy.[1] His father was a soldier, and he himself looked forward, as a boy, to the same profession. His heart, in

---

[1] Frederick W. Robertson, Suffolk, appears as second in the prize list of the Edinburgh Academy, 1832 : his friend George R. Moncrieff, standing first. There are two sets of verses—one in Latin, the other in English—attached to his name, but neither of remarkable merit.

fact, was passionately set on a soldier's career, and it was only with great reluctance that he abandoned the prospect. At first he especially recoiled from entering the Church—yet this seemed not only to his father, but to all who knew him best, the profession for which he was most fitted ; and at last his own heart, under a sense of duty, however, rather than enthusiasm, inclined in the same direction. The singular purity and devoutness of his character, his deep religious convictions which made him say, even while ardently cherishing the idea of entering the army, that his object was not ' to win laurels, but to do good ; ' his spirit of self-sacrifice and earnestness in all he did, led his friends, no doubt, to the conclusion which they impressed upon him and which he ultimately accepted. He was from a boy a prayerful student of the Bible, and sought to regulate by it his own life and the lives of others. When travelling with a companion in his twenty-first year, the same year that he entered the University (1837), he collected the servants of the several inns at which they stayed to prayer in the evening. At Oxford he established a society for prayer and conversation on the Scriptures. His direct study of the Scriptures and the confidence with which he read in them certain great principles, were evidently the main means by which he resisted the influence of Newmanism. He was carried, as he himself afterwards said, to the brink of the precipice,[1] but was held back by the force of his early training and a certain Pauline simplicity and severity of biblical thought characteristic of his youth.

[1] *Life*, vol. i. p. 120.

Robertson's first ministry was at Winchester, where he accepted a curacy in July 1840. He carried with him into his work, as his biographer says, 'a grave and awful sense of responsibility.' His religious character, always earnest, had deepened at Oxford. The death of one of his sisters and her happiness and peace in dying had affected him greatly. Amidst all the temptations of his young life at Paris (where he was for some time), as well as at Oxford, he had led a consistent Christian life and grown in Christian experience. Especially there were already developed in him two features of character which were afterwards very conspicuous—'hatred and resistance of evil, and a reverence and effort for purity.' There was something striking in the strength of his feelings in both these respects during all his life. Hs was never so moved as when he had 'to quell a falsehood or avenge a wrong.' Any injury to woman was especially resented by him. He had, as his biographer remarks, a singular chasteness of spirit which gave him, in a large degree, his insight into moral truth, and the fineness with which he could discriminate its more delicate shades. Vigorous in health when young, and with many soldierly qualities and great love of adventure, he was yet constitutionally of a sad temperament, the result of a singularly susceptible nervous organisation which vibrated acutely in response to every influence of nature and life. A more highly strung mind can hardly be imagined, reaching from intense enjoyment to painful depression. He seemed always haunted by an unfulfilled ideal, and yet his natural fulness of feeling went forth in a power of realising all the higher pleasures of life in a remarkable degree. 'The woof' of his own life 'was dark'—as he said of life in general—but it was 'shot with a warp of gold.'

During all the time of his ministry at Winchester he laboured more or less under a feeling of oppressive responsibility. He lived rigorously, frequently refraining from adequate food and sleep, compelling himself to rise early, and systematising his whole life under a sense of religious devotion. He gave certain days to prayer on definite subjects, and read daily books of devotion with scrupulous adherence to a plan. He read particularly such books as the lives of Martyn and Brainerd, and the *Imitation of Christ*. He continued his Greek and Hebrew studies; he visited the poor diligently; he grudged no self-denial to do the work to which he had been called. 'Only one thing was worth living for,' he said to a friend, 'to do God's work, and gradually grow in conformity to his image by mortification, and self-denial, and prayer. When that is accomplished, the sooner we leave this scene of weary struggle the better. Till then, welcome battle, conflict, victory.'[1] Men seldom think, and still seldomer write, in this way after the first years of youth; the words breathe the intense zeal of his youthful ministry.

From the first Robertson showed special, if not marked, gifts as a preacher. He spoke so that men listened to him. His voice was always musical and impressive; his heart was in what he said; and while he preached the ordinary Evangelical doctrines he was free from the peculiar phraseology of the school. There was, however, little or no play of thought in his Winchester sermons. They ran on the usual

[1] *Life*, vol. i. p. 61.

lines, were full of 'doctrinal analysis and general description of the love of Christ,' and in no way indicated his future power. Even his letters of this time are said to be 'scarcely worth reading.' All that he was yet to be remained dormant. The routine of his work absorbed him, and his rigorous abstinence and Puritan severity in dealing with himself laid the seeds of after disease. 'It is painful,' says his biographer, 'to read his diary, in which all his inward life is mapped out in divisions, his sins and errors labelled, selfishness discovered in all his efforts and resolves, and lists made out of the graces and gifts which he needed especially.' [1]

The result of all this was that after about a year he fell ill. He thought himself attacked by the family malady—consumption, which carried off his two sisters. He did not care to live long, and the sense of the shortness of his time only made him redouble his efforts. But his rector,[2] and others more considerate of his health than himself, at length forced him to take a continental holiday. He made a visit to the Rhine and Switzerland, which is chiefly memorable as serving to bring out his keen antagonism at once to Roman Catholicism and German Neology. He was bold in converse with men on spiritual subjects. He never shrank from making known his sentiments, and in his intense opposition to Popery sometimes indulged in a pugnacity of debate which was not without its risks. As unlike as possible to his later attitude, he was at this time

---

[1] *Life*, vol. i. p. 67.

[2] Mr. Nicholson, Rector of the united parishes of St. Maurice, St. Mary Kalendar, and St. Peter's, Colebrook.

a polemic on behalf of ordinary British Protestantism
in season and out of season.   At Geneva he plunged
eagerly into the religious questions which then agitated the city.   He had many conversations with César
Malan   and   others   less   orthodox,   and   maintained
always with zeal his own views.   ' I have just returned
from another long discussion with Malan before several
persons, which I do not like, because calmness in
argument is then always difficult.   You think of
your own victory instead of the truth.   However, I
only fenced, and allowed him to cross-question me.
He does it in the most affectionate and earnest
manner ; but I could not yield, because I believe all
I said leaned upon God's truth.   He said—and there
was much pathetic foresight in the prophecy, little
as young Robertson, in the midst of all his enthusiasm, felt it at the time—' Mon très-cher frère, vous
avez une triste vie et un triste ministère.'

Geneva proved the farthest point of his travels at
this time.   He there met a young lady, daughter of
a Northamptonshire Baronet, and after a brief
acquaintance married her.   It has always been supposed that the deep sadness of his life had something
to do with this sudden event ; but the veil has not been
lifted for us, and we have no right to try to lift it.
He returned almost immediately after his marriage.
and settled at Cheltenham ; and here, after a brief
interval, he began the second stage of his ministry in
circumstances that seemed to promise happiness and
usefulness.   He was greatly attached to his rector,
the Rev. Archibald Boyd, afterwards rector at St.
James's, Paddington, and latterly Dean of Exeter.
He looked up to him for a time with the greatest

respect, and was even disposed to learn from him as a preacher. His own preaching at Cheltenham from the first evidently struck a higher key than that of his Winchester ministry. There are many testimonies to this effect. One friend writes, 'I had a prejudice against him, through no fault of his, but I was not merely struck but startled by his sermon. The high order of thought, the large and clear conception, the breadth of view, the passion held in leash, the tremulously earnest tone, the utter forgetfulness of self in his subject, and the abundance of the heart out of which the mouth speaks, made me feel indeed that here indeed was one whom it would be well to miss no opportunity of hearing. From the first he largely swayed those minds that had any point of contact with him.' It seemed as if he had found a fitting sphere for his powers. But gradually he fell into his old depression. There were evidently external as well as internal causes for this, which are not fully explained ; the relations with his Rector, at first so cordial, seem to have altered. He took it into his head that his sermons were not intelligible to the congregation. The admirers of the Rector's preaching were plainly no admirers of his—the two men were quite different in their cast of thought, and the ladies who fluttered around the Incumbent did not care for the Curate. The idea that he was more or less of a failure assailed him. 'Sad and dispirited,' is an entry in his diary in 1845, after he had been about three years in Cheltenham.

During all this time his intellectual powers were rapidly growing. Carlyle's books became favourite studies. German literature and theology opened

up their treasures to him. ' He began to hew out
his own path to his convictions.' How far this new
spirit, which made itself felt no doubt in his sermons, may have had to do with his discomfort in the
discharge of his duty, is not said ; but there can be
little doubt that the change that was gradually passing over his thought was the main factor in the
mental disturbance that now overtook him. Since
1843, his attitude towards the Evangelical party
had begun to alter. Of this date he says, 'As
to the state of the Evangelical clergy, I think it
lamentable. I see sentiment instead of principle,
a miserable mawkish religion superseding a state
which once was healthy. Their adherents I love less
than themselves, for they are but copies of their faults
in a large edition. I stand nearly alone, a Theological
Ishmael. The Tractarians despise me, and the Evangelicals somewhat loudly express their doubts of me.'

This is the earliest indication of Robertson's decided
dissatisfaction with his old views. The change had
begun within a year of the commencement of his
ministry at Cheltenham. The three years which
followed were destined to see a complete revolution in
his thought. Doubts came to him in quick succession.
The study of German, the enlarged study of Scripture,
a deeper acquaintance with his own heart, dissatisfaction apparently with the Rector's teaching and modes
of action, which had at first so much attracted him,
seem all to have contributed to the result. His sermons altered, and it became painful for him to preach.
The reaction was violent in his case, in proportion to
the unhesitating acceptance which he had given to
the Evangelical doctrines. The whole system on

which he had founded his faith and his work fell away under him irretrievably, and after a struggle to maintain the old with the new, he gave way entirely, and plunged into a state of spiritual agony, so awful, that it not only shook his health to its centre, but smote his spirit down into so profound a darkness, that of all his early faiths but one remained, ' It must be right to do right.'

In such a state it was impossible for him to continue preaching. The state of his health alone forbade this; and there was nothing for him but once more to leave the scene of his ministry, and seek for some assuagement of his trouble in continental travel. There is no picture of the spiritual struggles of this time, when Froude, and Clough, and Sterling were all in the death-throes of their early faith, to be compared in touching interest with that of Frederick Robertson. He has himself told the story of it, and the tremulous depths of his language bring us very near his heart. He went down into the darkness, and all light for a time seemed to leave him—all save the sense of right and good. ' If there be no God and no future state, yet even then it is better to be generous than selfish, better to be chaste than licentious, better to be true than false, better to be brave than to be a coward.' So he felt, and from this moral basis he fought his way again upward towards the light.

Robertson's character stands singularly free in this great crisis from all trace of lower feeling or self-involution—from all that vanity, pride, or presumption which so frequently accompany such states even in large minds. There is no trace in him of mere intel-

lectualism, still less of sentimentalism, as if it were
something fine to be the victim of Divine despair,
nor is there, as we may see in George Eliot, any
sense of superiority over the logic of superstition,
—only a profound and unutterable misery, as of
one from whom a divine treasure had been stolen,
and to whom there had come 'a fearful loneliness of
spirit,' from which the stars of hope had gone out
one by one.   He was driven into the wilderness by
sheer force of spiritual perplexity ; he passed out of
sight of men and books, that he might fight with
his doubts in calm resolution.   'He did not seek for
sympathy.   He was accustomed, as he said, to con-
sume his own smoke.'   I know nothing more touching in biography than his lonely wanderings in the
Tyrol amidst scenery the excitement of which seemed
only for a time to deepen his mental unrest.   It is a
strange and painful yet exalting experience when the
weary heart carries with it the pressure of an intolerable self-consciousness into such scenes of solemn
beauty, and feels the glory around only to deepen the
awe of life and the burden of thought.   The clouds,
instead of being driven away, seem for a time only
to gather shape and consistency ; but all the while
Nature is doing its healing work, and the brain
once more rallying its exhausted forces, till, with the
return of health, it is found that the scenes through
which we have passed have wrought like magic,
bringing not only peace, but expansion and maturity
of intellect.[1]

[1] As he himself says in one of his letters, vol. i. p. 274—' The soul
collects its mightiest forces by being thrown in upon itself, and coerced
solitude often matures the mental and moral character marvellously.'

The autumn that Robertson spent in the Tyrol and at Heidelberg in 1846 was the turning-point of his life. His Evangelical faith was gone before he left England—worn out of his heart and mind by many causes. The great principles of morality, or *Ursachen*, as he called them, were alone left to him; all else was gone. 'Who was Christ? What are miracles? What do you mean by inspiration? Is the resurrection a fact or a myth? What saves a man—his own character, or that of another? Is the next life individual consciousness or continuation of the consciousness of the universe?' These and many other questions—to which he says 'Krause would return one answer, Neander another, and Dr. Chalmers another'—tormented him. They had come upon him not suddenly. He writes to a friend, the same apparently who had introduced him to Germanism, that he must not distress himself, as if he were responsible for his doubts. But if the sense of religious difficulties had been gradually growing in his mind before, it was his experience and ministry at Cheltenham that ripened them. He may have known something of them before; but there is nothing less like real spiritual perplexity than the sort of way in which young minds sometimes play with difficulties. And it was only when driven from Cheltenham in the autumn of 1846 that the rain descended and the floods came, and the wind beat upon his house till it shook to its foundations. It was only then certainly, and after much spiritual struggle, that he began to build again from the foundation. His whole spiritual and intellectual nature underwent a change. He laid hold of religious questions in a way he had never done before. His vision was enlarged, his grasp became stronger, richer, more penetrating. All the sermons and writings by which he is known are after this date. He had realised his own wish. As a friend and he looked at the summit of Skiddaw enveloped in a mist, on the eve of his departure to the Continent, he said to him, ' I would not have my head, like the peak of that mountain, involved in cloud for all that you could offer me.' 'I would,' rejoined Robertson quickly, ' for by and by the cloud and mist will roll away, and the sun will come down upon it in all his glory.' So it proved with him. The cloud rolled away : he emerged into a radiance, which did not always abide with him in its fulness, but which never again left him. Up to this point he was only a promising preacher. Henceforth he became, beyond all question, one of the spiritual thinkers of his time—strong in every fibre of intellectual and religious life. In the silence and solitude of the mountains of the Tyrol his ' soul, left to explore its own recesses, and to feel its nothingness in the presence of the Infinite,' had laid its foundations deep and sure.

He was two months at Oxford before settling at Brighton ; and here he enjoyed for the first time the full freedom of preaching. He began rapidly to draw attention. The undergraduates were thronging the church, and beginning to hang upon his words, when the sudden change to Brighton came. He began his ministry there in the autumn of 1847. He was still only 31 ; but his mind now opened at once to its full powers. His genius was never brighter or more 'productive' than during his first two years at Brighton. His inborn gifts of eloquence —of luminous intelligence—his capacity of swaying the human heart and of bringing light to the most difficult subjects, all came forth in their full development. He seemed as if he knew that his time would be short; and, 'unhasting, yet unresting,' he gave himself to make full proof of his ministry.

It was as a preacher that Frederick Robertson became one of the spiritual forces of his time. He was also active as a philanthropist—as a friend of working men, who gathered around him in numbers and with eager admiration. He delivered lectures on Poetry, and he published an analysis of Tennyson's *In Memoriam* of rare value. His literary powers were of the highest order, especially his faculty for poetic criticism. His theological learning was ample, and thoroughly his own, and at one time he projected a work on 'Inspiration.' But it was in the pulpit that he put forth all his intellectual and spiritual strength, and his 'Sermons' remain the permanent memorial of his genius and of the strong impulses of new and living thought that came from him. It is as a preacher, therefore, that we are alone called upon to estimate him.

What then were the elements of his rare and almost unexampled influence, not merely while he lived, but since his death? For of him, of all preachers, may it be truly said, that 'being dead, he yet speaketh.' His sermons, which, with a single exception, have all been published since his death, and many of them in an imperfect form, have not only perpetuated his fame, but spread the influence

of his thought far and wide beyond any bounds to
which his living voice could have extended. We
have already spoken of his impressive voice and
manner. His voice is described as 'low pitched,
deep and penetrating, seldom rising; but when it
did, going forth in a deep volume of sound like
a great bell,' thrilling from the repression rather
than excitement of feeling. Like many other men
with no ear for music, he was yet a subtle master of
sound, just as he was peculiarly susceptible to its
witchery in others. There were states in which it
would move him indescribably, and so 'linger upon
his ear that he could not sleep at night.' This was
only a part of his singular sensibility to all sense-
impressions—all influences of form and colour as
well as sound. Brightness, beauty of any kind,
affected him directly, and it made all the difference
in the world to him whether he had to compose in
a room facing to the north or the south. It was this
same sensitiveness that gave him such an exquisite
perception of natural scenery, so that its glow or
terror, its wildness or sweetness, touched him to the
very quick. There is nothing in his sermons and lectures more exquisite than some of his reminiscences
of his wanderings in the Tyrol. They are like bits of
sudden glory thrown upon a canvas, never for their
own sake merely, but as illustrating some hidden
chords of feeling or some fresh development of truth.
None but the eye of an artist could have seized the
picture, and no one but with rare gifts as a thinker
could have fitted the picture to the argument.

Apart from voice, Robertson's external characteristics as a preacher were not specially effective.

He was entirely without oratorical parade. He had hardly any gesture save a slow motion of his hand upwards, and when worn and ill in his last years, a fatal disease consuming both brain and heart, he stood almost motionless in the pulpit, 'his pale thin face and tall emaciated form seeming, as he spoke, to be glowing as alabaster glows when lit up by an inward fire.' ' When he began his sermon, he held in his hand a small slip of paper with a few notes upon it. He referred to it now and then ; but before ten minutes had gone by, it was crushed to uselessness in his grasp, for he knit his fingers together over it, as he knit his words over his thought.'

It was in all the nobler qualities of thought, insight, and feeling that he excelled, as it is these qualities that still live in his sermons and have made them such a marvellous power.. He was characteristically a Thinker in the Pulpit. He went straight to the heart of every subject that he touched, and with a rare combination of imaginative and dialectic power brought out all its meaning. He felt a truth before he expressed it ; but when once he felt it, and by patient study had made it his own, he wrought it with the most admirable logic—a logic closely linked, yet living in every link—into the minds of his hearers. This live glowing concatenated sequence of thought is seen in all his greater sermons. It could only have been forged in a brain stirred to its depths,—on fire with the ideas which possessed him for the time,—yet never mastered by, always mastering, his subject. This impress of creative force as he proceeded in his sermons gives them their wonderful perfection of form amidst all their hurrying energy.

They are many of them great as literary compositions with a living movement rare even in the higher
literature. The truth is, they were literally the creation of moments of inspired utterance. We cannot
imagine them written in cold blood. Their organisation shows a heated yet controlled enthusiasm. 'He
disentangled his subject, as he advanced, from the
crowd of images and thoughts which clustered round
it. He exercised a severe choice over this crowd,
and rejected what was superabundant. There was
no confusion in his mind. Step by step he led his
hearers from point to point till at last he placed them
on the summit where they could see all the landscape
of his subject in luminous and connected order. He
hated an isolated thought. He was not happy till he
had ranged it under a principle. Once there it was
found to be linked to a thousand others. Hence
arose his affluence of ideas, his ability for seizing
remote analogies, his wide grasp and lucid arrange-
ment of his subject, his power of making it, if abstruse,
clear, if common, great ; if great, not too great for
human nature's daily food. For he was not only
a thinker, but the thinker for men. All thought he
directed to human ends. Far above his keenness of
sympathy for the true and beautiful was his sympathy
for the true and beautiful in union with living hearts.'[1]

If the highest work of thought is to illuminate a subject—to pierce to its heart, and unfold in creative
order all its parts, and not merely to tell you about
it and what others have thought of it—to make alive
a new order of ideas and not merely explain an old
order—then Frederick Robertson is certainly the

[1] *Life*, vol. i. pp. 193-4.

greatest thinker who has appeared in the pulpit in modern times. Other preachers may have been more eloquent in the ordinary sense, more capable of swaying with delight varied audiences, but there are no sermons comparable to his in sustained elevation of thought. There are none that carry readers so steadily on the wings of spiritual and imaginative reason till they enter into the very life of the subject, and see eye to eye with the preacher. How vividly, for example, do we realise the contrasted attitude of Jew and Gentile to the Cross of Christ in his famous sermons 'The Jews require a sign, and the Greeks seek after wisdom, but we preach Christ crucified.' How does 'The Star in the East' assume meaning as he expounds it? With what a freshness does he discourse of 'Christ's Estimate of Sin,' and his creative vision of the Divine capacities that still lived in humanity amidst all its sinful ruin? How does the loneliness of Christ shadow us, and the sacrifice of Christ fill our hearts as he speaks of them? His thought was not only thorough. It not only went into a subject and round it, and embraced it in all its essential bearings, but it pictured it. It made it alive. It pierced it through and through at once with light and life.

But this divine rationality—rare as it is—would not have made Robertson's sermons all the power they have been apart from other and still higher qualities. With all his intellectuality he is never far from the depths of the spiritual life. And he touches these depths—the secrets of the heart, the sorrows of sin, aspirations after holiness, not only with an exquisite tenderness, sympathy, and penetrating knowledge,

but above all with a simplicity, directness, and honesty
that leave almost all preachers behind.   We know of
no sermons that search the heart, we do not say more
delicately, but with a straighter, clearer delicacy than
Robertson's.   Newman can play upon richer and
more tangled chords of spiritual feeling, he can
awaken and startle the conscience with more
solemnity, but there are intricacies and not unfre-
quently sophistries in Newman's most moving appeals.
It is the image of the Church or the authority of
dogma that plays with him the part of spiritual
judge.   You require to be a Churchman to feel the
full force of what he says.   He often deals obliquely
with the conscience, and delights to take it at a disad-
vantage.   In Robertson the play of spiritual feeling
is direct as it is intense.   There is not a trace of
sophistry in the most subtle of his spiritual analyses
or the most powerful of his spiritual appeals.   Our
common spiritual nature, and the great chords of
feeling that lie in it, and not mere churchly feeling
or over-drilled conscience, are the subjects with which
he deals.   Above all it is Christ himself, the living
Christ, and not any mere image of his authority
or notion about him, with which he plies the heart.
' My whole heart's expression,' he says in one of his
letters,[1] ' is "none but Christ," not in so-called evangelical sense, but in a deeper real sense—the mind of
Christ ; to feel as He felt ; to judge the world, and to
estimate the world's maxims as He judged and estimated.   To realise that is to feel none but Christ !
But then in proportion as a man does that, he is
stripping himself of garment after garment till his

[1] Vol. i. p. 154.

soul becomes naked of that which once seemed part of himself; he is not only giving up prejudice after prejudice, but also renouncing sympathy after sympathy with friends whose smile and approbation were once his life.'

There is in this last sentence a touch of exaggeration. He was apt to generalise too painfully from his own experience. But there was no exaggeration in the intensity with which he sought for himself nearness to Christ. The peculiar directness of his love to Christ was the root of all his life and effort. 'It was a conscious personal realised devotion,' too sacred to speak much about. It filled his whole soul and left him alone with the overpowering consciousness of the Divine Presence. It was this feeling that dictated his famous words when he spoke in the Town Hall of Brighton to the working men about infidel publications. 'I refuse to permit discussion respecting the love which a Christian man bears to his Redeemer—a love more delicate far than the love which was ever borne to sister or the adoration with which he regards his God—a reverence more sacred than ever man bore to mother.' This supreme feeling towards Christ pervades all Robertson's sermons. Every subject is brought more or less into direct relation with Christ, and glows or darkens in the light of His presence. It was his hold of the 'mind of Christ,' and the flashes of insight that constantly came from this source that made him so helpful as well as powerful a preacher. Above all he dealt with these two great realities—' Christ and the soul.'

Closely allied with this was his love of the truth in all things. To do and say the right thing because it is right—'to dare to gaze on the splendour of the naked truth without putting a veil before it to terrify any by mystery and vagueness—to live by love and not by fear—that is the life of a true brave man who will take Christ and his mind for the truth instead of the clamour either of the worldly world or the religious world.' He had no pet commonplaces to enforce either of tradition or doctrine. His aim was to see every question in the pure light of the gospel—to show how Christ had grasped the problems of thought and of society at their root, and given forth fertile principles applying to all time. He liked to be regarded as a teacher rather than a preacher. He hated using fine words about religion, or being supposed a fine talker. In the reaction which frequently came to him after preaching he was disposed to undervalue it altogether, and even to speak of it with contempt. He seemed to himself at times to do so little good, and the buzz that besets popularity in the pulpit rung painfully in his ears. It was impossible to offend him more than to speak of him as a popular preacher. He hated the idea. There was to him a sort of degradation in it ; and much of the indignant scorn and pride which rushed out sometimes in his words took their keenness from this source. There was a certain morbid feeling in this as in other points, but it all came of the deep truthfulness of the man, in whom the oratorical instinct, powerful as it was, never overpowered for a moment the higher qualities of sense, judgment, taste, and reason.

His theological standpoint is in some respects difficult to define. His biographer says 'he was the

child of no theological father. He owned no master
but Christ ; and he did not care, provided he fought
under him the good fight, to what regiment he
belonged.' The term 'Broad Church,' used as a distinctive party name, is used of him, as throughout,
with reserve. He was certainly neither Tractarian
nor Evangelical ; and in this sense he was ' broad '—
that he interpreted Christianity and the Church in
the widest sense both historically and spiritually.
All men who own their spiritual heritage in baptism
were to him the children of a common God and
Father. They were neither ' made the children of
God ' by baptism, nor was there any doubt as to their
position. He approved of the Gorham decision not
because he agreed with Mr. Gorham, but because it
left the question open. If he differed from Mr.
Gorham he certainly differed also from the Bishop of
Exeter. Baptism, he said, is the special revelation
of the great truth that all who are born into the world
are children of God by right. The truth or fact is
not dependent on the sacrament, nor on the faith of
the recipient. It is a fact before we believe it, else
how could we be asked to believe it ? But it must
be acknowledged and acted upon. We must believe
it and live it. When the Catechism says, 'My baptism, wherein I was made a child of God,' the
meaning is the same as in the saying, 'the Queen
is *made* Queen at her coronation.' She was Queen
before ; nay, if she had not been Queen, coronation
could not make her Queen.[1] Against this view he
set the Tractarian as implying the magical creation
of a nature at the moment of baptism ; and the

[1] See Sermons on Baptism, second Series, and Letters, vol. ii. *et seq.*

Evangelical as doing the same, but only in select cases. Either view appeared to him to destroy the essential nature of Christianity. His position was virtually the same as Mr. Maurice's, but he seized it with a healthier breadth. Maurice equally repudiated any magical efficacy in the rite, but he fell back into a species of ritualistic magic in attaching a special efficacy to the sacrament as administered in the Church of England. Robertson neither implies nor asserts any such restriction.

His explanation of baptism was closely connected with his whole view of dogma. He did not reject dogma even when its form repelled him. He tried to find its inner and comprehensive meaning. There was to him a certain verity underlying all dogma. The whole verity no dogma could express or measure. It only tried to do so. It was a proximate, tentative, or partial, but never complete or final interpretation of Divine Truth. So he always asked of a dogma, What does it really mean ? Not what did it mean in the language of those who spoke it. ' How in my language can I put into form the underlying truth—in corrected form if possible,—but in only approximate form after all ' . . . 'God's truth must be boundless. Tractarians and Evangelicals suppose that it is a pond which you can walk round and say, "I hold the truth." What, all ! Yes, all ; there it is circumscribed, defined, proved, quite large enough to be the immeasurable Gospel of the Lord of the Universe !'[1] There is wisdom as well as breadth in such words—a higher wisdom than many identified with the ' Broad

[1] Vol. ii. p. 41.

Church' knew. Neither Maurice nor Kingsley ever reached the true rational standpoint as to creeds and formulas. They failed to understand the profound distrust that a certain order of spiritual minds have of all statements, like the Athanasian Creed, which profess to sum up Divine Truth. Useful as 'aids to faith,' they are intolerable as limitations of faith. They are really water-marks of the Christian consciousness of the past. To make them 'ponds' enclosing that consciousness for all ages, is to mistake both their real origin and the nature of Divine truth. For this truth, as Robertson steadily maintained, is of the nature of poetry, 'to be felt and not proved.'[1] It is to be realised not as propositions addressed to the intellect, but as the witness of God's Spirit to man's spirit. And so all Robertson's teaching was suggestive rather than dogmatic. He sought to bring men face to face with the truth not in sharp doctrinal outlines, but in the fulness of its spirit and life, which,—allowing in his view differences of opinion,—united men by a pervasive spirit of love to Christ and to one another.' He had none of that dread of 'different sorts of opinion' that Mr. Maurice had,—which he and Newman alike stigmatised as 'Liberalism.' He did not shrink from the word 'Liberal' in religion. It expressed the generous recognition of difference and expansion of opinion here as in other things. He knew very well, that, whatever words we may use, it is simply a fact—which no theory whatever can alter—that men will differ in religious opinion, and that the higher view, therefore, is to admit the validity of dogmatic differences, and to point to the true Centre, the Spirit of Christ, in

[1] Vol. ii. p. 165.

which all differences, if they do not disappear, assume
their true proportion.   This aspect of Robertson's
teaching, we agree with his biographer in thinking,
will prove the most lasting of all.   It has radiated
upon all schools of Christian thought a softening
influence.   It has indicated the true point of contact
for diverse lines of Christian teaching.   Boldly
and confidently as he dealt with many Christian dogmas, the atonement, the doctrine of sin, the
doctrine of the sacraments, of absolution, of im-
puted righteousness, of apostolical succession, and
rich as is the light of thought which he has thrown
around many of them, he never supposed that he had
exhausted their meaning, or said the last word regarding them.   Such solutions as he gave he knew to be
partial like all other solutions.   'The time might
come when they would cease to be adequate.   The
solution that was fitting for one age might be unfitting
for another.'   He kept his mind open to still higher
and more comprehensive explanations.   He looked
forward 'to an advance of the Christian Church—
not into new truths, but into wider and more tolerant
views of those old truths which in themselves are
incapable of change.'

Robertson's genius was thus not only rich, but
eminently expansive.   It was generous and Catholic
to the core.   He might speak at times bitterly against
Evangelicalism.   If there was unfairness in his mind
at all, it was in some of his criticisms of Evangelical
doctrine.   But this was a natural reaction against
what he considered its injurious commonplaces, and
the suffering they had inflicted upon him.   He
was upon the whole highly just in speech as he was

fearless in thought.[1] He exhibited the combination so rare at all times of intense spirituality with a large critical and historical faculty. He had a true appreciation,—far more so than other teachers with whom he has been classed,—of the natural conditions underlying the development of Divine revelation and of dogmatic thought. He was no man of a school, with esoteric thoughts and private modes of inter-pretation destined to be swept away by the progress of criticism. He was Christian in the widest sense, with his mind alive to all the influences of knowledge, nature, or life. He stood in the van of critical as well as spiritual progress, content to vindicate re-ligion in the light of history and of conscience. He had no wish to disturb old dogmas in order to substi-tute dogmas of his own. He rather tried to make the best use of them he could—knowing how impossible is exactitude in matters of religious opinion. His aim was not to displace violently any central points of faith, but to make the old live as far as possible with the new. He sought to broaden down 'from pre-cedent to precedent,' recognising the universal truth hidden in the saying, 'I have many things to say unto you, but ye cannot bear them now.' His biographer testifies that he never brought forward in the pulpit an opinion which was only fermenting in his mind. 'He waited till the must became wine.' He endea-voured as far as in him lay, without sacrificing truth, not to shock the minds of any who were resting peacefully in an 'early heaven and in happy views.' He was tender of weak consciences, and all honest

[1] 'I desire for myself,' he says, 'that I may be true and fearless' (vol. ii. p. 249).

opinions.   Liberal, in short, in all the tendency of his thought, with a mind open to every fresh impulse of truth and progress, he was yet wise in his liberalism. He knew that the law of all progress is rooted in the past, and that men will advance in religion as in everything else not by displacement but by expansion, by building the temple of truth to a loftier height, not by subverting it and beginning once more from the naked soil.   Few minds have enriched Christian thought more in our time, or given it a more healthy or sounder impulse.

Robertson died in the summer of 1853.   Twelve years afterwards, when his sermons had spread far and wide,[1] a kindred spirit wrote of his *Life and Letters*, which had been sent to him by his daughter, that no 'present of thought' could be more valuable. 'Robertson helps me,' said Bishop Ewing, 'to a deeper realisation of that underlying life of the soul which is not dependent on externals, but which gives to all circumstances their true colour and significance, forming as it were God within ourselves.' Alexander Ewing had begun his ministry, a year or two before Robertson—in the Scottish Episcopal Church.   He was ordained a deacon at Inverness in the autumn of 1838.   But the former had nearly completed his brief career before the latter came to be known as a remarkable man.   Ordained a Priest in 1841, he became Bishop of Argyll and the Isles in

[1] Eleven editions of the first volume of his sermons had been published before his *Life and Letters* appeared.   Their circulation in America has also been very wide ; and their republication in theTauchnitz edition of English shows still more perhaps their wide-spread popularity.

1846 ; but it was not till nearly ten years later that he began to show any of that definite influence which he continued to exercise with growing effect, not only in Scotland and in his own communion, but throughout England, till his death. He cannot be said to have been an original force in the Christian thought of the century. If Thomas Erskine and Macleod Campbell had not lived, Alexander Ewing would certainly not have been the teacher that he was ; yet there was a sense in which he improved their teaching. With less power of thought and less theological knowledge—bishop as he was—he had yet upon the whole a healthier, manlier, and more natural turn of mind than either. He was more of a man among men, more free from the spirit of coterie, with a wider range of purely human feeling, more rational and broadly sympathetic, with bursts of poetry in his heart. He made Erskine's acquaintance in Carlyle's company in 1855, and an intimate friendship soon sprung up between them, in which Macleod Campbell shared. He expresses in his letters repeated obligations to both of them. The three friends especially met at Pollok, the residence of Sir John Maxwell, in the neighbourhood of Glasgow ; and Bishop Ewing has left us, in one of his *Present Day Papers*, a pleasant sketch of the charms of the old residence and its dignified, thoughtful, and genial host. The sketch might stand almost as a companion to that memorable one of Falkland, and his theological friends at Tew, near Oxford, so well known in Clarendon's description.[1] Here the friends discoursed of the greatness of

[1] Clarendon's *Life*, vol. i. pp. 42-50. Clarendon Press ed. See also *Rational Theology in England*, vol. i. pp. 118-29.

the Divine love, and how the Divine love was only another name for the Divine righteousness and holiness ; how all the attributes of God in one sense equally condemned the sinner and equally sought his salvation ; and how the popular theology had gone astray in arraying one attribute against another, instead of holding them closely in unity. Both Erskine and Campbell had by this time ripened in thought. Without changing their original standpoint, they had both grown in knowledge of men, and books, and theologies other than their own. Campbell had just published his great work on *The Nature of the Atonement,* which has affected so many minds far beyond his own school, and deepened and enriched, it may be said without exaggeration, the thought of Christendom on this great subject. We can easily understand how the youngest mind of the three was stimulated, and, as he says himself, ' bettered' by such high converse.

Happily there were elements of higher thought in Ewing from the first, and still more happily his intellectual and spiritual nature continued to grow with a healthy spontaneity. Notwithstanding all that he owed to both Campbell and Erskine, he did not allow himself to be confined by leading-strings of any kind. He sympathised with the freer tendencies of Robertson—and of Jowett, of whom he was an early friend,—no less than with the special universalism of the Row School. He had a truer appreciation of the limits of dogmatic authority and of the natural historical origin of dogma than either of his Pollok friends. The free air of history and of life was more congenial to him. Systems of any kind, new as well as old, were uncongenial. 'I do not think there is any vitality in the Athanasian formula,' he says in a letter to Archbishop Tait. 'It is holding up the skeleton of the dead amidst the living. To the great majority of those who attend our Churches, the technical phrases of the Creed are quite as unintelligible as are the special legal expressions in a legal deed, or the terms in a physician's prescription. I would keep it as an old and curious heirloom in a charter-chest.' The hyper-dogmatic language which has incrusted the great facts of the Atonement and of revelation was to him mere 'materialistic substitutions' for the facts themselves. 'Balances and equivalents,' he said, 'had made of none effect the direct revelation of the forgiveness of sins.'

With Bishop Ewing as with Robertson the centre of religious truth was the 'underlying life of the soul' in communion with God, the 'mind of Christ' within us. This was above all the teaching of his significant series of discourses, *Revelation considered as light.* All external authority—dogma, church, sacrament— is lower than this,—at the best only scaffolding to be taken down when the 'true light that lighteth every man' has shone into our hearts. 'Revelation,' he says, 'does not come from the Church, but to the Church. She is a witness, not a source. . . . Christianity is to be that which Christ was on earth. . . . It is the communication of a divine life through the manifestation of a divine life. It is the raising up of a divine life in our souls, through the knowledge of the divine life in the Son ; the spirit of the Son entering into our spirits, and we becoming sons also in our measure.' If there is any difficulty as to this inner authority—this light within us revealing the light of God—there is at least no substitute for it. No external authority,—no mere dogma,—can be anything to us till it has taken hold of us and become a part of the divine light within us. Or if we make it anything without its first having become this, we lose the very nature of religion in trying violently to seize its good. There is and can be no religion to any man in accepting any law but that which is 'written on his heart,' and to which his own spirit witnesses as divine. And so it is that 'Standards of Doctrine' do often more harm than good; and by their very definitions and externalities lead the mind away from God instead of to Him.

It was such growing spirituality and freedom that gave Bishop Ewing so much influence. He constantly proclaimed the power of Christianity to stand by itself. It was the 'light of life.' It was the highest thought and the highest ethic in the world, and able to vindicate itself. To cry after 'dogmatic authority' is to cry for the light of a candle when the sun is shining. Episcopacy and Presbytery have their respective merits. But they are only at the best 'material apparatus.' 'Let us rise to higher things,' he said in one of his Charges; 'let us live in that region which makes the face to shine, and where the heart says, 'I have seen the Lord.' In this spirit it lay very near his heart to promote something of the nature of a union between the Episcopal Church and the national Church of Scotland—a matter in which I, with some others, shared his confidence. Nothing came, or indeed could come, of this project at the time; but the spirit in which Bishop Ewing entered into it was in the highest degree liberal and praiseworthy. His idea as to church-government was the old rational idea found at once in Scripture and common sense, and alone verifiable from history, that while one form of government may be better than another —more calculated to insure the *well*-being of the Church—the form itself did not enter into the being of the Church. He himself believed Episcopacy to be the best form ; but this not only did not prevent his hearty co-operation with his Presbyterian brethren, but made him all the more seek for opportunities of such co-operation. Among his last desires was to testify in the College Chapel at Glasgow to the power of a common faith uniting his own Church and the Church of Scotland, and he was only prevented doing so by an act of Bishop Wilson of Glasgow refusing him permission to do so. He was much impressed and pained by what took place on this occasion. Writing to a friend, he expresses himself as follows :—' I cannot say how much it has impressed me with the feeling that these apparently innocent things—Apostolic Succession and High views (as they are called) of the Christian Sacraments—are really *antichristian* in their operation. When they take shape in actual life, they reveal their meaning to be a doctrine of election, which is just so much worse than the common one that it is external and official, and which, moreover, renders the sacraments themselves uncertain in their efficacy by demanding the co-operation of the will of the minister, if the reception of them is to be savingly beneficial. How destructive the doctrine must be of all simple and immediate fellowship between

man and man and between man and God, I need
not say.'

Bishop Ewing may not stand in the foremost rank
of Christian thinkers ; his theological education was
of too desultory character ; the mass of his thought
was too slight.   But his vivid intuitions of the Divine,
his broad Catholicity, his intensely human and
truth-loving aspirations, gave him a significant place
among those who have understood the needs of our
time, and who have laboured to promote a more
enlightened view of Christianity.   Resting in one
or two central truths, the light of his own life, his
mind was open on all sides to further light and
knowledge.   He was singularly progressive in all
the aspects of his thought, while holding firmly to
the Head and Centre of all Christian thought—
Christ.   There can be no higher attitude of mind.
What he said of his friend Dr. Macleod Campbell
was eminently true of himself, that he sought to
interpret Revelation 'in the light of its facts' rather
than of past theories.   So in all theology he got near
to God.   He was satisfied that the Divine substance
of Truth remained unimpaired however imperfect the
vehicle of it might be proved to be.   He and Campbell and Robertson did much to prepare the way for
the free exercise of historical criticism on the letter
of Scripture by showing how independent of all such
criticism is the essence of Divine truth—'how little
the treasure itself is affected by the nature of the
vessel containing it.'   This disengagement of the
spirit from the letter—of the heavenly treasure from
the earthly vessel, is destined to be a fertile principle
in the future of Theology, and to pave the way at

once for the free rights of criticism and the rightful demands of faith.[1]

With Bishop Ewing's name we might close our review. In even including him we have gone somewhat beyond our limits, inasmuch as his chief activity was towards the close of his life, and so beyond the period we have set to ourselves in these lectures. With the year 1860 at the latest a series of new lines of religious thought set in. There is a new outbreak of 'Liberalism' at Oxford, marked by the publication of *Essays and Reviews*. The note of this Liberalism is not merely a freer application of the principles of historical criticism to Scripture and

[1] Bishop Ewing was confessedly indebted—for the clearness of his views as to the distinction between Revelation and Theology, and the true character of Theology—to the Rev. Frederick Myers, whose *Catholic Thoughts on the Bible and Theology* were published in his series of *Present-day Papers*. Frederick Myers was incumbent of St. John's, Keswick, from 1838 to 1851, and may be known to some of our readers as the author of a remarkable book, *Lectures on Great Men*. But he deserves still more to be known as a Christian Thinker, the significance of whose position might well have occupied us in these Lectures if it had been of a wider or more public character. His *Catholic Thoughts on the Bible and Theology*, although written and privately printed as far back as 1848, were only published after Bishop Ewing's death, and have unhappily never attained to much popularity. This is greatly to be regretted, for there are few books at once so devout and enlightened—so spiritually penetrative and yet so rational in the treatment of the basis and structure of theology. What theology is and alone can be 'as a science;' its necessary imperfection and indeterminateness; its consequent liability to modification as time and knowledge advance; the distinction between the Bible and Revelation, and again between the facts of Revelation and the dogmas into which they have been woven, are all set forth with admirable perspicuity and grasp of thought. It is strange that a thinker so really wise and powerful should have attracted so little attention.

dogma, but specially the bearing of scientific discovery and method upon the study of Theology. And this 'scientific' note is more or less a characteristic of subsequent speculation down to the present time. The great idea of Evolution, underlying all processes of thought as well as of Nature, came into prominence. 'The side of the angels' became a party badge, and the conflict of opinion passed in the main away from such topics as had hitherto arrayed, on different sides, Evangelical, High Church,[1] and Broad Church, to far more fundamental questions,—the lines of which are not too strongly marked as Theistic on the one hand, and Atheistic on the other. It was not the intention of *Essays and Reviews* to stir such fundamental questions ; nor can it be said that they were in themselves fairly calculated to do so.[2] All will now admit that much of the panic which the volume created was false and unnatural—a panic of fashion as much as of sincere religion. Like all such panics it was little creditable either to the good sense, or the critical and historical knowledge of English Christendom. But the effect was nevertheless what we have stated. The volume was treated by the *Westminster Review* as a *reductio ad absurdum* of the Broad Church position. The insinuations of Negativism awoke the alarm and pro-

---

[1] The junction of High Church and Low Church in an unworthy assault against Free thought within the Church, which followed *Essays and Reviews*, of itself marks the difference of the times.

[2] I have the best reason for knowing that the editor of *Essays and Reviews* had no revolutionary intention in regard to English theology. It was the disturbance of the religious world, largely consequent upon Frederic Harrison's article in the *Westminster Review*, that alone gave such sinister significance to the volume.

voked the violence of orthodoxy, and so questions of criticism and history were transformed into questions affecting the very existence not only of Christianity but of religion,—such questions as the possibility of miracle, and whether any Divine theory of the world is tenable. It is in this deeper groove that religious thought has mainly run during the last twenty-five years, with thinkers like Herbert Spencer, and Professors Tyndall and Huxley, and Matthew Arnold on one side, and on the other a group of Theistic thinkers, of whom one of the most conspicuous and distinguished is certainly Dr. James Martineau, who has recently added a new and valuable contribution to the cause of Spiritual Philosophy.[1] This deeper conflict was no doubt opened by the Mills and their school within the earlier period we have reviewed, but it has recently passed into wider and larger phases. Materialism fights with bolder and more far-reaching weapons than it has ever before done, and the fight is one for life or death to Religion in the old sense of the word. It overshadows, therefore, every other controversy in minds who understand it, or who have any perception of the powerful forces at work.

But other forces have also been in active operation, and will remain to be described by any future historian of religious thought. Religion, so far from losing its hold of the higher consciousness of our time, has not only survived, but it may be said has gathered strength under all the assaults—scientific and literary—which have menaced it. Our Churches were never stronger in intelligence, in life, in the perception of difficulties to be encountered in the world

[1] *Types of Ethical Theory*, Clarendon Press, Oxford, 1885.

of thought and of action—of philosophy and philanthropy alike; in the restoration of faith and
the restoration of Society. Not only so; but there
has grown up in the wake of the Broad Church
movement a school of historical Criticism represented by such men as Bishop Lightfoot, with
kindred scholars in England and Scotland, who have
brought to the study of Scripture, and the problems
of Revelation, resources of learning and of insight
destined to large results. Different from the older
school of Maurice and Kingsley, these Christian
scholars—in the spirit of Bishop Ewing, but with
ampler knowledge—are seeking for the meaning of
Scripture not in any new theories, but in a closer
study of its own facts. They are making the Books
of the Old Testament and the New Testament alike
alive in the light of the circumstances of their origin,
and of the contemporary ideas of their respective
times. They are, in other words, resuscitating the
Divine Thought which has been the life of the world
in its original framework,—and in its growth and
progressiveness from lower to higher stages of development,—and so not only making this Thought
itself more living and intelligible, but laying the
foundation of some new and more living co-ordination of it in the future. This is a true spring of
advance, which will not wear out as the older form of
Broad Churchism has already almost done. That
Christian criticism, applying the same methods of
study to the Bible which have been applied to all
other ancient literature, has a great and fruitful work
before it, cannot be doubted by any who hold at once
to criticism and to Christianity.

Among those who led the way in this line of historical Criticism was undoubtedly Dean Stanley. Some have, consequently, expressed astonishment that we have not given to him a prominent place in our review. The astonishment was so far natural, as one at least of Dean Stanley's most significant books appeared within the fifth decade of this century, at the time when the Broad Church movement in its original form was acquiring prominence, viz., his *Sermons and Essays on the Apostolic Age.*[1] There is none of his many interesting writings which more distinctly indicates the line of thought which he followed throughout. It is instinct with a rare insight into the phenomena of the Apostolic time, and the bearing of these phenomena upon the true interpretation of Christian thought for all time. Like all his historic studies, it presents at once a picture of the past, and a mirror of the future. This volume and his biography of his great master, Arnold (1844), were undoubtedly among the most quickening features of the new movement of thought, which carried forward the Christian intelligence after the collapse of the 'Oxford' Tractarianism. But the new school of historical Criticism to which Stanley belongs has only made itself conspicuous since 1860, while by this date the earlier Broad Church movement had put forth all the freshness of its thought. Stanley's main work—his *Lectures on the History of the Jewish Church*—was only commenced to be published in 1862.

The new historical epoch in theology may be said to begin in 1855, with the publication of Stanley's

[1] Published in 1847.

second important work of historical criticism—*The Epistles of St. Paul to the Corinthians*—and Mr. Jowett's no less important volumes on the Pauline *Epistles to the Thessalonians, Galatians, and Romans*, in the same year. These volumes were hailed at the time as marking a new era in British Theological Literature, and they deserve to be reckoned in this light. They reproduced in a higher form all that was good in the Whately school, with a richer insight into the essential characteristics of New Testament thought, and a far clearer and more illuminating hold of the spiritual and historical position of the great Apostle,—of the true meaning of his teaching, and the development of his doctrine. From this time has greatly advanced that profounder study of the New Testament, which looks beyond its traditional to its real aspects, and its organic relations to contemporary usage and opinion—which sees in it a living literature, and not a mere repertory of doctrinal texts— and aims to separate the essential from the accidental of Divine Thought, untrammelled by later notions and controversial fictions. The text of Scripture has been studied in its own meaning, and not in support of dogmas which were the growth of long after centuries, and would have been wholly unintelligible to the writers credited with them. The spirit has been liberated from the letter, and the very form and pressure of divine truth as originally presented to the world, brought near to us. This has been especially true of the New Testament age and its marvellous phenomena. Other writers, whom we need not mention, have brought resources of exegesis to their task, superior to those of Stanley;

but no candid student can ever forget how much we owe to his vivid picture of Biblical history and of Christian Institutions in their rise and growth ; and much as he afterwards did, he never did anything better of its kind, than the picture which he gave in his volumes on the Epistles to the Corinthians, of the Apostolical time, with its conflicts of opinion and disorders of practice—particularly his sketch of the primitive eucharist, as ' we see the banquet spread in the late evening ' with its strange blending of the earthly and the heavenly. Nowhere is the first freshness of the Gospel seen in more living struggle with Greek intellectuality and Jewish obstinacy, taking colour and modification from both, yet under all hindrances changing the face of the world. Again the presentation of Pauline thought in its depth, range, and power, yet with the garments of Rabbinical scholasticism here and there encumbering it, was made hardly less vivid to us in Mr. Jowett's volumes. There were those who detected in these volumes traces of an underlying philosophy which tended to deflect here and there the straight spiritual meaning of the apostle—and also a tendency to minimise that meaning in its full scope : but no real student of the volumes can doubt that upon the whole Mr. Jowett tried faithfully to apply his own canon, that the true use of philosophy in reference to religion is ' to restore its simplicity, by freeing it from those perplexities which the love of system, or past philosophies, or the imperfections of language, or the mere lapse of ages, may have introduced into it.'

Both writers mark for us a turning-point in the criticism of Scripture and the *renascence* of Christian ideas nearly contemporary with the influx of new ideas in philosophy and science, which have also acted so powerfully in recent years. They fitly close, therefore, the older period and open the new. We have adverted to them only in this point of view, and with no intention of estimating their full importance. They will claim such an estimate from any one who may afterwards venture to review the more recent forces of thought which are still operating around us.

Meanwhile these lectures, desultory and imperfect as they have been, may help to awaken some intelligent comprehension of the movements of religious thought during the earlier portion of our century. They show how natural is the growth of this thought in its varying phases, springing up under manifold influences in the national consciousness; and how it is marked upon the whole by a character of advance. It is only stagnant in times of stagnation and low religious vitality. There are eternal truths, no doubt, in religion as in ethics ; but it is in the very nature of these truths, and the deeper inquiry which they continually excite, to take ever new expression. We have been slow in Scotland to recognise this inevitable law of development in religious thought, supposing ourselves a centre to which others moved rather than a part of the common movement. There was good in the old Puritan idea of religious immobility. It has kept us strong and righteous-minded in many things, but it has not been without evil consequences. It has made us the hardest religious controversialists in the Christian world—severe upon one another—repellent where we ought to have been sympathetic, and uncharitable where we ought to have held each other by the hand.

It is needless, however, to mourn the past. Let us try to build—if not for ourselves, for our children's children—some fairer temple of Christian thought and worship, in which they may dwell together in unity. But let us not deceive ourselves. Unity can never come from dogma, as our forefathers unhappily imagined. Dogma splits rather than unites from its very nature.[1] It is the creature of intellect, and the intellect can never rest. It remains unsatisfied with its own work, and is always turning up afresh the soil of past opinion. The spirit of Christ can alone bind together the fragments of Truth, as they mirror themselves in our partial reason.

If these lectures have brought home to any the conviction of how much larger the truth of God is than their own changing notions of it, and how the movements of Christian thought are for this very end—that we may prove all things, and hold fast that which is good—they will not be without fruit. We need not be afraid that any intelligent study of opinions differing from our own will make us indifferent to the truth. The truth itself can only be seen by a large vision. What we perhaps all need most to learn is not satisfaction with our opinions— that is easily acquired by most—but the capacity of looking beyond our own horizon; of searching for deeper foundations of our ordinary beliefs, and a

---

[1] 'Opinions are but a poor cement of human souls.'—George Eliot, —*Life*, vol. ii. p. 118.

more sympathetic appreciation of the beliefs of others. While cherishing, therefore, what we ourselves feel to be true, let us keep our minds open to all truth, and especially to the teaching of Him who is 'the Way, the Truth, and the Life.'

INDEX.

———

CORRIGENDUM.

Pp. 292, 293—*For* ' It was said of Novalis,' *read* ' It was said of Spinoza by Novalis.'